THE
HOLOCAUST

THE
HOLOCAUST
A NEW HISTORY

DORIS BERGEN

Front cover: Jewish children marked by the Star of David badge wait outside the soup kitchen in the ghetto in Łódz´, in German-occupied Poland, 1940 or 1941. (courtesy of USHMM Photo Archives. Photographer: Walter Genewein)

Back cover: German civilians conscripted by US troops from the surrounding area dig mass graves for the dead found in Kaufering IV, a subcamp of Dachau, 30 April 1945. (USHMM, courtesy of William O. McWorkman. Photographer: William O. McWorkman)

First published 2003 as *War & Genocide: a Concise History of the Holocaust*

This edition published 2020 by arrangement with Rowman & Littlefield Publishers, Inc.

The History Press
97 St George's Place, Cheltenham,
Gloucestershire, GL50 3QB
www.thehistorypress.co.uk

British Library Cataloguing in Publication Data.
A catalogue record for this book is available from the British Library.

ISBN 978 0 7509 9395 1

Typesetting and origination by The History Press
Printed and bound in Great Britain by TJ International Ltd.

MIX
Paper from
responsible sources
FSC® C013056
www.fsc.org

Contents

Preface: Race and Space   7

1   Preconditions: Antisemitism, Racism and Common
    Prejudices in Early Twentieth-Century Europe   11
2   Leadership and Will: Adolf Hitler, the NSDAP
    and Nazi Ideology   41
3   From Revolution to Routine: Nazi Germany,
    1933–1938   65
4   Open Aggression: In Search of War, 1938–1939   95
5   Experiments in Brutality: War against Poland and the
    So-called Euthanasia Programme, 1939–1940   115
6   Expansion and Systematization:
    Exporting War and Terror, 1940–1941   196
7   The Peak Years of Killing: 1942 and 1943   227
8   Death Throes and Killing Frenzies, 1944–1945   271

Epilogue: The Legacies of Atrocity   288
Sources and Suggestions for Further Reading   297
List of Illustrations   312
Index   322

Preface:
Race and Space

The Holocaust was an event of global proportions, involving perpetrators, victims, bystanders, beneficiaries and rescuers from all over Europe and elsewhere in the world. Any effort to grasp it in its entirety must begin with recognition of that massive scope.

This book attempts to address the enormity of the Holocaust by situating it in the context of the Second World War, the largest and deadliest conflict in human history. War and conquest delivered into Nazi German hands the Jews of Eastern and South-Eastern Europe – Poland, Ukraine, Belorussia, Hungary, Yugoslavia, Greece and elsewhere – as well as the smaller Jewish populations of the west, for example those of France, Belgium and the Netherlands. Approximately ninety-five per cent of the Jews killed between 1939 and 1945 lived outside Germany's pre-war borders. At the same time, war – in particular the Nazi war of annihilation to Germany's east – exponentially increased the numbers and kinds of victims, as brutal programmes of persecution, expulsion and murder, bloated on carnage, demanded and created even more enemies. Mass killings of non-Jews were also part of the Nazi German war effort, a war launched for the related goals of race and space: so-called racial purification and

territorial expansion. War provided killers with both a cover
and an excuse for murder; in wartime, killing was normalised
and extreme, even genocidal measures could be justified with
familiar arguments about the need to defend the fatherland.
Without the war, the Holocaust would not – and could not –
have happened.

Since the 1960s, the term 'Holocaust', from the Greek for 'a
burned offering', has been used to refer to the murder of approximately six million Jews by Nazi Germans and their collaborators
during the Second World War. Sometimes the Hebrew word
Shoah – catastrophe – is used as a synonym. There is no doubt
that hatred of Jews constituted the centre of Nazi ideology. Hitler
and his associates preached what the scholar Saul Friedländer calls
'redemptive antisemitism': the belief that Jews were the root
of all evil and that Germany could be saved from collapse only
by total removal of Jews and Jewish influence. Jews were the
main target of Nazi genocide; against the Jews Hitler's Germany
mobilised all its resources: bureaucratic, military, legal, scientific,
economic and intellectual.

Nevertheless, it was not Jews but the mentally and physically
disabled who became targets of the first large-scale, systematic
killings in Nazi Germany, under the euphemistically labelled
'Euthanasia Programme'. This programme, like the assault on
European Gypsies (Roma), shared with the genocide of the
Jews personnel, methods of killing and goals of so-called racial
purification. At the same time, Nazi Germany persecuted, incarcerated and killed millions of Slavic people – Polish Gentiles,
especially members of the intelligentsia; Soviet prisoners of
war; and others – and attacked communists, homosexual men,
Jehovah's Witnesses, Afro-Germans and other people considered
unwanted in the 'new European order'. Whether or not one
considers members of any or all of these groups to belong under
the label 'victims of the Holocaust', their fates were entwined
in significant ways with that of the Jews targeted and murdered
in the Nazi quest for race and space. This book seeks to identify
and explore connections between and among victim groups, not
in the interest of establishing some kind of hierarchy of suffering

but with the hope of coming to understand how state-sponsored programmes of violence and atrocity function and of offering at least a glimpse into how they are experienced by those who suffer their ravages.

This history is complex and I have tried to present it honestly and as fully as possible in a brief survey. I do not promise that this book will resolve the big questions that might be on your mind: Why did such horrible things happen? If there is a God, how could such atrocities have been possible? What are human beings that they can inflict such agony on other people?

This book addresses some more modest yet important questions regarding the history of Nazism, the Second World War and the Holocaust. Who was involved and in what ways? What motivated those people to behave as they did? How – through what processes – did large numbers of people, some of them 'ordinary', some less so, become murderers of larger numbers of other people? How did the targets of attack respond and what strategies did they develop in their quest to survive?

A list of sources and suggestions for further reading are included at the end of the book. Any synthesis such as this relies heavily on the work of other scholars and I am indebted and very grateful to all of those people whose research and interpretations have shaped and challenged my own.

Many people helped make it possible for this book to appear. My thanks go to Jim Harink and Christine Bergen, who loyally and critically read the first draft. I also appreciate the students and teaching assistants in courses on the Holocaust that I have taught over the past eighteen years at universities in the United States, Canada, Bosnia and Poland. Their insights constantly amaze me. Margarete Myers Feinstein, Daniel S. Mattern, Gary Hamburg, Laura Crago, Robert Wegs, Glenda Regenbaum, Gerhard Weinberg, Christopher Browning, Jürgen Matthäus and Geoffrey Giles provided invaluable comments and corrections. My friends Linda H. Pardo, Patricia Blanchette and Catherine Schlegel – a scientist, a philosopher and a classicist – always came through with insight and encouragement. Emily Elizabeth Fleming and Annamarie Bindenagel read the manuscript and gave me useful ideas; I especially appreciated Emily Elizabeth's astute judgments regarding photographs. A very special thank you to Sharon Muller and Judith Cohen at the United States Holocaust Memorial Museum Photo Archives, whose assistance was indispensable. They and the members of their staff were generous, patient and brilliantly creative in helping locate photographs for the original edition and this new edition. Thanks also to Marc Hardiejowski for advice on arranging images. I am grateful to Nicole and Karly Bergen for proofreading; to Nicole Thompson, who helped prepare the manuscript for press; and to Janine Rivière for the updated index. Notre Dame's Institute for Scholarship in the Liberal Arts and the Chancellor Rose and Ray Wolfe Chair in Holocaust Studies at the University of Toronto generously funded summer assistantships for the project. Steve Wrinn and subsequently Mary Carpenter and Erin McKindley at Rowman & Littlefield Publishing Group were supportive and Donald Critchlow offered editorial guidance. At Tempus, Jonathan Reeve has been persistent, encouraging and resourceful, as have Robin Harries and Simon Hamlet. Many thanks to them all.

Without my two scholarly mentors, Annelise L. Thimme and Gerhard L. Weinberg, I would never have come to work in this field in the first place. They have influenced me in ways that continue to surprise me and I am deeply grateful to them both. Of course, all errors and shortcomings in the book are my own responsibility.

1

Preconditions: Antisemitism, Racism and Common Prejudices in Early Twentieth-Century Europe

In order for a house to burn down, three things are required. The timber must be dry and combustible; there needs to be a spark that ignites it; and external conditions have to be favourable – not too damp, perhaps some wind. Hitler's Nazi regime in Germany provided the spark that set off the destruction we now call the Holocaust and the Second World War (1939–1945) created a setting conducive to brutality. However, without certain preconditions – the dry timber – mass murder on such a scale would not have been possible. People had to be prepared to accept the identification of other members of their society as enemies. In other words, a substantial part of the population had to be ready to consider it desirable, acceptable, or at least unavoidable, that certain other people would be isolated, persecuted and killed.

Hitler and his National Socialist German Workers' Party, now commonly referred to as the Nazis, came to power in Germany in 1933 and remained in place until the military defeat of Germany in 1945. More than half a century later, Nazism has become synonymous with the mass murder of millions of innocent people: Jews, above all, and also handicapped people, Gypsies, political opponents and others.

In their choices of target groups the Nazis reflected and built on prejudices that were familiar in many parts of Europe. Hitler and the Nazis did not invent antisemitism – hatred of Jews – nor were they the first to attack Sinti and Roma (Gypsies) or people considered handicapped. Their hostilities toward Europeans of African descent, Slavic people, Jehovah's Witnesses and homo-sexuals were not new either. The Nazis were extremists in the lengths to which they went in their assaults, but they were quite typical in whom they attacked.

Long-standing hatred alone did not cause the Holocaust. The world is full of old prejudices; only rarely do they erupt in genocide. Leadership, political will and manipulation of popular sentiments are needed to fan hostility into organised killing. Widespread nega-tive attitudes on their own do not create a holocaust, but they are a necessary condition for mass persecution – that is, the rest of the population must regard certain groups as legitimate targets in order for them to participate in or tolerate open assault. Nazi leaders could not simply have invented a category of enemies – for exam-ple, people between the ages of thirty-seven and forty-two – and then have expected the majority of the population to turn against them. Such a group would have been incompre-hensible to most people. The identities of those targeted for destruction during the Second World War were no coincidence; these people were already victims of prejudice.

This chapter surveys some of the widespread attitudes toward Jews and other groups in Europe prior to the Nazi rise to power in Germany in 1933. It outlines some ideas already in place in Europe by the early twentieth century that provided the ground in which the Nazi ideology of race and space – 'racial purifica-tion' and territorial expansion – could take root and grow.

The Holocaust originated in Nazi Germany, but it was by no means uniquely German in terms of its perpetrators, victims, bystanders, beneficiaries or heroes. They came from all over Europe and even farther away, swept into the deadly force field of developments with worldwide repercussions. By the same token, many of the ideas and attitudes that fed into the Holocaust had roots and branches outside Germany, particularly elsewhere in Europe. Although much of the discussion in this chapter focuses on Germany, it is important to keep in mind that scholarship, publications, opinions and prejudices flowed freely across national borders throughout the modern era; most Germans of the 1920s and 1930s were more typical than they were atypical for Europeans in their time.

Discussing the Nazi era raises some thorny problems of vocabulary. Should one say 'Nazis' or 'Germans' when referring to the people of Hitler's Germany? Some scholars have argued that using the term 'Nazis' in this general way is misleading. It implies that Hitler's supporters were not themselves Germans and that the 'real Germans' were somehow untouched by Nazism. On the other hand, simply saying 'Germans' suggests that all Germans marched in step behind Hitler. That was not the case either. German Jews were excluded from the Nazi movement by definition – that is, they were not permitted to join the Nazi Party or its affiliates – and the same was generally true of Germans deemed handicapped, Gypsies and other outsiders. Nevertheless, those people too were Germans. Moreover, some Germans also opposed the regime and tried to distance themselves from it. Throughout this book, I try to be as precise as possible in my use of terms, while recognizing the impossibility of avoiding over-generalisation.

A final introductory word of caution: prejudices always reveal more about the people who hold them than they do about those at whom they are directed. You will not learn much useful information about Judaism or Jews by studying antisemitism, but you can learn quite a lot about antisemites, their insecurities and their fears. By the same token, examining the lives of Jews in Europe before the Second World War is important in its own right, but it will not answer the question as to why antisemites hated Jews any more than studying African American history will explain why white supremacists hate black people. Prejudices are habits of thought; they are not reasoned responses to objective realities. The common prejudices described here were based on imaginings about people rather than on who those people really were.

To illustrate this point, it is useful to observe that Nazi prejudices against all of the target groups followed similar patterns. Proponents of Nazi ideas focused their attacks on people who were already suspect in the eyes of many Germans. They then echoed and enlarged familiar hatreds and linked them to current anxieties and concerns. For example, in the 1920s and 1930s, many Germans were distressed by Germany's defeat in the First World War. So, no matter which of their supposed enemies they described – Jews, homosexuals, communists, Jehovah's Witnesses – Nazi propagandists accused them of causing Germany to lose the war. Similarly, many Germans in Hitler's time were worried about decadence, criminality and supposed racial degeneration. Nazi thinkers charged every enemy group with promoting immorality, spreading crime and polluting the bloodstream. Whether they were talking about Slavic people, Gypsies, Jews, Afro-Germans or homosexuals, Nazi propaganda used similar slurs.

Antisemitism

Why begin a discussion of preconditions with the topic of antisemitism? Hatred of Jews was the centre of Nazi ideology. Nazi propagandists labelled all of Germany's supposed enemies as 'Jews' or judaised: they depicted Jews as deformed and criminal and compared them to handicapped people and Gypsies, whom they also described as monstrous and dangerous. Nazi ideologues linked communists, capitalists and liberals with a purported Jewish conspiracy; they described homosexuals, Eastern Europeans, the British and the Americans as nothing but cover groups for alleged Jewish interests. By examining the history of antisemitism and Nazi uses of it, we can begin to get a sense of how other Nazi ideas functioned and built on older traditions.

The term 'anti-Semitism' was coined in the 1870s by a German journalist who wanted to contrast his supposedly scientific hatred of Jews with religious forms of anti-Judaism. As a label, 'anti-Semitism' is misleading, because the adjective 'Semitic' describes a group of related languages, among them Hebrew, Arabic and

Phoenician and the people who speak them. Often you will see the word written with a hyphen – 'anti-Semitism' – a spelling I avoid. Use of the hyphen implies that there was such a thing as 'Semitism', which antisemites opposed. In fact, no one who used the term in the nineteenth century (or since) meant by it anything other than hatred of Jews.

Antipathy toward Jews in Europe dated back much further than the 1800s – as far as the ancient world. Roman authorities worried that Jewish refusal to worship local and imperial gods would jeopardise the security of the state. At times such unease, coupled with political conflicts, turned into open persecution and attacks. In 70 CE the Romans destroyed the Jewish temple in Jerusalem, the focal point of Jewish life up to that time; sixty years later they dispersed the Jews of Palestine, scattering them far from the region that had been their home.

The rise of Christianity added new fuel to anti-Jewish sentiments. Christianity grew out of Judaism – Jesus himself was a Jew, as were the apostles and important figures such as Paul of Tarsus. Nevertheless, early Christians tried to separate themselves from other Jews, both to win followers from the Gentile (non-Jewish) world and to gain favour with Roman imperial authorities. Some early Christians also stressed their loyalty to the state by pointing out that the Kingdom of God was not of this earth and therefore did not compete with Rome. Such efforts paid off: in less than four hundred years, Christianity went from being a persecuted branch of Judaism to being the dominant religion of the Roman Empire. It is significant that some early Christian accounts blamed Jews for Jesus' death even though crucifixion was a specifically Roman form of punishment commonly practiced during Jesus' time. The version of events that had Jewish mobs demanding Jesus' death while the Roman governor Pontius Pilate washed his hands allowed later Christians to emphasise their difference from Judaism and downplay the hostility that Roman authorities had shown toward Christianity in its early stages. All of the false accusations against Jews associated with the Roman imperial period – that Jews were traitors and conspirators, that they killed Christ – remained familiar in Europe into the twentieth century.

In many ways the Middle Ages – from around the ninth to the sixteenth centuries – were difficult times for Jews in Europe. Often crusades against Muslims and Christian heretics started or ended with violent attacks on Jews. Such attacks, later known as 'pogroms', a word that derived from Russian, were also common responses to outbreaks of plague or other disasters. For example, in many parts of Europe, the Black Death of 1348 sparked brutal pogroms, as Christians blamed Jews for somehow causing the epidemic of bubonic plague. Mobilised by such accusations, Christian mobs – sometimes spontaneously, sometimes urged on by state and church leaders – attacked Jewish homes and communities, plundering, destroying and killing. The scale of pogroms varied wildly, from brief local incidents to weeklong massacres that swept through entire regions. In their wake they left among Christians a habit of using Jews as scapegoats and among Jews, a sense of vulnerability and a repertoire of defences, such as paying protection money, sticking together and keeping a low profile.

In addition to sporadic waves of violence, Jews faced harassment and restrictions of various kinds from governments across Europe. In some cases, regulations forced Jews to live in certain areas or ghettos; sometimes Jews were required to wear identifying badges; elsewhere, state authorities drove Jews out of their territories altogether. In 1492, for example, King Ferdinand and Queen Isabella of Spain expelled all Jews and Muslims from Spanish soil except those who agreed to convert to Christianity. Throughout the Middle Ages, Jews everywhere in Europe faced limitations on the occupations in which they could engage as well as the kinds of property and titles they could hold.

Some church leaders and secular rulers tried to convince or coerce Jews to abandon their religion and convert to Christianity. But even conversion did not necessarily solve the problems of intolerance. Converts from Judaism to Christianity in sixteenth-century Spain found that they were still viewed with deep suspicion and regarded as somehow tainted by supposed 'Jewish blood'. Even the notion of Jewishness as a 'race' was not entirely original to the Nazis.

The Protestant Reformation did not improve the lot of European Jews. At first its leader, the German monk Martin Luther, hoped that his break with what he considered the corrupted Church of Rome would inspire mass conversions of Jews to Christianity. When the anticipated wave of baptisms did not occur, Luther turned against the Jews, whom he derided as stubborn and hard necked. In 1542 he wrote a pamphlet called *Against the Jews and Their Lies*. That tract, with its vicious characterization of Jews as parasites and its calls to 'set their synagogues and schools on fire', would later be widely quoted in Hitler's Germany. Other medieval images – the association of Jews with the devil, charges that Jews used the blood of Christian children for ritual purposes – also survived into the modern era. Even those Nazi leaders who hated Christianity and mocked it for its historical ties to Judaism found it useful to invoke these powerful, traditional notions about Jews. In other words, Nazi antisemitism was different from older religious forms of anti-Judaism, but its proponents still drew on those traditional hostilities. Ancient associations of Jews with deadly evil gave modern antisemitism a virulence that set it apart from other prejudices.

In the seventeenth, eighteenth and nineteenth centuries, European society became more secular, but bigotry toward Jews did not disappear. Instead, social, economic and political prejudices grew alongside and sometimes in place of older religious resentments. Enlightenment thinkers in eighteenth-century Europe favoured religious toleration and mocked the rigidity of institutionalised Christianity. But even such a self-consciously progressive thinker as the French writer Voltaire labelled Jews with contempt as 'vagrants, robbers, slaves, or seditious'. In the nineteenth century, Napoleon and other rulers introduced legislation to repeal old restrictions on Jews in Europe. This process is usually referred to as the emancipation of the Jews. Nevertheless, formal and informal limitations often remained in place.

Like every minority group striving to better its position while hampered by obstructions, European Jews ended up over-represented in some occupations and under-represented in others. Hostile non-Jews made much of the fact that in Germany by

around 1900, the field of journalism included a higher percentage of Jews than did the population as a whole. However, they
never mentioned the fact that Jews were almost completely
excluded from the higher ranks of the government bureaucracy
and the military. By the late 1800s, political parties that openly
championed antisemitism had sprung up in various parts of
Europe. Vienna's popular antisemitic mayor Karl Lueger would
make a deep impression on the young Adolf Hitler. In particular Hitler noticed how Lueger played on widespread anti-Jewish
sentiments to whip up enthusiasm in the crowds he addressed
and to boost his own support.

Modern antisemites claimed that their views were scientific,
based on the biological 'facts' of blood and race. In reality hatred
of Jews was no more scientific than were European attitudes
of superiority toward Africans, Asians or native peoples in the
Americas. Moreover the notion of 'Jewishness' as a race was
invented, as were the concepts of 'blackness', 'whiteness' and
'Orientalism' that became so central to how many Europeans and
North Americans viewed the world. Still, Social Darwinist ideas
about struggle between rival 'races' and survival of the strongest
provided fertile ground, not only for Nazi notions about Jews
but for an entire, interlocking system of prejudices against people
deemed inferior. Sexual anxieties and sexualised stereotypes fed
the racist mindset in powerful, pernicious ways. Notions about
Jewish and black men as sexual predators insatiable in their lust
for white women coexisted with charges that Jews and men of
colour were feminised weaklings incapable of soldierly honour.
In Medieval Europe, religion had served to legitimate and justify
hatreds. In the modern era science and pseudoscience played a
comparable role.

The Diversity of Jewish Life in Europe

Never more than a small minority – at most one or two per
cent of the entire population of Europe – Jews existed alongside Christians for centuries. Judaism was and is a religion and a

living community. Despite pogroms, massacres and expulsions, Jews survived in Europe. They thrived as individuals and as a community in different places at different times – in Spain before the Inquisition, later in the Netherlands, at times in Poland and Germany. Ever since ancient times the Jewish contribution to European life has been enormous.

European Jews, like European Christians, were and are a diverse group. By the early twentieth century many were highly assimilated; neither from appearance, habits of daily life, nor language could they be distinguished from their Gentile French, German, Italian, Polish, Greek or other neighbours. Some attended religious services several times a year; others, never. Some maintained a strong sense of Jewish identity; others, very little or none at all. Many Jews were intermarried with Christians; often Jews in intermarriages converted to Christianity and usually they raised their children as Christians. Karl Marx, the founder of communism, is frequently described as a Jew, but in fact he was the son of a couple who converted from Judaism to Christianity. Nazi law would not recognise such conversions but considered converts to Christianity, as well as the children and in some cases grandchildren of such converts, to be Jews.

In Europe in the early 1900s there were also more visible kinds of Jews. In some parts of Eastern Europe many Jews lived in small communities known as *shtetls*. Forced by the Russian tsars to remain in an area in the west of the Russian empire called the Pale of Settlement, these Jews developed a lifestyle of their own based on shared religious observance, the Yiddish language, a diet following *kashrut* – the Jewish dietary laws – and predominance of certain occupations. For example, many were small traders and craftspeople. Those lines of work did not require them to own land, something from which they were restricted and in some places prohibited altogether.

Jews in southern and south-eastern Europe tended to come from what is called the Sephardic tradition and to speak a language called Ladino, rather than the Yiddish of the Ashkenazic Jews of northern and central Europe. By the twentieth century, there were many strands of European Judaism. Some Jews were

strictly Orthodox, so that their mode of dress, adherence to dietary laws and other religious observances set them apart from the
Gentiles around them. Others were Reform, part of a branch of
Judaism that emerged out of early nineteenth-century Germany
and emphasised adapting rituals and practices for modern times.
Some Jews embraced the tradition of Hasidism, a movement that
started in Poland and emphasised joyous mysticism; others were
more austere. Some dressed distinctively, with the adult men
wearing beards and earlocks; other Jewish men might be distin-
guishable only by the physical marking of circumcision.

In short, there were wealthy Jews in Europe around 1930
as well as middle class and very poor Jews. There were Jewish
bankers and Jewish shopkeepers, Jewish doctors, nurses, actors,
professors, soldiers, typists, peddlers, factory owners, factory
workers, kindergarten teachers, conservatives, liberals, nationalists, feminists, anarchists and communists. Nazi propaganda
would create the category of 'the Jew', a composite based on
myths and stereotypes. Nazi persecution then reified that gross
generalisation, as violence and destruction rendered obsolete distinctions of age, sex, class and national origin among Jews, all of
whom where slated for annihilation. Before the Holocaust there
was no such thing as 'the Jew', only Jews who often differed as
much and in many cases much more, from one another than
they did from the Christians around them.

Perhaps the best way to capture the diversity of Jewish life is to
look at several individuals who experienced the assault of Nazism
as young people in Europe. One example comes from a memoir
by Peter Gay called *My German Question*. Gay was born in Berlin
in 1923 to a middle-class family named Fröhlich, which means
'happy' in German. (After moving to the United States, the name
would be changed to the English translation 'Gay'.) Peter's father
bought and sold glassware; his mother worked part-time as a clerk
in her sister's sewing notions store. Committed atheists, Fröhlich's
parents officially left the Jewish community. They had their son
circumcised but showed few other signs of Jewish identity.

Fröhlich's father fought in the First World War and was
wounded and decorated. An avid fan of all kinds of sports,

Fröhlich Sr. had many close friends who were not Jewish. Young Peter was one of a handful of Jewish boys at his school; he does not remember ever being ridiculed or harassed. He and his family considered themselves thoroughly German. Gay and his parents managed to get out of Germany in 1939 before the Second World War began. Gay eventually moved to the United States, where he became an important historian of modern Europe and a professor at Yale University.

As a young girl in Hungary, Aranka Siegal lived a rather different Jewish life in Europe before the Holocaust. She describes it in her book, *Upon the Head of the Goat*. Siegal, whose name at the time was Piri Davidowitz, was an observant Jew like her parents and her four sisters. Born in 1931, she went to a public school, where her friends included Catholic, Protestant and Russian Orthodox as well as Jewish children. Some of her fondest childhood memories are of the months she spent each summer on her grandmother's farm. It was from her grandmother that Piri learned the most about Judaism. With her grandmother she lit the Sabbath candles, recited the blessing for the new year on Rosh Hashanah and prepared traditional foods.

Siegal's grandmother also taught her about Jewish history. Old enough to have vivid memories of pogroms in Ukraine and Hungary in the 1910s and 1920s, she told her granddaughter how Christians had often used Jews as scapegoats in times of trouble. She also warned the little girl about a 'madman' called Hitler, who was terrorising Jews in Germany and Poland. Aranka Siegal's grandmother was right to be afraid. Almost everyone in the family would be killed in the Holocaust. Miraculously Piri and one sister survived being sent to the Nazi killing centre of Auschwitz. After some time in Sweden, Aranka Siegal moved to New York. She speaks to many audiences every year about her experiences during and after the Second World War.

A third, very different Jewish life is that of Jack Pomerantz, which is recorded in his memoir *Run East*. A native of Radzyn, a small town near Lublin in Poland, Pomerantz was born in 1918 during a pogrom, a violent attack on the Jewish community by their Christian neighbours. His mother was hiding in a barn when she

gave birth to Yankel, one of eight children. (He would later angli-
cise his first name to 'Jack'.) Yankel's father was a peddler; he wore
a long beard, dark clothing and often a prayer shawl. Although the
family was desperately poor, Yankel's mother still always tried to
have a special meal for *Shabbat*, the best day of the week. Like all
married Orthodox women she wore a wig. For the Jewish holidays most of the women in the *shtetl* made wonderful food, but
sometimes Pomerantz's mother had nothing to cook. She would
boil rags just to steam up the windows of their shack and create the
impression that they too were preparing a feast.

Pomerantz spoke Yiddish at home and was very conscious of
himself as a Jew. His town was about half Jews and half Polish
Christians and there was considerable tension between the
two groups. As a boy Yankel heard people say they hated Jews
because they 'killed Christ'. Once, in a fight, a Polish Catholic
boy cut Yankel's cheek with a knife, right through into his mouth.
Pomerantz was no stranger to antisemitism.

Like Peter Gay and Aranka Siegal, Jack Pomerantz survived
the war and went to the United States, where he worked as a
builder and contractor in New Jersey. He died a few years after
publishing his memoir. Gay, Siegal and Pomerantz are only three
of millions of examples of the immense range of living situations
experienced by European Jews before the Holocaust.

Eugenics and Attitudes Toward People Deemed Handicapped

When one considers the long history of anti-Jewish attitudes
and actions in Europe and the dramatic, destructive ways that
Nazi antisemitism disrupted the lives of people like Peter Gay,
Aranka Siegal and Jack Pomerantz, one might conclude that
Jews must have been the first targets for systematic murder in
Hitler's Germany. That, however, was not the case. Instead, the
first category of people slated for mass killing were individuals deemed handicapped. Perhaps Nazi leaders believed they
would encounter less opposition to attacks on that segment of

the population; perhaps they thought it would be easier to keep such a programme secret. Certainly initiatives came from within the scientific and medical communities, whose members played key roles in carrying out the killings. These are all matters open to research and discussion. What is clear is that attitudes toward people with disabilities in Europe developed in a manner rather different from what we have seen with regard to antisemitism. Nevertheless, here too Nazi ideology and practice built on existing prejudices in ways that were extreme but not unique.

It is hard to know exactly how the majority of the population regarded people with mental and physical handicaps in Medieval and Early Modern Europe. Christianity, like Judaism, out of which it grew, taught compassion for the afflicted and church as well as state law provided some protections for those who could not protect themselves. But there is also evidence, including many literary accounts, that the able-bodied often ridiculed, took advantage of and abused those weaker than they were. Nevertheless it seems that in various ways society found places for those with mental and physical disabilities. The village idiot, court dwarfs, fools, beggars and cripples were all familiar characters. They showed that, although life might not always be fair or good to those with handicaps, at least everyone recognised their existence and assumed that they, like the poor, were a permanent part of society.

By the nineteenth century the assumption that the handicapped would always be present had begun to change, at least for many people in Europe and elsewhere. Scientific and medical advances together with Social Darwinist notions led to the idea that society could be engineered so that only the supposedly healthiest elements would reproduce. This way of thinking and the pseudoscience that grew up around it is often referred to as eugenics.

Eugenics became popular all over Europe and North America in the early twentieth century. Many places introduced programmes to sterilise people considered undesirable. Even though the proponents of such plans claimed to be objective and scientific, they tended to identify people already viewed as outsiders as the least desirable 'breeding stock' and to label them 'feeble-minded' or 'degenerate'. For example, eugenics programmes in some parts of the United States disproportionately targeted African Americans; elsewhere in North America native people were prime subjects. Europeans often focused on Gypsies and other itinerant people and everywhere poor people came in for the closest scrutiny. In the wake of the First World War, many political leaders, interested in boosting the size and health of their populations – and their armies – promoted eugenics programmes. Meanwhile, perennial problems such as crime seemed solvable to people who believed that criminal tendencies were inherited and that their carriers could be identified by physical characteristics. Even many scientists, medical experts and social workers who considered themselves progressive reformers supported programmes to attempt to 'raise' the quality of the population by 'selective breeding' with or without the consent of those involved. For example, in the 1910s and 1920s the British sex reformer Marie Stopes helped thousands of men and women learn about birth control and gain access to necessary technologies and supplies. One of Stopes's arguments in support of legalising birth control was the assumed need to curb the reproduction of people considered burdens on society. When a deaf man wrote to ask Dr Stopes a question about reproductive rights she fired back an angry letter demanding to know why someone like him would even consider having children. Of course such efforts to 'improve' humanity, even at the expense of those considered inferior, were different from attempts to build a Nazi-style 'master race' that would rule the world. Still, by the 1920s, as notions about building a 'better race' entered the mainstream, they served to legitimate more extreme schemes of exclusion, manipulation and domination.

A look at one influential publication illustrates the radicalisation of eugenic ideas after the First World War. In 1920 Karl Binding, former president of Germany's highest court and Alfred Hoche, a German professor of psychiatry, wrote *Permission for the Destruction of Worthless Life, Its Extent and Form*. Binding and Hoche believed that the First World War had produced a marked increase in the number of 'mental defectives'. As a result, they said, Germany was weighed down with people they called 'living burdens'. They expressed shock at the tremendous care that was devoted to inmates of mental hospitals at a time when the country had lost so many young men in war. In their view the mentally ill were 'completely worthless creatures'.

Binding and Hoche did not explicitly say that people who wanted to live should be killed, but their ideas still had radical implications. According to them, every human being's worth could be measured in terms of contribution to the community and the nation. Some people, they suggested, did not really have any value. Although Binding and Hoche's book was controversial, the mentality it expressed was widely shared in Europe and North America in the decades before the Second World War. Given this background, it is perhaps no surprise that Hitler's regime would begin its programme of mass murder with attacks on people deemed mentally or physically disabled.

Prejudices Toward Sinti and Roma (Gypsies)

Hitler and his followers intended to wipe out the Gypsies of Europe, whom they associated with criminality and degeneracy. The Jews, people deemed handicapped and the Gypsies were the groups toward which the Nazis most consistently followed a policy of annihilation that included murdering even babies and old people. Anti-Gypsyism, like antisemitism, was an old, familiar hatred in Europe, so with regard to the Gypsies too, Nazi Germany could draw on long-standing prejudices.

The origins of the European Roma remain somewhat contested, but many scholars agree that they moved into Europe from India during the Middle Ages. The English word 'Gypsy', often applied as a pejorative term of insult, developed from the mistaken idea that the people in question originated in Egypt. The German term for Gypsies is *Zigeuner*, but it too has taken on negative connotations, so that many people now try to avoid using that label. Instead they prefer to speak of 'Roma', 'Rom people', or 'Roma and Sinti'. The Sinti are a group of Gypsies primarily based in German-speaking Europe. It is hard to pin down whether Roma/Gypsies are a racial, ethnic or social group, that is, whether they are defined by family relationships with one another, language and traditions, or lifestyle. Perhaps that difficulty itself is a useful reminder of how arbitrary such categories are. It is probably most useful to think of Gypsies as a group that includes elements of all those criteria.

When Gypsies first arrived in Medieval Europe, they encountered hospitality from some European courts. Soon, however, they became targets of hostility from Europeans who were suspicious of these newcomers. Whether from habit or because of coercion, many Gypsies were itinerant and their mobile lifestyle further roused the antagonism of others. The rest of European society labelled them thieves and tricksters who used their musical abilities and physical charms to lure the unsuspecting to their ruin.

A number of common attitudes toward Roma in the medieval period echoed anti-Jewish notions. Non-Jewish Europeans falsely accused Jews of stealing Christian children in order to use their blood; likewise non-Gypsies charged Gypsies with kidnapping children for evil purposes. Like Jews, Gypsies were easy scapegoats in times of disaster, such as plague or earthquakes. Their opponents claimed that they poisoned the wells, practised magic and consorted with the devil. European folklore did not accuse Gypsies of killing Jesus, but because the Roma were known for their skills as metalworkers, it charged them with forging the nails that pierced his flesh.

According to European myths, Gypsies, like Jews, had been condemned by God to wander the earth without ever finding a homeland. One popular version of events held that while still in Egypt, the Gypsies had tried to prevent Joseph, Mary and the baby Jesus from gaining refuge from King Herod, and God punished them with eternal homelessness. Probably by the twentieth century few Europeans would have accepted such myths as the literal truth. Nor would most non-Gypsies have realised that in some parts of south-eastern Europe, Roma had been enslaved until the mid–nineteenth century. Nevertheless what remained was a widespread sense that Roma were somehow evil outsiders who did not merit the respect or protection awarded to other members of society.

Nineteenth- and twentieth-century notions about heredity and criminality also contributed to attacks on the Roma in Europe. If criminality was inherited and Gypsies were criminals, 'experts' reasoned, then one could fight crime by preventing Gypsies from having children. Social scientists, medical specialists and criminologists tended to regard Roma as if they were some kind of disease, as evident in references to the 'Gypsy plague'. Public authorities introduced all kinds of restrictions on where Gypsies could reside and what activities were permitted them and police all over Europe were especially diligent when it came to enforcing such laws and 'controlling' Gypsies. Years before Hitler came to power in Germany Roma in that country were required to carry photo identification cards and to register themselves with local police. France, Hungary, Romania and other European countries had anti-Gypsy measures of their own.

It is even harder to make meaningful generalisations about the lives of people considered disabled and the Gypsies in Europe prior to the Second World War than it is about Jews. There is certainly much less published about members of these two outsider groups. Many disabled people were not in a position to leave written records. For that matter, many probably did not think of themselves as members of a special group whose particular experiences should be preserved. Romany tradition, it seems, has always been more connected to the present than the past, more oral than written, and centuries of persecution produced a tendency to be secretive with people outside the immediate group.

Even something that seems as obvious as the numbers of people in these categories cannot be pinned down with any precision. Who was considered handicapped, mentally or physically, could vary enormously from place to place and time to time. For their part, Gypsies were skilled at evading such formalities as government censuses. Experience with various bureaucracies had taught them that they had little to gain and much to lose by being counted. The European officials who introduced restrictions on Gypsies and the police who enforced them were often unclear about who exactly was a Gypsy. Non-Gypsies tended to assume they could recognise Gypsies by their appearance: many Roma had darker hair, skin and eyes than most people in Northern, Western and Eastern Europe, but by no means were there always physical markers. In some areas Gypsies were associated with certain trades, such as working with metal or leather. Most Europeans thought all Gypsies were wanderers who made a living from fortune-telling, music, dancing and theft. In fact, not all Roma were itinerant and many held regular jobs, for example, as civil servants. Nor were all wandering people in Europe Gypsies in any sense of the word. Sometimes, however, police and other authorities treated people who were not ethnic Sinti or Roma at all as if they were Gypsies, because they fit the stereotype of homeless, petty thieves.

Just as Nazi ideologues invented the category of 'the Jew', as if all Jews were somehow the same, they created the stereotypical, deformed 'life unworthy of living' and the monolithic 'Gypsy', In actuality people deemed handicapped represented the full range of European society: they were Christians, Jews, Gypsies, women, men, children, rich, poor, beautiful, dependent, self-reliant and anything else you might add. As for Sinti and Roma, they too varied considerably from one another in terms of religion, lifestyle, language, appearance, name and occupation. Many were Christians; some intermarried with non-Gypsies. Some spoke a language known as Romani, which linguists believe is linked to languages on the Indian subcontinent; others spoke the languages of the people around them. As would be the case with European Jews, the shared experience of Nazi persecution created a degree of commonality among Gypsies that would not have existed otherwise.

Imperialism and Racism

European imperialism, especially its nineteenth-century forms, was also indirectly part of the preconditions to the Holocaust.

Through the experience of ruling over subject peoples in their overseas colonies and other conquered territories, Europeans gained habits of behaviour and thought that lent themselves to developing hierarchies among peoples within Europe. From their experiences in Africa, Asia and elsewhere, Europeans learned methods and technologies for oppressing and enslaving large groups of people. Ways of thinking about subject peoples whom Europeans considered inferior to themselves were also transferred onto targets of abuse within Europe, such as Jews. The notion that humanity was divided into races that struggled with one another for survival and dominance was in large part a product of the colonial experience.

Over the course of the nineteenth century, Europeans divided almost the entire continent of Africa among themselves. The British and French had large colonial holdings in Africa, as did the Portuguese, Belgians, Italians and Germans. These and other European powers already dominated vast territories around the world. In Asia, the British controlled India, for example, and the Russians, Central Asia. The Dutch held Indonesia and various Europeans had colonies in the Pacific, the Caribbean and the Americas. The rule of law and protections of citizens' rights that had been introduced in many European jurisdictions by the late 1800s usually did not apply in the colonies, so missionaries, entrepreneurs, administrators and military men often had very few limits on their behaviour once they were overseas. They could and did use flogging, torture, and even death for offences committed by native peoples that could never have been punished so severely at home. In the Belgian Congo, for example, European rubber magnates sometimes ordered that the hands be cut off of Africans whose production did not meet certain quotas.

Europeans' technological and military advantage enabled them to carry out such acts more or less with impunity. A massacre known as the Battle of Omdurman provides a graphic illustration. In 1898, a small group of British military on an expedition south of Egypt encountered resistance from local Sudanese tribesmen. The British, armed with machine guns, opened fire. The Sudanese, mounted on horseback and equipped with swords and

other weapons for hand-to-hand combat, rode wave after wave
into the barrage. The British killed an estimated 11,000 Sudanese
and lost only twenty-eight of their own men. Such events must
have contributed to a sense among many Europeans that human
life – at least the lives of people they considered inferior – was
extremely cheap. Notions of racial superiority were by no means
unique to Germany.

Nevertheless, Germans did engage in their own atrocities
overseas during the imperial era. Since 1883, Germany had a
protectorate over Southwest Africa, the modern-day country of
Namibia. By 1904 white pressure on native lands led to a revolt
of the largest tribe in the area, the cattle-herding Herero. A
smaller group called the Nama joined the rebellion. It took some
14,000 German soldiers three years to crush these uprisings. By
1907, fifteen hundred German men had died in the Southwest
African conflict, half of them from illness.

But the Herero and Nama suffered far more. In what developed into an act of genocide, the Germans slaughtered more
than 50,000 Herero and 10,000 Nama. They shot many, especially adult men; hunted women, children and old people into
the desert, where they died of thirst and starvation; and forced
others into concentration camps, where disease, inadequate
food and horrendous conditions took a terrible toll. In the end,
between seventy-five and eighty per cent of all Hereros died;
among the Nama the death rate was over forty-five per cent.
This carnage was not ordered by German authorities in Berlin
but evolved out of specific military goals: a demand for 'total victory' and a drive to annihilate the enemy in order to prevent any
possibility of resurgence. German accusations that the Africans
were irregular combatants who shot from concealed positions,
used women and children as warriors and mutilated the bodies of
their victims served to legitimate ruthless acts of 'retaliation' that
treated soldiers and civilians with equal brutality. Such practices
left a violent legacy that would be evident in both the First and
the Second World Wars.

Many Nazi ideas about what a race was grew out of ways
of thinking about people of colour that were common among

white Europeans and Americans in the early twentieth century. An obvious illustration of some of these ideas comes from Germany in the 1920s. After the First World War, the French occupied the Rhineland, an area in the western part of defeated Germany. The occupation forces included some indigenous troops drawn from France's overseas territories in Africa and Asia. Many Germans were horrified at the presence of these men of colour on German soil.

Stereotypes about African men as sexual predators on white women were widespread in Europe, and German racists and nationalists played on such fears and fantasies to stir up resentments against the French occupation. Judging from the hysteria in the German press in the early 1920s, one might have thought that hordes of Africans were raping and pillaging all over Germany. In fact there were at most about 5,000 black men stationed in the Rhineland at any given time between 1919 and 1923 and perhaps another 20,000 non-white forces. Among these men of colour were Senegalese and a small number of Sudanese; Frenchmen, Arabs and Berbers from Morocco; Malagasies from Madagascar; Annamese from Indochina and others. They seem to have gotten into no more trouble than any other French units. Nevertheless, Nazi propagandists would return to this topic in the 1930s in their own efforts to whip up German anxieties about supposed racial defilement.

Some of the French African troops in Germany in the 1920s became involved with German women and in some cases those liaisons produced children. These few biracial individuals – who in 1924 may have numbered only seventy-eight – also attracted a great deal of attention. Fanatical German nationalists and racists of various kinds referred to these people as the 'Rhineland bastards'. Throughout the 1920s some Germans claimed that the existence of those biracial individuals proved there was a vast conspiracy – controlled by the French, the Jews, or simply by the unnamed enemies of Germany – to befoul German blood and weaken the German nation. It is no surprise that once in power, Hitler and his Nazi regime took steps against Germans of African descent, too.

Anti-Slavic Attitudes in Germany

Hindsight, they say, is twenty-twenty. Looking back on European history more than half a century after the Second World War, it is clear that certain widespread German attitudes toward Eastern Europeans, especially the Slavic peoples – Poles, Russians, Ukrainians, Czechs, Serbs and others – were also a pre-condition for the atrocities of the Second World War.

The origins of these negative ideas are hard to identify. Certainly nineteenth-century German nationalists commonly contrasted what they considered their culture's unique achievements with the supposed primitivism and barbarism of their neighbours to the east. Even the German language included slurs against Slavs. For example, a common German expression for a chaotic situation was a 'Polish economy'. In general many twentieth-century Germans considered Slavic people to be backward, uneducated, slovenly, brutish and childlike. The fact that Eastern European industrialisation lagged behind that of the west seemed to confirm those stereotypes for many Germans who conveniently ignored the artistic, cultural and scientific achievements of their eastern neighbours.

Developments in the early twentieth century added new dimensions to German notions of superiority over the Slavs. After the First World War, for the first time since the late 1700s, an independent Polish nation was established. Until the war, territories in which many Polish people lived had been ruled by the German, Austro-Hungarian and Russian empires. With the defeat of Germany and the collapse of the old Habsburg Empire in Austria-Hungary in 1918, the way was cleared for return of an independent Polish state. Many Germans resented this new neighbour and the loss of territories formerly under German control to Polish rule.

Instead of disbanding at the end of the First World War, some German soldiers reformed themselves into units called the *Freikorps* (Free Corps) to fight communists and others they considered Germany's enemies. *Freikorps* activities included attacks on Poles both inside Germany and across the border in Poland.

During the decades before Hitler came to power, Germans inside Germany also encouraged the ethnic Germans who lived in Poland to provoke clashes with Polish authorities.

A similar situation existed with the German minority who lived in Czechoslovakia. Like Poland, Czechoslovakia was a newly created state after the First World War. Politically and economically weak, it was no match for its powerful German neighbour. Some members of Czechoslovakia's German-speaking population were happy enough to live in a country where they were far fewer in number than Czechs and Slovaks, but others resented their minority status. Here too Nazi agitators in the 1930s would find fertile ground for their notions of German superiority and their plans to rearrange the borders of Europe in Germany's favour.

Developments in Russia also added a new dimension to German suspicion of Slavs. Germany won some of its most dramatic victories during the First World War against Russia. In fact, the Russian military effort collapsed in 1917 and as soon as Lenin and the Bolsheviks had claimed control of the country, they sued for peace with Germany. It was all the more humiliating for the Germans a few months later in 1918, when, still flushed with their successes in the east, they had to concede defeat in the west and abandon all claims to the territories they had won from Russia.

The Russian Revolution of 1917 and the civil war that followed were extremely violent. Accounts of the bloodshed reached Germany and, at least for some, seemed to add more reasons to fear and hate Russians. After the First World War, many Germans believed they were surrounded by enemies who conspired for Germany's destruction. The fact that communist ideology called for world revolution and the existence of a very visible Communist Party in Germany itself after 1918 seemed proof that such a conspiracy was indeed underway.

Antisemitic Germans often linked their fear of the Soviet Union with their hatred of Jews. They pointed to some prominent communists who were Jews or had Jewish names as evidence that Jews were somehow responsible for the Russian Revolution. Of course there were some Jewish communists,

but there were also many non-Jewish communists as well as
many anti-communist Jews. Sometimes antisemites imagined
or invented Jewish identities for powerful individuals, such as
Lenin, who was often described as Jewish but in fact came from a
Russian Orthodox family. This tangled web of prejudices toward
Slavs, communists and Jews would emerge in a more massive
and violent but still recognisable form in Hitler's Germany.

Common Prejudices toward So-called Asocials, Homosexuals, Jehovah's Witnesses and Freemasons

Historians often fail to mention some of the additional groups
persecuted by the Nazi regime. In some cases, such as the Jehovah's
Witnesses and Freemasons, their relatively small numbers make
them easy for outsiders to forget or ignore. In other cases, such as
homosexuals, the persistence of prejudices against them long after
collapse of the Third Reich may have blocked recognition of their
suffering at Nazi hands. As for people who came under the vague
label of 'asocial', they have been criticised and attacked so often
that their victimisation is sometimes almost taken for granted.
Study of the Nazi era, however, demonstrates that assaults on such
people also grew out of a particular ideology.

Nazi officials created a category called 'asocials' into which
they put all kinds of people they considered problematic: Gypsies,
the homeless, criminals deemed incurable, people with certain
mental disorders, or those accused of sexual perversions. One did
not have to be a Nazi in twentieth-century Europe to be afraid of
'asocials'. Explosive population growth in the nineteenth century
and rapid urbanisation in many parts of Europe in the twentieth
century contributed to a perception among many people that the
world was becoming a more dangerous place, full of bizarre and
threatening people. In the decade before Hitler came to power
in 1933, the Nazi Party in Germany played on such anxieties to
present itself as the force that would 'clean up' a society supposedly degenerating into lunacy. Propagandists, and after 1933, Nazi
policy makers, used the catchall label 'asocial' to stigmatise people

who did not fit the norms and pretensions of their ideal Germany. The unemployed became criminal 'shirkers'; women suspected of sexual improprieties – lesbian relationships, promiscuity, prostitution – became vulnerable to incarceration as 'asocials'.

Pre-Second World War prejudices against homosexuals are hard to summarise, because scholars disagree as to when the category of 'homosexual' even became recognisable in Europe. It seems evident that in the ancient world certain forms of intimacy between people of the same sex did not carry any stigma or preclude sexual relations with members of the opposite sex. By the modern era much of this flexibility was gone, although even the supposedly prudish society of Victorian England showed considerable tolerance for at least some kinds of same-sex intimacies. For example, many people considered sexual experimentation among boys in boarding schools to be a normal part of development; loving relationships between women who often became lifelong companions were not uncommon either.

Nevertheless, by the late nineteenth century many parts of Europe had introduced laws against homosexuality. The German criminal code of 1871 explicitly forbade sexual relations between men. The state prosecuted some cases and public interest in such 'scandals' ran high. For example, it was an enormous sensation when Prince Eulenburg, a member of the inner circle of the German Kaiser Wilhelm II (1888–1918) was charged with homosexual activities and forced from public life. Somewhat paradoxically, an increased openness around the subject of human sexuality in the decades after the First World War served to make homosexual men and women more visible in Europe and to increase the panic some heterosexuals felt about them.

Political changes in Germany after the First World War made it possible for the first time for Berlin to develop a gay scene that included clubs, restaurants and bathhouses frequented by homosexual men. Lesbians, it seems, tended to attract less public attention, although there were also some clubs popular with homosexual women. Laws against sex between men were still on the books in Germany's first democracy, the Weimar Republic, but enforcement was slacker than it had been before the First

World War, especially in the major cities. Many heterosexual Germans, however, disapproved of what they considered their overly permissive society.

Magnus Hirschfeld (1868–1935), a sex reformer and homosexual rights leader in Berlin, made an international reputation for his research in sexology, the new field of studies of sex and sexuality. Hirschfeld regarded homosexuality as the 'third sex', a natural and legitimate variant between masculine and feminine. Homosexuals, he pointed out, looked and behaved normally and should be treated accordingly. For many people the work of researchers and activists such as Hirschfeld offered new possibilities for human freedom. For others it seemed to represent the decadence of a society that had abandoned its traditional values. Hitler's Nazis capitalised on such fears as well; they forced Hirschfeld out of Germany and his research institute was one of the first casualties of their new regime.

As European outsiders, the Jehovah's Witnesses were relative newcomers. Founded in the United States in the late 1870s, the Jehovah's Witnesses, or International Bible Students as they were initially called, were not a large group. By the early 1930s they had about 20,000 members in Germany. A number of beliefs and activities important to Jehovah's Witnesses made them stand out in European society. Because Jehovah's Witnesses considered themselves citizens of Jehovah's Kingdom, as a principle they did not swear allegiance to any earthly government, nor did they serve in any nation's military. The world, they believed, would soon enter a peaceful, thousand-year heavenly rule, but not until it had gone through the battle of Armageddon. In order to teach others and prepare for the end times, Jehovah's Witnesses emphasised door-to-door preaching and distribution of literature, especially their periodical, *The Watchtower*. Such efforts made them publicly visible in large German cities and even some smaller towns, to an extent far out of proportion to their numbers.

Jehovah's Witnesses were not popular with mainstream European society in the early decades of the twentieth century. Members of the established Protestant and Catholic churches labelled the Jehovah's Witnesses a 'sect' or a 'cult' and discounted their interpretations of Christian scripture. Some critics considered the Jehovah's Witnesses' emphasis on the Old Testament suspect and intimated that they might be somehow connected with Judaism. Many people found their proselytising efforts and handing out of tracts to win converts annoying or offensive. Public officials were suspicious because most Jehovah's Witnesses refused to serve in the military or acknowledge state authority if it clashed with their understanding of God's commands. The group's international ties and strong connections to the United States were also suspect to some ardent nationalists in Germany and elsewhere. Jehovah's Witnesses would be easy targets for the Nazis, who made them the first religious group to be outlawed in 1933.

Nazi authorities were also hostile to members of the Freemasons, a European association dating back to the eighteenth century and devoted to the ideals of the Enlightenment: progress, freedom and tolerance. Many well-known Europeans in the age of the French Revolution and afterward belonged to the Freemasons. Mozart was an enthusiast, for example and he incorporated some of the ideas and rituals of the Masons into his opera *The Magic Flute*.

Over the years the Freemasons had developed some secret rites and the air of secrecy that surrounded the group made it seem all the more threatening in the eyes of its critics. Especially in central and Eastern Europe, conservatives and nationalists regarded the Freemasons with suspicion, accusing them of spreading atheism, liberalism and disobedience to authority. People fearful of Freemasonry associated it with the 'decadent' West, especially France, and with French traditions of secularism and anticlericalism. There were rumours of bizarre, illicit sexual rituals, too. Not surprisingly, opponents of the Freemasons also often hinted that the organisation was run by Jews as part of some supposed international Jewish conspiracy. When they attacked the Freemasons too, the Nazis chose a familiar target.

In fact, the number of Freemasons in twentieth-century Germany was always very small and the organisation neither wielded any significant power nor posed a threat to the state. Nevertheless, after 1933, under Nazi rule, men who belonged to the association would face a whole range of discriminatory measures. Some lost their jobs; others ended up in prisons and concentration camps.

The First World War and the Cheapening of Human Life

It is important to conclude this survey of some common attitudes in Europe with reflections on the influence of the First World War (1914–1918). This cataclysmic event had a profound impact on Europe and on the world as a whole. In significant ways it too formed part of the preconditions that set the stage for the Nazi era, the Second World War and the Holocaust.

The connections between the First World War and the horrors of the Nazi era, however, are rather different than is often claimed. It is sometimes charged that the victorious French and their allies imposed such a humiliating peace on the defeated Germans after 1918 that the Germans had no choice but to seek the restoration of national honour at any price. Also common is the claim that the victors in the First World War, in particular the French, forced the Germans to pay crushing reparations, thereby sparking hyperinflation in the 1920s and destroying the German economy. According to this line of argument, the desperate Germans turned to Hitler to rescue them and turned on the Jews as a scapegoat for their suffering.

Both of these common sets of assumptions are deeply flawed. The Germans did lose the war – in fact, it was their military leaders Generals Paul von Hindenburg and Erich Ludendorff in October 1918 who convinced the civilian government that it was necessary to sue for peace. And the Germans did have to accept the terms of the Treaty of Versailles in 1919, without having been part of the negotiations that drew up that accord. Still, the treaty was not exceptionally harsh. In fact, compared to the Treaty of Brest-Litovsk, which the Germans had imposed on the defeated Russians just a year earlier, it might almost be called generous.

In March 1918 the Germans had demanded that the Russians cede about thirty per cent of their territory, including much of their agricultural, industrial and mineral wealth. Under the terms of the Treaty of Versailles the Germans lost about ten per cent of their territory, much of it fairly recently acquired: Alsace and Lorraine, for example, taken in 1870 from France. Contrary to what is often said, the Treaty of Versailles did not blame the Germans for the war itself. Article 231, often referred to as the 'war guilt clause', was in fact not a moral judgment but a general, legal statement stipulating that Germany was responsible for paying for damages in the places outside Germany where most of the fighting had occurred. A similar clause appeared in the treaties with Germany's former allies Austria, Hungary and Turkey.

As for reparations, the Germans paid only a very small amount of the bill originally presented to them, which was repeatedly adjusted downward. The victorious nations, above all the British and the French, had neither the ability to make Germany pay nor the will to risk another war after all the suffering and loss they had experienced between 1914 and 1918. Certainly the payments that were made imposed hardships on the Germans and especially in the aftermath of a devastating war, the notion of reparations itself was psychologically harsh. All of Europe, however, faced terrible economic problems after what had been an extremely costly war and the Germans were by no means alone in their difficulties, although admittedly the knowledge of widespread hardship probably provided little comfort to anyone.

The First World War did not cause Nazism or the Second World War in such direct ways. Its impact was both less obvious and perhaps even more insidious. Although the Germans ended the First World War in better shape economically than many of the actual victors, they cultivated a politics of resentment that promoted a bitter sense of humiliation and poisoned the chances for the new German democracy that was formed in 1918. Refusal to accept the reality of defeat led many Germans to search for people to blame for what they perceived as a betrayal.

That climate of scapegoating, in turn, created a kind of open season on many familiar outsiders. For example, old accusations that Jews had crucified Jesus dovetailed with the popular stab-in-the-back myth that blamed treacherous Jews for Germany's loss of the war. Communists, homosexuals and hostile neighbours were blamed too, especially by German military leaders who falsely claimed that their forces had been undefeated in the field.

The First World War brought tremendous bloodshed and disastrous implications that extended far beyond Germany. An estimated twenty million Europeans died in the war and its aftermath; it wiped out almost an entire generation of young men. Those who made it home again included many wounded, crippled and shell-shocked. In addition to combat, blockades, food shortages and disease took their own toll. From the Russian steppes to Belgium, from England to Serbia, by 1918 there would be scarcely a European family without casualties.

In many cases soldiers, their families and their political leaders emerged from four years of carnage with a deep fear of ever risking another war. In other cases, however, they took away different and more dangerous lessons: the notion that only in warfare could a man prove himself a real man; the conviction that the sense of camaraderie between fighting men was the most perfect form of human communion possible; the belief that sheer force was in the end the strongest thing in the world.

Perhaps most important, the Great War, as it was called at the time, seemed to many Europeans to prove that human life was cheap and expendable. It sparked a cult of violence that flourished in the brutality of the revolution and civil war in Russia, in the paramilitary groups that sprang up around Europe in its wake and in the nihilistic pessimism of so many Europeans in the 1920s and 1930s. The First World War did not lead inevitably to the rise of Nazism, the outbreak of the Second World War or the Holocaust. However, the massive legacy of death and suffering it left behind did constitute one of the preconditions that made possible an unprecedented explosion of violence just two decades later.

2

Leadership and Will: Adolf Hitler, the NSDAP and Nazi Ideology

The previous chapter described some preconditions for developments in the Nazi era: historical antisemitism, eugenics, racism, negative German attitudes toward Slavs and the cheapening of human life after the First World War. If historical prejudices made the timber of European and German society combustible, Hitler lit the match that set the house on fire. This chapter examines the leadership provided by Adolf Hitler and the NSDAP – National Socialist German Workers' Party. Who was Hitler and what was his view of the world? How did he come to power in Germany?

Adolf Hitler

Any discussion of Adolf Hitler (1889–1945) raises both general and specific questions about the role of the individual in making history. Do personalities shape events? Would the Nazi era, or the Second World War, or the Holocaust have occurred without Hitler? Certainly common wisdom assumes that Hitler was central to the shaping of those sets of events. There is no denying that Hitler has caught the popular imagination like no other tyrant – the evidence is ubiquitous. Fascination with Hitler seems to cut across all kinds of lines: nationality, age, gender, level of education.

Is so much interest in Hitler justified? Scholars in fact disagree about just how crucial Hitler was. One group, often referred to as intentionalists because they emphasise Hitler's intentions and consider the Holocaust the result of long-term planning, describes Hitler as the mastermind of mass murder. These scholars point to the consistency of Hitler's views from the early 1920s right down to his final testament in 1945. They emphasise the direct, hands-on way he made the major decisions in Nazi Germany.

Others, sometimes called functionalists because they describe the Holocaust as a function of other developments, especially during the war – something that evolved over time in an improvised way – downplay the role of Hitler. Some functionalists argue that Hitler was actually a 'weak dictator', more a pawn swept along by forces outside his control than the orchestrator of colossal events.

Scholars influenced by Marxism have also tended to pay little attention to Hitler. In their interpretations, Nazism was an extreme form of capitalism that had much more to do with broad, economic structures than with the ideas or actions of any one individual.

These debates about Hitler have moral as well as historical implications. Some people criticise the intentionalist stance because they think it focuses too much on Hitler and lets everyone else off the hook. Others attack the functionalist and Marxist positions for depersonalising the past. They say that functionalists, who describe the Holocaust and other crimes of Nazism as the result of developments or events, draw attention away from the people who in fact made the decisions and took the actions involved in genocide. Still other people reject both the intentionalist and the functionalist positions and argue that we should pay less attention to the perpetrators altogether and concentrate instead on the victims of Nazi crimes.

In this book I proceed on the assumption that in order to understand the causes of Nazi crimes we need to study those who initiated and carried them out. With regard to Hitler I take what might be called a modified intentionalist position. Hitler was an essential factor in Nazism and the genocide it produced. He did not have complete power – even dictators depend on popular support – and a programme as massive as the crimes of Nazism required many accomplices. Nonetheless, Hitler's leadership was essential in setting the agenda. Hitler was no mere opportunist; he operated from a consistent view of the world. He could be flexible, pragmatic and responsive to the situation 'on the ground', but he took the initiative and provided much of the drive and the will that proved crucial in setting Germany on the path to war and genocide. Without Hitler, Nazism, the Second World War and the Holocaust would have taken very different forms, if they had occurred at all.

A Brief Biography

Adolf Hitler was born in 1889 in the small Austrian border town of Braunau am Inn. Not much is known with certainty about Hitler's childhood, because the most detailed source – his auto-biographical book *Mein Kampf* ('My Struggle') – was a work of propaganda intended to depict him as someone who had been marked from his earliest days for greatness. In fact, Hitler's early life seems to have been fairly typical for a middle-class boy in late nineteenth-century Central Europe.

Adolf was the fourth child of an Austrian customs official and his third wife, but the first to live past infancy. The family was comfortable although not wealthy and did well enough to afford a cook and a maid. Adolf's father, Alois, was a strict, authoritarian man with a bad temper, who seems to have taken little interest in his family. For reasons now unknown, Alois changed his last name from Schicklgruber to Hitler, more than a decade before the birth of the son who would make the new name notorious. Alois Hitler died in 1903, when Adolf was still an adolescent.

Adolf's mother, Klara, was much younger than her husband, whom she met when she worked as a maid in his household. According to the account of her doctor, Klara Hitler was a gentle, pious woman devoted to her children, especially her one surviving son. Adolf returned the affection and later wrote in *Mein Kampf*, 'I had honoured my father, but loved my mother'. Other than his mother, Hitler does not seem to have been close to anyone in his family. Even decades after his death the rumour persists that Hitler had 'Jewish blood'. That claim is false. It is true that Hitler did not know the identity of his paternal grandfather, because his father, Alois, was born to an unmarried woman. Alois was baptised into the Roman Catholic Church, as his son Adolf would be, too. In the 1920s and later, rumours circulated that Adolf Hitler's grandmother had been a maid in a Jewish household and had become pregnant by one of her employers' sons. Those allegations were unfounded. In fact there were no Jews in the town where Hitler's grandmother lived, because Jews were prohibited from living in that part of Austria at the time.

What is the significance of this rumour? First of all it shows the extent to which people in Hitler's time became obsessed with issues of blood and race. In Nazi Germany, accusations of so-called Jewish blood were a sure way to discredit someone. It is no surprise that similar rumours circulated about many top Nazis and about other people. The persistence of such a rumour may also tell us something about our own society. What would it actually explain even if the rumour of Hitler's 'Jewish blood' were true? Obviously nothing, just as it would explain nothing if there were any truth to the claims that Hitler was secretly homosexual or that he had only one testicle. (Both of these common allegations, to the best of anyone's knowledge, are false as well.) Such claims reflect a desire to find easy explanations for historical processes that in fact have many complicated causes. Rumours of that kind also reflect a widespread tendency to blame the victims for their misfortunes, as if someone who was 'part Jewish', or 'secretly homosexual', or in some way physically deformed might somehow be expected to initiate programmes to murder Jews, persecute gay men, or kill people deemed handicapped.

An honest understanding of history requires a critical – and self-critical – response to such simplistic notions.

As a child Hitler was a mediocre student. Later, in *Mein Kampf*, he would claim that he led his class in geography and history. That was not the case, although he did better in those subjects than in some others, where he received failing grades. When he was sixteen he dropped out of school. Young Hitler spent the next two and a half years in the Austrian city of Linz, idling, dreaming, drawing and redesigning the city on paper. He always had a penchant for grandiose plans.

In 1907 Hitler relocated to Vienna, where he planned to study art. He failed to get into art school, however, a fact he concealed from members of his family and even close friends for as long as possible. Hitler's many drawings, paintings and architectural sketches showed some technical ability but little creativity. It is not surprising that years after his death an ambitious forger would have no trouble cranking out many convincing fakes. Hitler later made much of his dire poverty during his years in Vienna and he did face some hard times when he could not afford lodgings and had to live in a men's shelter. His means of support included selling cards on which he painted local scenes. During most of his young adult years in Vienna, however, Hitler received funds from his family that enabled him to live quite comfortably without ever being employed. For example, he could afford to see Richard Wagner's opera *Lohengrin* and other favourites over and over again.

While in Vienna, Hitler picked up on many ideas and trends around him. He was interested in Pan-Germanism – the conviction that Germans should be unified in one state instead of dispersed throughout Central and Eastern Europe – as well as in ultra-nationalism and antisemitism. He admired Karl Lueger, mayor of Vienna from 1895 to 1910 and a member of the anti-Semitic Christian Social Party. Lueger's use of propaganda particularly impressed Hitler.

In Vienna Hitler began to fuse his ideas into a worldview and to get acquainted with political extremists of various kinds. He became enthusiastic about Social Darwinist theories that described life as a struggle between races. His reading consisted mostly of popular tracts about mythology, biology and even the occult. Hitler preferred to read summaries and pamphlets rather than the actual writings of people such as the philosopher Friedrich Nietzsche. Enthusiasm for the operas of Wagner encouraged Hitler's tendencies toward a grandiose style. Wagner's operas with their huge casts, imposing music, exaggerated passions and powerful depictions of Germanic myth, inspired Hitler as he developed his own vision of politics and power.

In 1913 Hitler left Vienna for Munich. He crossed the border from Austria to Germany in violation of Austrian law, which required him as an able-bodied young man to perform military service for his homeland. Hitler's motivations for moving are not known for certain, but he had never made a secret of his contempt for the Austrian government and his conviction that the future lay with Germany.

In Munich Hitler's self-education was interrupted by the outbreak of war in 1914. He volunteered for the German army, where he reached the rank of corporal. Wounded in action, he served with distinction as a runner who relayed messages from the rear to the front. It was a dangerous job, although not exactly the combat role Hitler would later imply he had played, and he received an Iron Cross for his bravery. Nevertheless, a report by one of his superiors – in hindsight tinged in irony – commented that Hitler lacked leadership qualities.

It is not completely clear when and how Hitler developed his fanatical antisemitism. He certainly came into frequent contact with antisemites in Vienna, although he also had acquaintances, associates and even what might be called friends who were Jewish. In any case, Hitler's experience of Germany's defeat in the First World War deepened and hardened his hatred of Jews, or at least he would later claim that his conversion to antisemitism came in 1918. To his mind, the Jews were somehow to blame. That reaction was completely unfounded; German and Austro-Hungarian Jews had fought and died loyally alongside fellow citizens in their countries' armies. But as he would do with every disappointment he faced throughout his life, whether

it was failing to get into art school or losing a war, Hitler considered the Jews at fault.

In 1919, a year after the war ended, Hitler got involved in a
political organisation called the German Workers' Party. It would
soon change its name to the National Socialist German Workers'
Party. The German acronym was NSDAP. English-speakers
commonly use the abbreviation 'Nazi', taken from the first two
syllables of the German pronunciation of 'National'. Within a
year Hitler had become a full-time agitator and extremely popular speaker for the group.

On 9 November 1923, Hitler and a group of co-conspira-
tors that included the war hero Erich Ludendorff launched
what became known as the Beer Hall Putsch in Munich. They
intended to overthrow the government of Bavaria in order to
install a regime that would be the beginning of a national revival
in Germany. Poorly planned and organised, the Putsch failed;
Hitler was captured and sentenced to five years in prison for high
treason. He served only thirteen months in Landsberg Prison,
where he was treated like a celebrity by most of the staff and
many of his fellow inmates. So many admirers flocked to visit
him that he eventually stopped receiving them in order to have
time to write the book he had begun. By the time Hitler was
released in 1925, he had written and published *Mein Kampf*, a
combination memoir and propaganda tract. The book did not
become a best-seller until Hitler became chancellor of Germany
in 1933.

In this early phase of his career, Hitler was still relatively
obscure, part of the fringe elements that proliferated in German
society after the First World War. Most Germans outside
Bavaria knew little about him and did not take him seriously.
His modest background, his relatively unremarkable military career and his lack of education and experience with the
wider world all made him seem almost laughable to some of
the people he encountered. For example, one German aristocrat, a Bavarian baron called Fritz Percy Reck-Malleczewen,
described his early impressions of Hitler with contempt. He
once saw Hitler in a deserted restaurant in the early 1930s,

Reck-Malleczewen recorded in his diary, later published as *Diary of a Man in Despair*. Reck-Malleczewen had a pistol in his pocket and could easily have killed the future dictator. 'But I mistook him for a cartoon character', the baron said, looking back on the event, 'and I did not shoot'.

Because of the tremendous fascination with Hitler the person, we know quite a bit about some details of his daily life. He was a vegetarian who loved animals and hated cigarette smoke. He liked to watch movies, especially comedies and enjoyed reading westerns, like those by the popular German writer Karl May. May, like Hitler, never set foot in the Americas. Hitler's most intense emotional attachment after the death of his mother seems to have been his relationship with his niece Geli Raubal, the daughter of his half-sister Angela. Hitler had invited Angela to live with him to supervise his household in Munich.

Evidence points toward some kind of affair between Hitler and his much younger niece. Proud of the vivacious young woman and possessive of her time and attention, Hitler was often seen with her in public. Geli seems to have chafed under the control of her domineering uncle and some observers later claimed she was trying to get away from him. In 1931 Geli died under suspicious circumstances. The official verdict was suicide, but rumours of foul play persisted for years. The young woman was found in her uncle's Munich apartment, shot with his pistol. Stories circulated – Geli was pregnant, people whispered; she had a Jewish lover, some hinted; her jealous uncle had her killed, others speculated. Given the few documents and wit-nesses available and the years that have since passed, it is unlikely that we will ever get to the bottom of events surrounding Geli Raubal. Scandalous and intriguing as the whole affair is, it does not seem to have played a major role in shaping Hitler or his view of the world.

Indeed, none of the details of Hitler's life that can be found have managed to provide the clue needed to explain the strengths of his obsessions or his ability to realise his convictions. The magnitude of the crimes he initiated remains oddly out of proportion to the banality of his person and his life.

Hitler's Worldview

It is impossible to talk about Nazi ideas without borrowing Nazi terminology, most of which, even translated into English, is offensive, nonsensical, or both. Words like 'Aryan', 'race' and 'blood' had particular meanings within the Nazi system of thought, but those terms do not describe objective realities. However, once Nazi ideology became enshrined in laws and regulations and implemented in practice, such labels would take on very real implications of life and death.

The main elements of Hitler's ideology developed during his years in Vienna, his time in Munich and his years with the German army during and immediately after the First World War. Those ideas remained remarkably constant from the beginning of his political career in the early 1920s to his death in 1945.

Hitler's core ideas can be summed up in the phrase 'race and space'. Hitler was obsessed with two notions: that humanity was engaged in a gigantic struggle between 'races', or communities of 'blood'; and that 'pure Germans', members of the so-called Aryan race, needed space to expand, living space that Hitler called by the German term *Lebensraum*. For Hitler, these two notions of race and space were intertwined. Any race that was not expanding, he believed, was doomed to disappear. Without living space – land to produce food and raise new generations of soldiers and mothers – a race could not grow. Hitler saw the potential living space for German 'Aryans' to Germany's east, in the territories of Poland and the Soviet Union. The 'races' that he considered prime threats to the survival and dominance of his 'Aryans' were the Slavs who occupied that land and the Jews, who, in his theory, sought to infiltrate, weaken and destroy German strength.

What was an 'Aryan'? Like all races the category 'Aryan' was an invention, a social construction rather than a physical fact. Hitler did not coin the term 'Aryan' but borrowed it from eighteenth- and nineteenth-century European racial theorists who used various labels for the categories into which they divided humanity. The word 'Aryan' originally referred to a group of people in ancient India. Hitler drew on vague theories that these people, supposedly taller and lighter-skinned than their neighbours, were a superior group who somehow ended up in Europe, where they continued to be the bearers of all cultural creativity. Hitler and other Nazi writers tended to be rather vague when it came to the details of their theories and they were not troubled by internal contradictions. Thus Hitler considered the ancient Greeks to have been Aryans; so, at least in his mind, were the best elements in ancient Rome as well as the Germanic tribes that finally destroyed Roman power.

Using the term 'Aryan' to describe his supposed master race gave Hitler a degree of flexibility that proved very useful. Had he simply preached the 'German' master race he would have had to find some way to exclude German Jews, many of whom were certainly as German as their fellow citizens in terms of language and ethnicity. Had he drawn exclusively on terms like 'Nordic', which tended to describe physical appearance rather than less visible qualities of blood and character, he might have had some explaining to do with regard to the inclusion of many loyal Nazis in the privileged category. As it was, Germans would tell jokes during the Nazi years about the less-than-perfect specimens who were their leaders: 'What does the ideal Aryan look like? As tall as Goebbels, as slim as Göring, as blond as Hitler'. In fact, propaganda minister Joseph Goebbels was short and had a club foot; Hermann Göring, commander of the German air force, was a fat man and Hitler had dark hair. In general the label 'Aryan' combined the ring of scientific authority with the vague, elastic quality of a new invention. It could be and was redefined as needed to fit the imperatives of race and space. The only reliable constant was the claim that 'Aryan' was the opposite of 'Jew'.

By the early 1920s, hatred of Jews was a fixed point in Hitler's ideology. No mere opportunist, he maintained until his death a fanatical antipathy to anything he considered Jewish. Hitler's antisemitism incorporated all of the strands of previous generations. It had religious and metaphysical dimensions: he regularly spoke of Jews as evil enemies of virtue and honour. It was political, too: his theory of a Jewish conspiracy extended in every direction. At various times Hitler described communism, capitalism, liberalism, anarchism, atheism, Christianity, Great Britain, the United States and France as parts of some international Jewish plot. There were cultural elements to Hitler's antisemitism: he considered jazz, abstract art and many other forms of modernism somehow degenerate and 'Jewish', because, in his view, they distorted reality and lured people away from racial purity. Of course, Hitler's hostility included familiar social and economic resentments. He shared all the stereotypes of Jews as greedy bankers, legalistic pedants, lecherous males and seductive, destructive females. 'Jewish' to him meant everything he considered negative, the antithesis of the supposedly perfect Aryan. Hitler regarded Jewishness as a race, a biological fact that could not be altered by any change of religion, name, or habits. The sheer multidimensionality of Hitler's antisemitism gave it a kind of mass appeal. Many Germans could find something in it they shared, even if they did not buy the whole package.

Hitler drew on old forms of antisemitism, but he combined them in ways that produced something new. The historian Saul Friedländer has labelled Hitler's particular strain of hatred 'redemptive antisemitism'. By this phrase Friedländer means that Hitler combined a murderous rage with an idealistic goal. Hitler and the hardcore Nazis who accepted his views had a religious fervour, a fanatical conviction that attacks on Jews were necessary to save the world for Aryan Germany. Hitler stated his faith at the end of the second chapter of *Mein Kampf*: 'Today I believe that I am acting in accordance with the will of the Almighty Creator: by defending myself against the Jew, I am fighting for the work of the Lord'.

Hitler's view of 'the Jew' was full of internal contradictions. He called Jewish men effeminate and weak yet also characterised them as sexual predators. He denounced Jews as inferior idiots yet believed they had a cunning intelligence, which made them a diabolical threat to the supposedly superior 'Aryans'. Certain images enabled him to reconcile these contradictory accusations, at least rhetorically. One of his favourites was that of the germ. A germ or a parasite, Hitler was fond of pointing out, was very small, even invisible and yet it had an incredible, superhuman ability to kill. He claimed that Jews were similar: they might seem few and weak, but according to Hitler's paranoid view, they had enormous powers of destruction.

Another important feature of Hitler's ideology was its sense of urgency. According to Hitler, time was running out: it was five to midnight for the Aryan race, he warned, and the clock was ticking. The race was already dangerously polluted, he insisted; if it were not saved immediately it would perish. That notion of impending doom added an apocalyptic dimension to Hitler's thought. His belief in the necessity – and desirability – of war gave that mythical struggle concrete form. Only war would redeem the Aryan race, Hitler maintained: war in the name of racial purity and in the quest for living space. Other traits of Hitler's worldview were also connected to his key notions of race and space. Hitler was passionately anti-communist, although once in power he would show himself willing to make at least temporary concessions toward communism in favour of his more central goals. Hitler blamed German communists as well as Jews for the loss of the First World War. By the late 1920s he regularly linked communism and Bolshevism with Jews and he accused Jews of creating communism as part of a plot to destroy Germany. During the Second World War, Hitler would return repeatedly to the idea of some diabolical Jewish–communist plot in order to rally Germany against the Soviet Union. One of Hitler's typical terms of derision was 'Bolshevik Jewish internationalist'.

Hitler's ideas about women and men also fit into his worldview. He claimed that he would restore women to what he called their rightful place in the home. He regarded women's bodies as important to the state, because they produced new generations of soldiers and breeders. But women's bodies in Hitler's view could also be the floodgates to racial impurity, the means through which supposed pollutants entered the Aryan bloodstream. Some German women found such theories appealing, because they seemed to offer women a powerful position as mothers and guardians of the master race. Others recognised the misogyny inherent in Nazi ideas. Hitler's sexism and antisemitism were mutually reinforcing. He used sexist images and vocabulary to belittle Jews and other so-called enemies. At the same time, he equated feminists with Jews and derided Jewish men as defilers of Aryan womanhood and champions of homosexuality and other supposed perversions. Such sexual images caught the attention of Hitler's audiences and played on many of their own anxieties.

Hitler endorsed a position that he and other National Socialists referred to as the '*Führer* principle'. The German term 'der *Führer*' means 'the leader' in English. Hitler would later take that title for himself. The *Führer* principle meant commitment to uncontested leadership. When individuals in the Nazi organisation grew powerful enough to pose a potential threat to Hitler's position, he found ways to clip their wings, even if it meant temporarily weakening the Nazi Party's base of support. Hitler believed power had to be focused in order to be effective; the crucial focal point, in his view, was himself.

As *Führer*, Hitler demanded total loyalty from his followers. One of his most devoted associates turned out to be Joseph Goebbels, later minister of propaganda, who wrote in his diary: 'I love you, AH'. Hitler rewarded faithful subordinates with privileges, powers and, in special cases, access to him and his inner circle. Admittedly, spending time with the *Führer* had disadvantages even for the most dedicated Nazis: his impromptu speeches, lectures and dinner diatribes could last for hours and often put his listeners to sleep. Nevertheless, the Nazi focus on Hitler as leader gave the movement and subsequently the entire system a powerful dynamic that the historian Sir Ian Kershaw calls 'working toward the *Führer*'. Once his position and power were assured, Hitler did not need to issue specific orders in most cases. It was enough to let his wishes be known in general terms, and his underlings would rush to fulfil and even anticipate them, in the hope of winning his favour and advancing their own careers. In the words of one Nazi functionary: 'It is the duty of every single person to attempt, in the spirit of the *Führer*, to work towards him'.

The *Führer* principle was also linked to the goals of race and space. Hitler was convinced that he needed unquestioned power to complete his historical mission. Democracy, he claimed, was a product of Jewish-Bolshevik-liberal-internationalism; in his opinion, democratic institutions obstructed the work of 'great individuals'. Hitler's *Führer* principle was both a means to achieve his policies of race and space and an end in itself.

Adolf Hitler was not a brilliant, original thinker. There was nothing really new about his ideas or even about the way in which he combined them. His ideology was a mix of nineteenth-century racial theories, Social Darwinism, post–First World War resentments, antisemitism, anti-modernism and sexism dressed up in familiar symbols drawn from nationalism, mythology and even Christianity, although Hitler and many of his closest associates actually detested Christianity, which they considered a religion for the weak. What was different was the intensity with which he held his views and his ability to captivate large audiences in such a way that many who heard him speak felt he gave voice to their own feelings and beliefs. Above all, what differentiated Hitler from the many other demagogues and ideologues in Europe between the wars was the tremendous power he achieved after he became chancellor of Germany in 1933. From that position he was able to harness an entire government – its military, diplomacy and bureaucracy – behind implementation of his notions of race and space.

Old Fighters and True Believers – The Inner Circle

Hitler neither rose to power alone nor developed his ideas in a vacuum. A rather motley crew of men formed his inner circle. Three individuals who stuck with Hitler throughout his political career were Hermann Göring, Joseph Goebbels and Heinrich Himmler. All of them would play key roles in the Nazi regime.

Hermann Göring (1893–1946) was a hero of the First World War who rose through the air force to become commander of the famous Richthofen Squadron. Somewhat at a loss after the war ended with Germany's defeat and massive demilitarisation, he joined the Nazi Party in 1922. One of Hitler's oldest associates, Göring had the distinction of having been wounded at the Beer Hall Putsch in 1923. Nazi lingo reserved the label 'old fighters' for those of the faithful who had been members before the failed Putsch.

Hitler often presented Göring as one of Nazism's more respectable figures. Göring's father had been a judge and consular official and he had ties with conservative and nationalist circles. Göring senior had even served as resident minister plenipotentiary in German Southwest Africa, site of the German genocide of the Herero and Nama people in 1907 and 1908. In fact there is a street named after him in Windhoek, the capital of Namibia. Throughout the 1930s Hitler showered appointments on Hermann Göring: when the Nazi Party became the largest party in the German parliament, Göring became president of the Reichstag (as the German parliament was called). Göring established the Gestapo, a political police force and was named commander-in-chief of the *Luftwaffe* (air force). In 1936 Hitler chose Göring to head the Four-Year Plan to prepare Germany for war. A swaggering, flamboyant individual who relished luxury and excess, Göring was also an ambitious schemer and a vicious infighter.

Joseph Goebbels (1897–1945) was a rather different kind of Nazi. A journalist and writer, he had a Ph.D. and wrote a novel called *Michael*, although it remained unpublished until the Nazi Party press picked it up in 1929. Goebbels first came into contact with members of the Nazi Party in 1924; by 1928 Hitler had made him head of propaganda. In 1933 Goebbels became minister for popular enlightenment and propaganda. He kept that post throughout the entire Third Reich, although his ambitious, energetic nature meant that he was always trying to find ways to play even bigger roles.

Goebbels was a master propagandist who excelled in stirring up hatred and orchestrating gigantic extravaganzas, such as the annual Nazi Party rallies. He was the only one of Hitler's early associates who stayed with him right to the end. When Hitler committed suicide in 1945, Goebbels did so, too: he and his wife Magda had their children poisoned before he had her and himself shot. Goebbels's extensive diaries, large parts of which have been published, reveal him to have been a 'true believer', committed to Hitler as a person and to realisation of his ideas.

Heinrich Himmler (1900–1945) would become, next to Hitler, the most powerful man in the Third Reich. Head of the elite Nazi guard known as the *Schutzstaffel* (SS) from 1929 to 1945, by 1936 he had also become chief of all German police. In these positions he presided over a vast network of offices and agencies that implemented terror and mass murder all over German-occupied Europe.

Himmler was neither flashy like Göring nor educated like Goebbels. Awkward and homely as a young man, he read voraciously and had developed his own conspiratorial view of the world even before he met Hitler in 1926. Like Hitler, Himmler feared and hated Jews and believed in the superiority of the so-called Aryan race. Himmler too was convinced that Germany had to expand to the east. Dogged and capable of meticulous attention to detail, Himmler involved himself directly in projects that targeted homosexual men and Gypsies as well as Slavs and Jews. With justification the historian Richard Breitman and others have labelled Himmler the 'architect of genocide'.

There were no women in Hitler's inner circle, nor did any women wield direct political power. The closest was Gertrud Scholtz-Klink (b. 1902), national women's leader from 1934 until 1945. A true believer in Hitler's worldview, Scholtz-Klink described herself as fighting for Hitler's cause with the weapons of a woman. According to Scholtz-Klink, the crowning achievement of a Nazi woman was motherhood. Her own three marriages produced eleven children. Hitler referred to Scholtz-Klink and her Nazi women's organisations when it suited him to do so, but he did not consult her or for that matter seem to take her seriously. Like many women in the Third Reich, she played the role of the enthusiastic supporter and beneficiary of Nazism.

The Nazi Rise to Power

How did Hitler come to power in Germany? It is important first to note some common – and mistaken – answers to this question.

Hitler's rise to power was not inevitable. It was neither an automatic product of Germany's defeat in the First World War nor the unavoidable result of the Great Depression. Hitler was not swept to power by a stampede of German voters hypnotised by his oratorical skills, nor did he seize power in an illegal coup d'état. The road that brought Adolf Hitler into the chancellor's seat by 1933 was both less direct and more mundane than these standard interpretations suggest. Briefly put, it was a combination of difficult circumstances, political manoeuvring, luck, treachery and miscalculation on the part of many people that catapulted Hitler into power.

What was the situation in Germany prior to Hitler's rule? In the wake of military defeat in 1918, Germans introduced a form of government new to them: a republic based on a democratic constitution. It was called the Weimar Republic, after the city of Weimar, which served as its temporary capital until the situation in Berlin was stable enough for the government to set up shop there.

In hindsight it is easy to dismiss the Weimar Republic as a failed experiment in German democracy, nothing more than a chaotic prelude to Nazism. In fact, although novel in many ways, the Weimar Republic built on longstanding political parties, legal and bureaucratic structures and even electoral practices in Germany. Moreover, it lasted two years longer than the Nazi regime Hitler and his followers promised would be a 'Thousand-Year Reich'. The Weimar Republic persisted in some form for fourteen years, from its proclamation in November 1918 to Adolf Hitler's appointment as chancellor in January 1933.

The Weimar Republic witnessed considerable achievements in the political and cultural spheres as well as in foreign policy and economics. Antidemocratic Germans often complained that the victorious powers of the First World War had forced democracy on a defeated Germany. The Weimar Republic, however, was based on liberal and democratic tendencies within Germany that predated the war. Under the Weimar Constitution of 1919, Germany became the first major European power to give women the vote, not counting the short-lived Provisional

Government in 1917 Russia. Weimar Germany produced the most modern, innovative film industry in the world at the time and it returned Germany to international respectability with the country's incorporation into the League of Nations in 1926. In short, the existence of the Weimar Republic by no means made Hitler's rise inevitable.

It may come as a surprise that Weimar Germany had the strongest economy in continental Europe for most if not all of its history. Its post-war recovery was eased by the fact that very little of the fighting in the First World War had taken place on German soil. As a result Germany's infrastructure and industry remained mostly intact. In contrast, Germany's neighbours to the west – France and Belgium – had been demolished by the war. They sought reparations, but the Germans managed to avoid paying most of the sums charged by negotiating the amounts downward, by falling behind on payments and eventually by ceasing payments altogether. To the east, the territories of Poland and the Soviet Union had been on the whole less industrialised than Germany already before 1914. The enormous costs and devastation of years of war put their struggling economies even further behind the Germans.

Of course Weimar Germany faced very real economic problems, the most dramatic of which was inflation. In 1923 inflationary tendencies spiralled into a hyperinflation that saw the value of the German Mark plummet to impossible levels. The situation got so bad that people needed enormous quantities of banknotes merely to buy a loaf of bread or a glass of beer. Images of desperate Germans demanding their pay hourly before it could become worthless and moving their petty cash in wheelbarrows have become standard features in histories of the Weimar years.

The hyperinflation of 1923, however, was not simply the result of crushing reparations payments, as is often assumed. Instead it was irresponsible fiscal policies on the part of the German government during the war and an attempt to thwart French and Belgian efforts to seize reparations directly from Germany afterward that destroyed the value of the German currency. Moreover, all of Europe experienced inflation after the war, although the months of massive inflation in Germany in 1923 were especially dramatic.

As in any inflation, some Germans lost a great deal. Those on fixed incomes, such as pensioners and people who had loaned out money, were particularly hard hit. Yet there were also big winners in 1923, as is true of every inflationary situation: people with property in forms other than money, speculators and above all debtors who could pay back what they owed in currency worth a fraction of its value when they borrowed it. Currency reform in 1923 halted the hyperinflation and began a period of economic stabilisation in Germany that lasted until the end of the decade. By the time Hitler came to power, the hyperinflation of 1923 was ten years in the past.

Weimar Germany's situation in terms of national security was also much stronger than is often recognised. The old Habsburg Empire, once Germany's rival for power in central Europe, disappeared completely in the war, leaving a small, weak Austria as Germany's neighbour to the south. Before the First World War, the Habsburg Empire had ruled large parts of central and Eastern Europe, including territories that lie in modern-day Austria, Poland, Hungary, the Czech Republic, Slovakia, Croatia and other countries. After the war, those lands were organised as much smaller, independent countries that often had reasons to focus their animosities on one another rather than competing with or challenging German power in Europe.

After the First World War, Germany's former rival to the east, the once formidable Russian Empire, was gone too, replaced by Lenin's new Soviet Union. Racked by civil war until the early 1920s, the Soviet Union was in no position to threaten German interests. In any case, the post-war settlement in Europe meant that Germany no longer shared a border with Russia, because the creation of an independent Poland created a buffer between the two larger nations. After 1918, Germany's immediate neighbours included Poland in the east and Czechoslovakia in the southeast – tenuous, new nations engaged in their own struggles for stability.

In short, all of Europe faced enormous economic, political and social challenges in the 1920s. Even Great Britain, with its massive empire, was weakened after years of war. The British retained wartime rationing of bread longer after hostilities ended in November 1918 than did the Germans. The Weimar Republic had as good a chance to survive as did most of its European counterparts. Being surrounded by neighbours poorer and weaker than itself gave it some significant advantages.

But what about the shame of defeat? Many people assume that Germans who wished to return their nation to greatness naturally turned to Hitler to lead them out of humiliation. This view is oversimplified. Military defeat need not usher in tyranny and destruction. In fact it can generate reassessment and reform, as was the case after 1806, when Prussia's defeat at Napoleon's hands led Prussian reformers to introduce remarkable changes to their country's military, bureaucracy and system of education. Likewise Russian defeat in the Crimean War of 1854–1856 prompted the tsar to free the serfs. In Germany after 1918, however, such positive change was blocked by a widespread refusal to accept the reality of defeat.

In the autumn of 1918 Germany's military leadership – Generals Paul von Hindenburg and Erich Ludendorff – had insisted on suing for peace. Germany simply did not have the resources to fight on, its top generals realised. Even before the armistice was concluded in November, however, they began to spin the account of events to save their own reputations. It was not the military but the German civilians who had lost their nerve, the generals claimed. It was the disloyal, revolutionary home front, they conjectured, that had stabbed the fighting men in the back and betrayed them to their enemies.

The myth of a stab in the back spread quickly. Many Germans needed an explanation for defeat in a war that their military leadership and the press it partly controlled had never let on it was losing. The fact that the war ended with almost no foreign troops on German soil lent credence to the idea of betrayal from within Germany. And the notion of an undefeated military fit with comforting myths about national greatness. In the eyes of many Germans, their new, democratic government symbolised the civilian weaklings who had supposedly betrayed Germany's fighting heroes. This perception in turn undercut the authority of the Weimar Republic.

Hitler would later capitalise on the stab-in-the-back myth. He was able to do so because, by the time he appeared on the national scene, the idea had been propagated within Germany for more than a decade: by military leaders who refused to take responsibility for defeat; by nationalist professors, schoolteachers and clergy; and by antidemocratic politicians and publicists who found it easier to live in a glorified past than to face the challenges of the present. Defeat in the First World War did not make Hitler's rise to power inevitable, but the way that many Germans, particularly those in positions of power, chose to respond to the challenges of defeat weakened the base of support of their own government and prepared the way for even more extreme manipulation of public opinion.

From its beginnings, the Weimar Republic faced a crisis of legitimacy. Its critics on the left wanted a revolutionary, communist regime instead of a liberal, democratic republic. Conservatives and those further to the right considered the whole idea of democracy to be weak, ineffective and non-German. Beset by extremists of all kinds, Weimar authorities tended to crack down hard on the left but treat the right with leniency.

The new government in 1918 had not purged the judiciary or the civil service, so the republic's judges, lawyers and bureaucrats were the same people who had served the German Kaiser before the First World War. Many of them were less than enthusiastic about the democratic constitution they supposedly upheld. When faced with illegal actions or revolutionary efforts by communists, they dealt out long prison terms and imposed death sentences. Rightwing extremists charged with criminal acts or caught in plots to overthrow the government received much lighter penalties. Critics of the Weimar system often fault its liberal constitution for tolerating antidemocratic movements such as the National Socialists. But there were laws that might have curbed the growth of Nazism; they were simply not enforced.

Hitler's early career is a case in point. In 1923 he was arrested for his role in the Beer Hall Putsch and charged with high treason. Instead of being a setback, the trial gave Hitler a chance to gain national publicity. He was sentenced to five years – a rather light term for someone caught in the act of trying to overthrow the government – and served a total of only thirteen months. Communists in the Weimar Republic charged with similar offences regularly received much harsher treatment: life terms and even death sentences were not uncommon for them.

Hitler spent the decade after the failed Putsch building his party. He presided over a two-pronged approach. On the one hand there was the paramilitary, street-fighting wing of the movement: the SA (*Sturmabteilung*), or storm troopers. On the other hand there was the legal, political party, the National Socialist German Workers' Party (NSDAP). The brown-shirted storm troopers, modelled after Benito Mussolini's Fascist Black Shirts in Italy, brawled with communists and Social Democrats, harassed and attacked Jews and homosexuals and generally used terror tactics to intimidate the public. At the same time, the existence of the Nazi Party allowed for legal actions: collecting funds, organising local support, putting forward candidates for election and hosting rallies and other events.

Until 1928 the NSDAP was just one of many splinter political groups vying for the attention of voters. That year brought some local and regional electoral breakthroughs in northern Germany, and for the first time the party established a presence in the Reichstag, the German parliament. This first evidence of national popularity preceded the Great Depression; it was not simply economic hardship that brought some Germans to support the NSDAP, although hard times certainly brought many new voters and activists. Indeed a general climate of political polarisation meant that all parties at the extremes – Nazis and ultranationalists on the right, communists on the left – gained at the expense of the moderate middle. Over the course of the 1920s, the NSDAP became a genuine mass party with voters in all social classes: workers, members of the lower middle class, students, academics, clergy, the wealthy, women as well as men.

The U.S. stock market crash of 1929 was felt all over the world, not just in Germany. It is with good reason that the depression associated with that event has been called a world depression. Germany faced growing unemployment as did much of the industrialised world. German farmers, like their counterparts elsewhere, faced falling commodity prices and shrinking markets. Economic hardship did not make the rise of a Nazi dictator inevitable, but it did add to the challenges of the Weimar Republic.

By early 1930 economic difficulties had brought Germany into a political crisis. High taxes, increased tariffs, cuts in government spending and deflationary policies did nothing to ease the situation. In the midst of that misery and strife, few people even noticed the evacuation of the last French troops from German soil in June 1930.

The chancellor, Heinrich Brüning, was unable to get the backing of the Reichstag for his measures. So he convinced the German president, the old war hero Paul von Hindenburg, to invoke Article 48 of the constitution. Article 48 allowed the president to govern by decree in a state of emergency. Brüning had no problem convincing Hindenburg. Never a fan of democracy, Hindenburg had long believed that parliamentary government was too chaotic. By 1930 he was an old man – some say he was senile. A joke made the rounds, one aide to another: 'Don't put your sandwich paper down in front of the president. He might sign it!'

From 1930 until the end of 1932, Hindenburg and his various chancellors ruled by decree rather than relying on the democratically elected Reichstag. Democracy was essentially dead in Germany, but there were still alternatives to Hitler: some people awaited a military coup; others expected some kind of conservative, authoritarian rule.

In that climate Hitler and the Nazi Party ran in a number of important elections. In one, the presidential election of 1932, Hitler lost his bid for the presidency to the aged Hindenburg. In another, in July 1932, the Nazi Party won thirty-seven per cent of the votes cast, its highest return in a free election ever. Although some Germans later would claim that no one could resist the magnetic force of Hitler's oratory, more than sixty per cent of German voters had no trouble doing so in 1932. Some of them are on record as having found his style braying, annoying, low-class and offensive. Nevertheless, the July election brought the Nazis more seats than any other party in the Reichstag.

In the third election of the year, in November 1932, support for the Nazis dropped and the party lost two million votes. With 196 seats, it was still the strongest party in the Reichstag, but the communists, with 100 seats, were not far behind. Some observers thought the Nazis had peaked. In his disappointment Hitler contemplated suicide and wondered whether he had missed his opportunity.

Hitler was saved, not by his own ingenuity but by the miscalculation of his rivals. Former chancellor Franz von Papen, a conservative and a nationalist, convinced Hindenburg to name Hitler chancellor. Papen reckoned that giving Hitler the post would buy popular support for his own cause – he planned to make sure it did so by getting himself named Hitler's vice chancellor. From that position, he told Hindenburg, he and others loyal to the president would be able to control the Nazi upstart.

Other conservatives and some industrialists backed Hitler as well. They hoped to defuse discontent among workers and prevent any increase of communist strength. Hitler could not do much harm, they told President Hindenburg, as long as he was surrounded with members of the cabinet who were not Nazis. Hitler for his part said he would accept the chancellorship only if he could name two of the Nazi Party members of the Reichstag as government ministers. Hindenburg agreed and on 30 January 1933, Hitler became chancellor of Germany. Like all the members of his cabinet he swore an oath to the constitution. A photograph widely distributed in the German press showed him shaking hands with President Hindenburg. The Bavarian aristocrat Reck-Malleczewen described the look on Hitler's face as that of 'a head waiter as he closes his hand around the tip'. Hitler did not need to seize power. It was handed to him.

3

From Revolution to Routine: Nazi Germany, 1933–1938

Looking back it is easy to forget that half of the Nazi era occurred before the Second World War began. Those first six years proved crucial. Between 1933, when Hitler became chancellor and 1939, when German forces invaded Poland, Nazi rule revolutionised Germany. During those same years, the 'Third Reich' or third empire, as Hitler and his followers called their new Germany, became routine for many Germans. This chapter examines those two phases of Hitler's rule: first, the Nazi revolution and second, the routinisation of Nazism that followed. How did Hitler begin to implement his ideas of race and space during the peacetime years of Nazi rule? How did the German public respond and what was life like for Germans under the Nazi system?

Examination of Hitler's worldview and rise to power reveals an imbalance between the ordinary aspects of his life and the extraordinary impact he had. There was nothing so unusual in Hitler's background, nor were his ideas original. Even the factors that brought him to power – misfortune, opportunism, mis-calculation – were unsensational. And yet the destructive role that Hitler would play was far from ordinary. Even today, when asked to name one individual who has dominated the past millennium, many people say 'Adolf Hitler'.

That same dichotomy or gap between the extraordinary and the ordinary is evident throughout the entire Nazi period. On the one hand, Hitler revolutionised Germany, but on the other hand, the ways in which he did so seemed far from dramatic to many participants and observers at the time. Between 1933 and 1938, Nazism became everyday and ordinary for many Germans, but that routine normalised terror and legalised extraordinary persecution.

Phase I: The Nazi Revolution, 1933–1934

Hitler's appointment as chancellor in January 1933 was in itself unspectacular. Since 1918, Germany had seen many chancellors from a range of political parties and many of their governments had been short lived. Yet that seemingly unremarkable event on 30 January 1933 marked the beginning of a revolution that would transform German politics and society. The new chancellor lost no time in attacking the elements of the population he despised, but he did so in ways that expanded his own power even as he isolated his enemies.

Hitler's political position in early 1933 was not especially strong. His party's support had dropped from its July 1932 peak and even then it had received only thirty-seven per cent of the votes cast. The Nazi Party faithful themselves were divided into factions with very different visions for Germany's future. Some favoured a social revolution that would redistribute wealth and property in radically egalitarian ways; others wanted to bolster traditional elites. Meanwhile, Hitler's cabinet included only two members of the Nazi Party besides himself: Hermann Göring and another long-time associate, Wilhelm Frick, as minister of the interior. The rest of the cabinet posts were assigned to conservatives and nationalists, members of the Catholic Centre Party and military men who thought they could control their inexperienced new chancellor. Instead he proved skilled at manipulating them.

Hitler made his first major move in early 1933 against the communists, a target he chose with care. Communism could have posed a real threat to Nazi power. Like the Nazi Party, the Communist Party had local cells throughout Germany. It was well represented both in the Reichstag and in the streets, where its men had fought the Nazi storm troopers for more than a decade. The communists, however, were an ideal first target for another reason as well; Hitler was guaranteed to have allies against them. Precisely those elements in German society that had helped Hitler into the chancellor's seat – conservatives, nationalists, industrialists and military men – hated and feared communism. They were unlikely to protest any anti-communist measures, no matter how unconstitutional or harsh.

On 27 February 1933 the Reichstag – the German parliament building – burned down. The Reichstag fire gave Hitler the opportunity he wanted. His spokes-people insisted that communists had torched the building and the German press, relying on information from Nazi sources and reluctant to speak against the new regime, echoed those accusations. At the time some non-Nazi Germans assumed that Hitler's own people had started the fire, but they could do little except grumble in private, unless they were willing to risk being accused of sympathising with the communists. Historians are still debating this issue. For a long time, research seemed to indicate that the blaze was, in fact, the work of a lone, Dutch arsonist named Marinus van der Lubbe, who was linked to neither the Communist nor the Nazi Parties. Subsequent work, however, points back to the Nazis as the instigators.

Hitler ordered massive reprisals against German communists in response to the fire. He had thousands arrested, tortured and beaten; hundreds were 'shot while trying to escape'. That phrase was an indirect way of saying that police or soldiers had shot them in the back. Thousands more fled into exile. Shortly after the Reichstag fire, in March 1933, German newspapers announced the opening of the first official concentration camp – at Dachau, near Munich. Among the first prisoners sent there were many communist men. With the actions of late February 1933, Hitler crippled communist power in Germany. That assault was only the beginning: by the end of the Nazi regime, about 150,000 German communists would be arrested and many of them would be killed by 1945.

The Reichstag fire gave Hitler a pretext to dismantle what was left of Germany's democratic institutions. Pointing to the supposed risk of disorder and to his now proven ability to act decisively, he convinced the members of the Reichstag to pass the Enabling Law of 23 March 1933. The Enabling Law allowed Hitler to put through any measure without approval from the Reichstag. He no longer even needed to have the president declare a state of emergency or sign a decree. Social Democratic representatives opposed the Enabling Law, but they were the only mainstream party to do so. The Communist Party, of course, had already been outlawed. In effect the Reichstag was now defunct; its own members had voted it out of existence. Their reasons for doing so varied: quite a few welcomed the new regime they thought would replace the cumbersome parliamentary system they hated with authoritarian order; others felt intimidated by Nazi attacks on communists and Social Democrats; some hoped to curry favour with Hitler and his people by proving how willing they were to cooperate.

By the end of the summer of 1933, Hitler had used his authority to dissolve or outlaw all political parties except the NSDAP – the National Socialist German Workers' Party, or the Nazi Party. Even the facade of German democracy was gone. Hitler's political revolution was not without violence, but he established his dictatorship through means that were, at least in a narrow sense of the word, legal.

The Nazi revolution had immediate effects on those groups Hitler had described as enemies for years. It was not only political opponents like the communists who felt early blows; homosexuals, Jehovah's Witnesses, German Jews, people considered physically or mentally handicapped and Afro-Germans all experienced attacks within the first year of Nazi rule.

Hitler and his associates in the new German leadership struck in dramatic, decisive ways, but they always tested the public response to each move before proceeding further. This mixture of boldness and caution would be typical of Nazi tactics throughout the Third Reich, from its inception in 1933 to its collapse in 1945. Public opinion was very important to Hitler. A firm believer in the stab-in-the-back myth, he was convinced that a disgruntled German public had lost Germany the First World War. He was determined to avoid a repeat of that situation under his rule.

In *Mein Kampf* Hitler had made it clear that he planned to 'deal with' the Jews. He started his social revolution, however, with attacks on a group that was even less likely to receive public support: homosexual men. In the 1920s and early 1930s, Berlin and other major German cities had become centres of a small but vibrant gay culture. Even before the Nazis came to power, police had sometimes harassed men known or suspected to be homosexual; many Germans regarded homosexuality as deviant and decadent and urged their government to crack down by imposing what they considered moral and sexual order.

Since 1871, Paragraph 175 of the German criminal code had outlawed sexual relations between men: 'A male who indulges in criminally indecent activities with another male or who allows himself to participate in such activities will be punished with jail'. The prohibition did not mention sexual acts between women. Hitler built on this law in early 1933 to ban homosexual rights organisations in Germany. According to National Socialist teachings, homosexuals were an abomination because they opted out of the reproduction of the so-called Aryan master race. Moreover, according to Himmler and others, homosexual men in public positions of any kind were dangerous because they were always vulnerable to blackmail. Antagonistic Nazis focused on gay men; they seemed for the most part not to see lesbians or bisexual women as posing a particular threat, because women did not exercise public power by serving in the military or the high ranks of the bureaucracy. In any case women, some Nazi activists presumed, could always be forced to bear children for the German *Volk*, regardless of their own sexual orientation. Nevertheless, in some individual cases lesbians were persecuted as so-called asocial elements.

Leadership from above prompted initiatives by people acting out their own hostility. In 1933, Nazi storm troopers and other thugs raided gay bars and clubs in German cities and forced many of them to close. A few managed to remain open longer – some intermittently until the end of the Second World War – but under constant threat of raids and violence. In May 1933, a group of Nazi students stormed and destroyed the Institute for Sexual Research in Berlin. Its director was the gay rights activist Magnus Hirschfeld. For the most part the German public was indifferent to or cheered such offensives.

There was likewise no protest within Germany in the spring of 1933, when Nazi regulations banned the Jehovah's Witnesses. In fact, leaders of the official German Protestant and Catholic churches actively encouraged state measures against a religious group they considered a dangerous cult. Many mainstream Christians in Germany disliked Jehovah's Witnesses for their efforts to win converts; German nationalists inside and outside the churches found Jehovah's Witnesses suspect because they neither swore allegiance to the state nor in many cases served in the military.

Most Germans were just as unlikely to complain when the new regime used existing laws and conventions to bear down hard on Gypsies. Stereotyped as shiftless wanderers, Roma and Sinti had suffered police harassment and public prejudice for decades, even before Hitler came to power. Nazi persecution in its early stages hardly seemed new.

Germans of African descent were easy targets as well. They were few in number – probably only hundreds in the early 1930s – and vulnerable in their visibility; those with dark complexions stood out in a nation of white people. Some had come from Germany's former colonies in Africa – territories in modern-day Cameroon, Togo, Namibia, Burundi and Tanzania – or were children of colonials. Some were the offspring of African soldiers or other men of colour stationed in the Rhine area after 1918 as part of the French occupation forces. Many Germans had responded with panic to the appearance of black troops in their midst and the children some of them left behind seemed to many racist Germans to be living examples of Germany's humiliation. Even before he came to power Hitler had spoken of his desire to see all Germans of African descent – people he, like others, called the 'Rhineland bastards' – sterilised. The early months of Nazi rule brought attacks, official as well as spontaneous, on these people as well. Compulsory registration of all Germans deemed 'half-breeds' revealed 385 such individuals, 370 of whose fathers had been part of the French occupation. In 1937 most of those 385 people were sterilised.

One German woman named Doris Reiprich recalls how her landlord evicted her and her African father, white German mother and sister from their apartment after Hitler came to power. She lost her job and fellow students tormented her sister, Erika, in school. Teachers were no better; they forced Erika to take part in a course on 'race' and listen to such statements as 'God made all whites and blacks; half-breeds come from the Devil'. The authorities tried to convince the girls' mother to divorce their father, but she refused.

Both Afro-German sisters would make it through the war by acting in films. They recount their experiences in the book *Showing Our Colours: Afro-German Women Speak Out*. German filmmakers needed a few people of colour to make movies promoting German colonialism in Africa. Throughout the Nazi years most Afro-Germans had no such protective positions. Like Doris Reiprich and her sister, they suffered a whole range of indignities and abuses and many of them experienced even harsher treatment – sterilisation, incarceration and death.

Of course the Nazi revolution also meant assault on German Jews. In 1933 Germany's Jewish population was small: about half a million people, less than one per cent of the total population. New regulations in April banned Jews from the German civil service. That same month the Nazi Party organised a boycott of Jewish businesses throughout Germany, although the boycott was not the success its planners had anticipated.

Hitler's Nazis used a combination of intimidation and legislation to create a mood of hostility toward Germany's Jews, a kind of open season for abuse. During the boycott storm troopers stood outside Jewish businesses to frighten potential customers. Some Jewish children experienced vicious harassment in school from teachers as well as fellow students. Nazi activists staged public humiliations of Jews and friends of Jews. Especially singled out were German Jews and non-Jews who were involved in intimate relations with one another. In one case, for example, Nazi toughs forced a Gentile woman and her Jewish boyfriend to stand in the street wearing sandwich boards. Hers read, 'I am the biggest pig in the place and go around only with Jews'. His said, 'As a Jewish boy I only take German girls to my room'.

The civil service ban and the boycott were less successful for Hitler's new regime than Nazi leaders and activists had hoped. For one thing, there was no concrete definition of who exactly counted as a Jew. So it was not always clear to whom the ban applied. Given Hitler's sensitivity to public opinion, it was important not to antagonise potential 'Aryan' supporters by mistaking them for Jews. Moreover, by April 1933, German Jews had not yet been isolated from the rest of population. The Nazi government did not dare impose measures against Jewish veterans of the First World War, for example, or against Christian spouses of Jews. There was also uncertainty around how to regard people who had converted from Judaism to Christianity. Outraged German Jews who did not yet know how far the regime would go in attacks on them deluged authorities with petitions and requests for exceptions and sometimes non-Jews supported their efforts.

Some non-Jews, however, went even further than the civil service law to introduce anti-Jewish measures on their own. Some Gentile spouses quietly divorced 'undesirable' Jewish mates. In many universities, Gentile administrators fired scholars who were not in fact targeted by the law, for example, Christian men with Jewish wives or people whose parents had converted from Judaism to Christianity. Removing such individuals made those supervisors look especially eager to cooperate with the new government. Students and the other professors were not too likely to complain, because they hoped to benefit from the situation. After all, professorial positions were in high demand in German society, with its many educated people, high level of unemployment and great respect for academics.

In the Protestant church, pro-Nazi clergy who belonged to a group called the German Christian Movement tried to expel from the pulpits any pastors who had converted from Judaism to Christianity or who were the children or grandchildren of such converts. Only a handful of clergy actually fell into those categories. Uneasy as to how Protestant church people inside Germany and abroad would respond, Nazi government authorities decided in 1933 not to back that scheme. Public opinion was still more important to Hitler than complete thoroughness. There would be time to widen the net later. Meanwhile, individuals and organisations were free to develop anti-Jewish initiatives that suited their own purposes. German municipal governments, strapped for cash, found it expeditious to drop Jewish recipients of public support from their welfare lists, before authorities in Berlin had even thought of the idea.

As for the anti-Jewish boycott of April 1933, it did not really catch on. Some German Gentiles complained that the ban on Jewish businesses disrupted their lives and created public disorder. Many continued to frequent Jewish shops out of habit or convenience. Outside Germany there was considerable negative publicity around the anti-Jewish measures. In the United States, Britain and elsewhere, Jews and people who generally opposed abuses of human rights threatened to organise a counter-boycott of German goods to pressure the German government into curbing antisemitic behaviour. Aware that the anti-Jewish boycott was damaging his public image at home and abroad, Hitler ended it.

Nazi leaders learned some lessons from these early anti-Jewish experiments. First, they realised that it was easiest to attack people who were already marginalised. Second, they learned that members of the general public were more likely to participate in or at least tolerate attacks on minorities if they stood to gain rather than to lose from such initiatives. In any case, leading Nazis found out that unanimous approval was not required. As long as there were some activists, indifference of the majority was all that was needed to carry out many plans.

How did German Jews respond to Nazi attacks? Like communists and homosexuals, some left the country. Departure, however, was not a simple proposition, especially for people with families and deep roots in Germany. There had been Jews in German territory for some sixteen hundred years; many Jews were at home in German society in ways that made leaving almost unfathomable. Moreover, some of the people who anti-semites considered Jews did not regard themselves as Jewish at all. Over the centuries Jews had intermarried with Christians and some had converted to Christianity, but because Nazi ideology was based on the notion of blood, its adherents claimed all such people were still Jews.

Unlike communists, who could (mistakenly) expect a haven in the Soviet Union, there was no obvious place for Jews to go. No State of Israel existed yet in the 1930s and the traditional countries of immigrants – the United States, Canada, Australia – all had very restrictive immigration policies. Economic problems linked to the Great Depression and a climate of protectionism made governments and public alike hostile to immigrants, especially those who were not Christian or did not come from Western Europe.

Many German Jews tried to find new ways to pull together within Germany. They organised self-help efforts and sought to combat social isolation by providing educational and cultural opportunities for themselves. To these ends, in September 1933 a group of Jewish leaders created the Reich Representation of the German Jews to unify attempts to preserve Jewish religious life and offer practical assistance to Jews from all over Germany. The group's president, Berlin Rabbi Leo Baeck (1873–1956) would steadfastly refuse to leave even when he had opportunities to do so. As long as any Jews remained in Germany, Rabbi Baeck believed, he belonged with them.

Once German officials began deporting German Jews to the killing centres in late 1941, the Reich Representation of the German Jews lost its already very limited ability to do anything to help its members. Its leaders too were sent to camps and killing centres. In 1943 German police sent Rabbi Baeck to the ghetto and transit camp at Theresienstadt, also known as Terezin, near Prague. Rabbi Baeck survived the war and moved to London.

In 1933 some German Jews joined Zionist associations. The Zionist movement had emerged in the late nineteenth century. Its members believed that Jews were not only a religious group but a distinct people who deserved a country of their own. Zionists took their name from the biblical name 'Zion', the hill in Jerusalem on which the Jewish temple had stood. They worked to establish a Jewish national homeland and some even moved to Palestine. Before the 1930s Zionism had been rather unpopular among German Jews, but Nazi measures made many Jews in Germany think it was their only alternative. After Hitler came to power, some German Zionist leaders who promoted immigration to Palestine found ways to work out arrangements with Nazi authorities who wanted Jews out of Germany. Other German Jews continued to wait and hope that somehow the storm would pass.

The Nazi revolution advanced on all fronts in its drive for so-called racial purity. In May 1933 Hitler introduced a law to legalise eugenic sterilisation, that is, sterilisation to prevent reproduction by people deemed unworthy on the basis of mental or physical conditions. More radical legislation followed just two months later.

In July 1933 Hitler proclaimed the Law for Prevention of Hereditarily Diseased Offspring. It ordered sterilisation of people with certain physical and psychiatric conditions. The list included people characterised as severe alcoholics, epileptics, schizophrenics and a number of other loosely defined categories such as the 'feeble-minded'. Roma and Sinti were targeted too, as 'asocials'. Nazi minister of the interior Wilhelm Frick went so far as to suggest that twenty per cent of the population should be sterilised. Ultimately the number of Germans sterilised under this law would come to less than one per cent of the German population, but that still meant destroying the reproductive capabilities of some 400,000 people without their consent and in many cases against their will.

There was some criticism of the sterilisation law, especially from Catholic clergy. Nevertheless proponents of the measure also found a few Catholic theologians who were willing to endorse it. Meanwhile enforcement required the participation of many people: lawyers who drafted the legislation; medical and social workers who reported people to be sterilised to the authorities; bureaucrats who handled the paperwork; doctors, nurses and aides who performed the procedures. As the Nazi regime established and reinforced its power, it involved ever larger numbers of people, who in turn developed a stake in its continuation. Through this dynamic, Nazi ideas gained acceptance, even among people who might earlier have opposed them.

Rewards and Punishments in the Nazi Revolution

The Nazi revolution brought rewards for those who cooperated as well as attacks on those deemed undesirable. Many Germans of all ages enjoyed participating in an exciting, dynamic movement that welcomed them as long as they were 'the right kinds of people'. In 1933 Hitler and his accomplices introduced a process called *Gleichschaltung*, which means 'coordination', literally 'shifting into the same gear'. In the name of national unity, new Nazi organisations swallowed up other, independent groups and clubs. For example, the Nazi-run German Labour Front replaced the old trades union. Nazi organisations of farmers, women, boys, girls, writers and artists absorbed associations of people in those categories. These new groups had monopolies over their clienteles and did not tolerate competing organisations.

Local cooperation and leadership were essential to the success of 'coordination'. So was a bombardment of propaganda from party-controlled newspapers and publicists enthusiastic about the 'national awakening'. For at least some Germans the surge of group activities provided an exciting sense of belonging. Melitta Maschmann, a teenager in 1933, later described how she loved being part of the Nazi League of German Girls. It gave her a chance to assert independence from her parents, she said, and to feel like someone important, part of dramatic new developments. Testimonials collected from Nazi Party members in the 1930s by the American social scientist Theodore Abel echoed those sentiments: joining the Nazi movement empowered many Germans. Hitler's government introduced all kinds of programmes to win favour with the majority of the population. Enormous publicity was devoted to job creation and massive public works programmes. Many people still claim that Hitler 'saved' Germany from the depression and indeed, Nazi policies did accelerate the process of economic recovery. At the same time, many of Hitler's schemes continued what his predecessors had begun and in any case, by 1933, the depression seemed to have bottomed out in Germany. Of course Hitler took credit for all improvements and the Nazis even set up an agency called Strength Through Joy to organise workers' leisure activities and plan holiday trips. Strength Through Joy set up package tours, such as cruises to the Mediterranean and Scandinavia or short trips within Germany. It also sponsored plans to mass produce the 'people's cars' – Volkswagens – and set up savings plans so that workers could arrange to buy them. Even fun was to appear to be a gift of the *Führer*.

The Nazi revolution claimed to restore order, but from the beginning it was enforced with terror. In March 1933, not even two months after Hitler became chancellor, Nazi authorities opened the first official concentration camp. Located at Dachau, just outside Munich, its initial prisoners were political – communists arrested in the wake of the Reichstag fire – but it also held common criminals and men charged with homosexuality. Dachau Concentration Camp was no secret. To the contrary, the Nazi press covered its opening in detail, on the theory that mere knowledge of its existence would serve as a public deterrent.

Dachau and the network of similar camps that followed were under the control of Heinrich Himmler, one of Hitler's long-time associates and the SS, the Nazis' elite paramilitary force. By July 1933 German concentration camps held an estimated 27,000 people in what was euphemistically called 'protective custody'.

Violence itself served the Nazi regime as a form of propaganda. In May 1933, Hitler's minister of propaganda, Joseph Goebbels, organised public book burnings that presented intimidating spectacles of Nazi might. Thousands of pro-Nazi students proved especially eager to participate. They and other Nazi supporters made huge bonfires of books by such Jewish authors as Albert Einstein and the satirist Kurt Tucholsky. They also burned works by communists and others associated with left-wing positions – for example, the playwright Bertolt Brecht and the writer Heinrich Mann; liberals such as Thomas Mann; and foreigners, including the American Jack London. Such scenes must have communicated a clear threat to outsiders and to critics of Nazism.

Pageantry was the flip side of Nazi terror, another show of strength. The first months of Hitler's rule featured endless torch-light parades with columns of marching men. Observers after the fact often interpret footage of those events as evidence of the unanimity of Germans behind Hitler. It would be probably more accurate to see those demonstrations as efforts on the part of the new regime to create an image of unanimity that itself worked to prevent opposition. It must have been a lonely and terrifying experience to be on the outside of a torchlight march looking in. What chance would one feel one had against that monolith of power?

The columns of Nazis often sang as they marched. Supporters adapted old songs and wrote reams of new ones, everything from sentimental folk songs to outright vicious fighting songs, with lyrics about 'Jewish blood' spurting from German knives. The most famous Nazi song was the *Horst Wessel Lied*. It was named after its lyricist, a young Nazi storm trooper who had been killed in a brawl with a communist in the 1920s. Set to a familiar folk tune, Horst Wessel's lyrics extolled the Nazi flag, called for unity against the foe and praised the comrade heroes who had died for the cause. During the Third Reich the Horst Wessel song became part of Germany's official national anthem. It was always sung with the right arm outstretched in the 'Hitler salute'.

As he had at home, Hitler used a combination of boldness and caution to bring about a revolution in foreign policy. He was a master of making his aims look safely conventional, even while his intentions were dangerously radical. Hitler railed against the Treaty of Versailles, but so had almost all German politicians since the war. He talked about restoring German boundaries to their 'rightful' location; so had many German nationalists. Hitler's plans, however, were far more ambitious and he wanted nothing short of world domination. Nevertheless, in the first stage of his rule he used diplomacy to work toward achieving his goals.

In this regard too Hitler chose his priorities carefully. His first major foreign policy success came in July 1933 shortly before announcement of the new sterilisation law. That month Hitler's representatives signed an agreement called the Concordat with the Vatican in Rome. In exchange for recognition of his regime's legitimacy from the pope, Hitler promised to respect the rights of Catholics and the Roman Catholic Church in Germany. The pope, for his part, hoped to protect Catholic interests within Germany and to use Hitler's Nazi regime as a defence against communism all over Europe. For Hitler the Concordat turned out to be an extremely effective way to buy support both at home and abroad.

Germany's population in 1933 was almost forty per cent Roman Catholic and Hitler himself was raised in the Catholic Church. Nevertheless many German Catholic clergy were initially suspicious of Nazism. They saw Nazi ideas as anti-Christian, especially the emphasis on race and blood and the obvious disrespect for human life. Before the Concordat, some priests in Germany had refused to administer the sacrament of communion to church members in storm trooper or SS uniforms.

The Concordat pulled the rug out from under potential Catholic opposition in Germany. How could parish priests criticise a chancellor who had been recognised by their pope? What possibility remained for a united Catholic front against the sterilisation programme? Meanwhile, abroad the Concordat added to the prestige of Hitler's new regime. Even if the pope no longer wielded much political power, he still had moral authority with Catholics all over the world.

Other foreign policy successes followed. By January 1934 Hitler's diplomats had negotiated a Non-Aggression Pact with Poland that was supposed to last for ten years. Hitler had no intention of keeping that promise, but such deals bought precious time. Meanwhile, Germany withdrew from all its multilateral arrangements; most notably, in October 1933, it left the League of Nations.

Under Hitler Germany began to rearm. Because the Treaty of Versailles restricted German military power, rearmament at first had to be secret. In 1933 Hitler's government set up a phoney initiative called the Agricultural Tractor Program, which was a cover for a project that in fact built tanks. By 1934 Germany was producing explosives, ships and aircraft in quantity. In 1935 Hitler dropped even the pretence of secrecy. Germany had become a military power once again, with an air force, a navy and an army based on conscription.

The Nazi revolution was difficult to oppose because it occurred with a mixture of subtlety and force. The regime did not snap into place in January 1933 as a full-blown totalitarian prison. There was still room for Germans – at least those who were not considered handicapped, Jewish, or otherwise unwanted – to manoeuvre, even to criticise. Precisely those mainstream members of society, however, were the least likely to recognise the revolutionary nature of the new regime. Many of them stood to gain from the measures it introduced and others were apathetic. What did any of it have to do with them? Sadly it was exactly those in the most vulnerable positions – Nazism's targets – who were the first to recognise what was at stake. They, however, had little power to do much about it, other than to warn people like them, who often preferred to hope for the best instead of heeding alarmists, or to try to convince a busy and often hostile world of their impending doom.

An incident recounted by a German waiter and recorded in Bernd Engelmann's book *Inside Hitler's Germany* captures the dynamics of the early months of Nazi rule. In early 1933, the man worked at a restaurant in a small town. One day a group of Nazi enthusiasts came in. The editor of the town's Nazi newspaper was there, so were the chief storm trooper and the local party leader. At another table all alone sat an elderly, Jewish lawyer who had lived in the town all his life. The group of Nazi functionaries got louder and drunker. Suddenly they summoned the waiter, a young man at the time, to their table and told him to deliver a note to the lawyer. Afraid to refuse, the waiter complied, but as he put the note down on the table he saw that it said something like: 'Get out, you Jewish swine'.

The lawyer read the note and began trembling with rage and shame. He stood up at his table and addressed the three men. How dare you, he challenged them: 'I am a veteran of the World War. I risked my life for this country'. The restaurant became deathly still. No one at any of the other tables spoke or even seemed to breathe.

The waiter remembered being able to hear the sounds of pots and pans in the kitchen. The three Nazis broke the silence. They taunted the lawyer again and turned back to their beers. The lawyer summoned the waiter and, still shaking, handed him money to cover his meal, then left the restaurant.

Later the waiter realised that the man had given him far too much money for his bill. He went to the lawyer's home to return the extra. There he found the man dressed in his hat and coat with a suitcase in his hand. He was leaving, he told the waiter, because there was no future for him in Germany.

What would have happened to any of the other Germans at that restaurant if they had spoken in defence of their Jewish neighbour? At that point, in early 1933, probably very little. The aggressors were drunken bullies new to their roles. The observers likely knew them personally, as they did the lawyer. So why did they say nothing? Perhaps they did not want to risk an unpleasant, embarrassing scene. Maybe they would have taken the chance for someone else, a woman, say, or a Christian clergyman. In any case, they were silent and their silence emboldened the ruffians. All over Germany the silence of others like them sent a message back up to Hitler: it was safe to keep pushing.

The end of Nazism's revolutionary phase can be marked with reference to a specific event – the so-called Night of Long Knives, also known as the Röhm Putsch, of 30 June 1934. Ernst Röhm (1887–1934) a veteran of the First World War, had been Hitler's associate since the early 1920s, when he had been instrumental in building up the storm trooper organisation. By 1934 Röhm was head of 2.5 million storm troopers. Röhm and his storm troopers had played a powerful role in destabilising the Weimar Republic and consolidating Hitler's new regime. After some professional setbacks and personal scandals, Röhm emigrated to Bolivia in

1928, but Hitler brought him back to Germany in 1930 to reorganise the storm troopers.

After Hitler became chancellor, he began to view the storm troopers as a liability. Restless for action and disgruntled with what seemed a slow pace of change, many of them thought Hitler had sold out their movement's ideals for the sake of respectability. The SS, or *Schutzstaffel* (protective staff), Nazism's elite guard headed by Himmler, had grown more powerful and wanted the upper hand over its rival organisation, the storm troopers. Meanwhile the army and Hitler's new conservative friends considered the storm troopers disreputable thugs who disrupted public order.

Hitler had to choose. Would he cast his lot with the SS and the army or be loyal to his old brown-shirted storm trooper allies? He decided to move against the storm troopers. On the night of 30 June 1934, on Hitler's orders, the SS struck.

It is often said that a revolution devours its own children. Hitler's revolution was no exception. In a bloody rampage, SS men fanned out to kill Röhm, other old allies of the *Führer* such as the Nazi ideologue Gregor Strasser and Hitler's rivals, including former chancellor General Kurt Schleicher and, for some reason, Schleicher's wife. In general, Hitler and SS leader Himmler used the purge to get rid of people they found problematic. The list of dead even included a Catholic priest who had helped write *Mein Kampf* when Hitler was in prison. Perhaps that man was a victim of mistaken identity, or Hitler may have thought he knew too much to be trusted.

The total number of people killed is unknown. Some place it as low as 150; others estimate it in the thousands. At least eighty high-ranking storm troopers were shot. The numbers of more lowly individuals killed on local initiatives, that is, not on direct orders from Hitler or Himmler, may have been much higher. Hitler did not dismantle the storm troopers completely after the purge, but he clipped the organisation's wings and subordinated it directly to his authority.

Hitler dressed the bloodbath in the guise of conventional morality. Ernst Röhm was openly homosexual. Hitler had known about Röhm's sexual preferences for years and never seemed to have considered them a problem. Now, however, in his bid for legitimacy, Hitler publicly reviled Röhm. The killings, Nazi press reports contended in lurid detail, were part of a cleanup of the movement, a necessary measure against decadence and perversion.

How did the German public react? One might expect shock or horror. In fact there was little of either expressed in Germany, at least in public. President Hindenburg sent Hitler a telegram of congratulation for restoring order and German military leaders likewise praised what they considered appropriate measures in the interest of public safety. Members of Hitler's cabinet declared the purge retroactively legal. Many observers believed that now the Nazi regime had become an ordinary government, its dangerous, extremist days behind it.

Victor Klemperer, a German professor of Jewish background in Dresden, had a different opinion. After such blatant criminality, he was certain that the regime of brutes had to fall. Surely the old German elite would come to its senses and throw out the upstarts, he hoped, but Klemperer was wrong. The Night of Long Knives left Hitler stronger than ever.

Phase II: Routinisation, 1934–1937

June 1934 marked a turning point in the Nazi regime. By no means did it signify the end of brutality, but it did usher in a new phase of routinisation. Instead of uncontrolled, revolutionary shows of force, Nazi authorities concentrated on systematising violence and normalising coercion. They did so by centralising power in the hands of a few and passing laws to make their measures at least look respectable. Inventing rituals and convincing people to police their own behaviour in keeping with Nazi regulations were also parts of the process.

One component of routinisation was centralisation, which took many forms. One of the most significant was the centralisation of police power under Heinrich Himmler and the SS. The Night of Long Knives brought the storm troopers under Himmler's jurisdiction. In 1934, Himmler, along with his associate Reinhard Heydrich, who ran the intelligence office known as the Security Service, took over all political police, known in Germany as the Gestapo. By 1936 Himmler had pulled the criminal police into his orbit as well, so that the head of the SS and the concentration camps was now in charge of all police forces in Germany.

Himmler and his tens of thousands of SS men were crucial to the Third Reich. Unlike the German military, the SS was officially linked to the Nazi Party organisation, not to the government of Germany. Throughout the Third Reich, the Nazi Party retained its own separate hierarchy with headquarters in the Brown House in Munich. Its status as attached to the party gave the SS an unprecedented degree of independence from any kind of authority that predated Hitler's rise to power. The SS was an ideologically dynamic organisation that combined the functions of a conventional, repressive political police with a drive to implement the '*Führer*'s idea'. Himmler saw his goal as defending 'purity of the blood' and persecuting those who he believed threatened it: communists, Freemasons, Jehovah's Witnesses, homosexuals, Jews, Gypsies and others.

In August 1934 President Hindenburg, the man who had appointed Hitler chancellor of Germany, died. In another act of centralisation, Hitler united the offices of president and chancellor in his own person. That change did not substantially alter Hitler's actual duties, nor did the president's death remove a major obstacle to the expansion of Hitler's power. Hindenburg had done little to check Hitler's activities in the first year and a half of Nazi rule. Nevertheless, for some Germans the death of the old man Hindenburg meant the end of any hope that Hitler and Nazism would be stopped.

There were also practical repercussions to the uniting of the offices of chancellor and president in the person of the *Führer*. According to the German constitution, still officially in force, the president was the supreme commander of the German armed forces. Hitler now claimed that position for himself and used it to require members of the military to swear an oath of personal allegiance to him.

A second component of routinisation involved legalising Nazi measures. The goals of Hitler and the Nazi 'true believers' were twofold: 'racial purity' and spatial expansion. In this phase of development after the Nazi revolution of 1933–1934, pursuing those goals meant revamping German law. Members of all professions – teachers, journalists, doctors – served the Nazi cause, but lawyers and judges played an especially important role in giving the regime and its measures a veneer of legitimacy that was important to international observers and at least some Germans. As he consolidated and expanded his power, Hitler had to operate within the prevailing view of Germany as a state governed by law.

The first minister of justice under Hitler, Franz Gürtner, was not a Nazi, although he supported authoritarian rule. Gürtner was prepared to sanction the blatant illegalities of the revolutionary phase, including attacks on communists and the Röhm Putsch massacre. Justice Minister Gürtner also presided over laying the legal foundations for what would become mass murder of people considered handicapped and of Jews.

The key pieces of legislation when it came to attacks on Jews were the Nuremberg Laws, passed in the autumn of 1935. The laws had two parts. First was the Law for Protection of German Blood and Honour, which forbade marriage or sexual relations between Jews and 'Aryan' Germans. Jews could not fly the German flag, nor could they employ German Gentile women under the age of forty-five in their households. Such measures were intended to isolate German Jews from the rest of the population and stigmatise them as disloyal, destructive outsiders.

The second component was the Reich Citizenship Law of November 1935. This legislation defined, for the first time, who was to count as a Jew in Nazi Germany. According to Nazi ideology, Jewishness was a racial trait, but in fact there was no way to measure distinctions of blood, because they did not actually exist. In other words, there were no reliable markers of appearance, blood type, or any other physical traits that Nazi 'experts' could use to separate Jews from 'Aryans'. Instead the Nuremberg Laws fell back on religion as the only way to define Jews.

Under the law it was not one's own religion but that of one's grandparents that mattered. People with three or more grandparents of the Jewish faith counted as Jews. Most Germans defined as 'Jews' under the law lost the rights associated with German citizenship.

The Nuremberg Laws considered people who had two grandparents of the Jewish faith to be *Mischlinge*, or 'mixed bloods', a category that would remain in dispute throughout the entire Third Reich. *Mischlinge* who were Jewish by religion or who married people categorised as Jews also counted as Jews. Some *Mischlinge* who had no contact with Judaism or Jews likewise ended up being treated as Jews, perhaps because they looked like the stereotype of Jewish or had especially hostile neighbours or co-workers. There were, however, *Mischlinge* who managed to continue living in German society throughout the Nazi period and some of them even served in the German military in the Second World War. The law did not address people with one Jewish grandparent, but in practice some of them would also face disadvantage and discrimination of various kinds.

The Reich Citizenship Law offered no definition of 'Aryan' other than the implied opposite of 'non-Aryan' or 'Jew'. Thus, by default, Germans with four grandparents who were baptised into a Christian church were generally assumed to be 'Aryans'.

Most non-Jewish Germans gave little thought to the Nuremberg Laws. They seemed just one more bureaucratic measure that would have little direct impact on their lives. Nor did the international community regard the laws as especially significant. After all, every nation reserved for itself the right to determine who counted as its citizens, on what basis and what rights they received.

Their mundane appearance notwithstanding, the Nuremberg Laws proved to be a crucial step toward the destruction of Germany's Jews. All kinds of attacks on Jews were now directly sanctioned, even mandated, by law. Moreover, once Jews were defined, it would be much easier to isolate, rob, deport and eventually kill them.

Although focused on Jews, the Nuremberg Laws had repercussions for other target groups as well. Regulations that followed meant that under certain conditions, Gypsies, as 'alien to the Aryan species', could also lose the rights of German citizens. They too faced prohibitions on marrying so-called Aryan Germans. Eager German racists applied measures described in the Nuremberg Laws to Afro-Germans as well. One woman remembers how as a small girl she was sent home by a teacher who forbade her, as a 'non-Aryan', to march behind the German flag.

The phase of routinisation also brought increased measures against homosexuals. In June 1935, Paragraph 175 of the German criminal code was revised to expand the definition of 'criminally indecent activities between men'. Now sexual relations did not have to be established; any physical intimacy assumed to lead to sexual arousal could be grounds for prosecution. It became easy for denouncers to lay charges of homosexuality and the courts used their power to impose a crackdown that brought thousands of men accused of homosexual behaviour into prisons and con-centration camps.

Meanwhile, Nazi sterilisation developed its own routines and new regulations extended the assault on those considered handi-capped. For example, a 1935 law required any pregnant woman who should have been sterilised under the 1933 law but had not been to have an abortion. The laws and regulations already intro-duced against people deemed handicapped routinised worsening conditions in institutions and hospitals around Germany. What kind of treatment would you expect healthcare workers to mete out toward people whose government labelled them 'useless eaters' and 'unworthy lives'?

In addition to centralisation and legalisation, a third com-ponent of Nazi routinisation was ritualisation. After the first year, Nazi pageantry developed a ritualised rhythm. The largest event was the annual Party Rally, held each year in the southern German city of Nuremberg. It was an enormous spectacle, cho-reographed by propaganda experts to the smallest details. As with the early torchlight marches, these imposing shows of strength were supposed to create a sense of unanimity and invincibility so that any opponents of the system would feel isolated and help-less. In 1934 the German director Leni Riefenstahl filmed the rally and released it under the title *Triumph of the Will*. It has become one of the most famous propaganda movies of all time.

Later some Germans would describe their participation in these Nazi extravaganzas as among the high points of their lives. In particular children seemed very impressed. Alfons Heck, a member of the Hitler Youth from a small town near the French border, described his trip to the Nuremberg Party Rally in 1935 in his book *A Child of Hitler*, which he wrote many years later. Heck was awed by the pageantry, the uniforms and the scale of the whole affair. No doubt those sensations contributed to his own devotion to the Nazi cause and his desire to share in such amazing power.

Of course, for others inside Germany Nazi spectacles brought other kinds of routines – predictable harassment and the drudgery of confinement. In preparation for the 1936 Olympics in Berlin, an event that Nazi organisers used to showcase the 'new Germany' in all its splendour, police forced about six hundred Gypsies out of Berlin into detention in a camp near a sewage dump and the cemetery in the nearby suburb of Marzahn. Guarded by police and their dogs, the camp had only three water pumps and two toilets. Under those conditions, contagious diseases ran rampant. Otto Rosenberg, a Sinto from Berlin, had just turned nine when police shipped him, his grandmother, a teenaged aunt, and a brother and sister to Marzahn. The smell of sewage was terrible, he recalled, and people lived in huts knocked together from sheet iron they scrounged for themselves. The glories of the Third Reich looked rather different from the vantage point of what amounted to an overcrowded, filthy, open-air prison.

A fourth important aspect of routinisation might be called self-coordination. In the years between 1934 and the beginning of the war, Nazism lost much of its momentum. Some people became disillusioned or bored with the new system, but most of the population, even those who were not overly enthusiastic, fell into the habit of going along with the regime. They grumbled in private, perhaps, or expressed their criticism in ineffective forms, such as jokes. In either case they posed no real threat to Nazi control.

One popular joke that poked fun both at Hitler's pretensions and at public gullibility went as follows. Hitler and Goebbels were driving through the German countryside when their car struck a dog. Hitler, who loved animals, was devastated. 'Go and find the masters of that loyal German dog', he ordered his minister of propaganda. 'Apologise to them in the name of the *Führer*'. Some time later Goebbels returned, beaming and bearing all kinds of gifts: bread, sausage and beer. 'What happened?' Hitler demanded. 'Were they unhappy?' 'Not at all, mein *Führer*', Goebbels answered. 'All I said was '*Heil Hitler! Der Hund ist tot*' [The dog is dead] and they began to celebrate'.

Self-coordination also involved self-policing. Since 1933 a law called the Malicious Practices Act had banned remarks that offended or subverted Nazi authority. Such prohibitions can only be effective if people report one another and they did so in Nazi Germany. Throughout the 1930s denunciations poured into the offices of the Gestapo, the political police in charge of crimes against the state. Some people denounced others in order to demonstrate their own loyalty to the Nazi cause. Others sought to better their positions, attack outsiders, or just carry out old grudges. The prevalence of denunciations and police raids inspired German wits to invent two new national 'saints', Maria D'enunciata and Marie Haussuchung – that is, Holy Mary the Denouncer and Mary of the House Searches.

Fear of denunciation led people to develop what became known as the 'German glance' – the quick look over the shoulder before one spoke to see who might overhear. The SD or Security Service employed an elaborate network of infiltrators and informers whose job it was to report in detail on the public mood across Germany. Nazi routinisation depended on consensus and co-option as well as coercion.

Nevertheless Nazi Germany cannot simply be characterised as a 'police state'. Indeed, as the historian Robert Gellately has shown, there were relatively few police per capita in Germany in the 1930s. A high level of cooperation from the general public, not an unusual number of men in uniform, made Nazi control possible. Smooth functioning of the system did not require all Germans – or even most – to share every tenet of Nazi ideology. Enough enthusiasts could always be found to stage enormous public shows of support, such as the annual Nuremberg Party rallies. On a day-to-day basis, the Nazi regime only needed most people to obey the law, try to stay out of trouble and promote their own interests as best they could under the current circumstances.

Preparations for War

Even during the period of routinisation Hitler did not lose sight of his goals of race and space. In various ways he presided over Germany's preparation for war. After two years of secret rearmament, in 1935 Hitler's government went public. It reintroduced conscription and revealed its new military machine to the world.

No one had altered the Treaty of Versailles, but German contravention of its terms had become routine under the Nazis. The victors of the First World War were not in a position to risk a new conflict in order to check German violations. Impoverished by the war and the difficult years that followed and faced with their own problems at home, the British and the French had no desire to play the role of international police. The United States had retreated into isolationism and most of its people opposed its government involving them again in the turmoil of European affairs.

In 1936 Hitler took his biggest foreign policy gamble so far. Under the Treaty of Versailles, the westernmost part of Germany along the Rhine River had been demilitarised to provide a buffer zone for France. A year after reintroduction of conscription, rumours began to circulate that Hitler intended to reoccupy the Rhineland with Germany's new military. For some months he seemed to waver, waiting until the Winter Olympics in Berlin had ended and collecting the views of his inner circle, Germany's diplomats and military leaders. By the beginning of March, he had made his decision and prepared to act.

Hitler made the announcement in a speech on 7 March to the Reichstag and, by radio, to the people of Germany. It was a lengthy and in places emotional speech, which denounced

Versailles and railed against communism. Hitler saved the punchline for the end. 'In the interest of the primitive rights of a people to the security of its borders and safeguarding of its defence capability', he proclaimed, 'the German Reich government has therefore from today restored the full and unrestricted sovereignty of the Reich in the demilitarised zone of the Rhineland'. The six hundred deputies in the Reichstag, all in Nazi uniform, went wild, stretching out their arms in the Nazi salute and screaming 'Heil!'

Meanwhile, German troops were approaching the Hohenzollern Bridge across the Rhine River in the city of Cologne. Propaganda minister Goebbels had arranged for planeloads of journalists to be on hand to record the event and thousands of Germans crowded into nearby streets to cheer the soldiers as they crossed into the demilitarised zone. Even in this moment of national euphoria, Hitler and his advisers retained some caution. They made sure that the forward troops were instructed to withdraw and fight if they met military resistance from the French. As Hitler had expected, the French did not respond by sending in troops to engage the Germans. Instead the gamble paid off by giving Hitler's prestige at home its most enormous boost yet.

Even as he publicly pledged his commitment to European peace, Hitler announced to his inner circle in 1936 that Germany must be ready for war within four years. To that end he named his old associate Hermann Göring head of a 'Four-Year Plan' to prepare the German economy and military for war. Göring took over economic planning and the old minister of the economy resigned.

In the winter of 1937–1938, Hitler completed the routinisation and consolidation of his rule by dumping the old elites who had been so instrumental in bringing him to power. Those old-fashioned conservatives had been useful throughout the phases of Nazi revolution and routinisation. They had lent respectability to the regime when it needed it and had provided expertise and continuity as it consolidated its power. Now, as Hitler prepared to move to a more aggressive phase, they had become a burden.

In November 1937 Hitler met with leaders of the German army, navy and air force. It had been two years since Germany had announced its rearmament. Since 1936 German forces had been involved in the Spanish Civil War on the side of General Francisco Franco and the enemies of the Spanish Republic. Hitler had pushed German intervention even though many Germans opposed it. Because the Soviet Union backed the Republic in Spain, support of Franco gave Hitler a way to attack communism. Moreover, Mussolini was actively behind Franco as well. So Spain offered a chance for Germany and Italy to practice cooperation in the spirit of their leaders' mutual admiration. For the Germans the Spanish Civil War was also an opportunity to try out new military equipment. In particular they broke in their new air force by bombing Spanish towns and cities. Now Hitler was ready to risk more. Hitler gave those gathered at the November meeting a lengthy harangue on Germany's need for more space. They were sceptical. How could Germany be ready for war? Hitler's response to their misgivings was typical. In early 1938 he launched a purge of the military leadership, replacing old conservatives with men more amenable to Nazi plans. He retired fourteen senior generals, replaced or pensioned approximately sixty others and assumed command of the armed forces as minister of war. Hitler made a clean sweep of all positions directly related to his plans for war. He replaced the conservative foreign minister Constantin von Neurath with the loyal Nazi Joachim von Ribbentrop. The Nazi general Walter von Brauchitsch became head of the army in place of Werner von Fritsch. There were new Nazi ambassadors to Rome, Tokyo and Vienna.

Hitler's methods in early 1938 were quite different from those he had used to purge the storm troopers less than four years earlier. This time he employed less violent means, in keeping with the stature of the individuals involved and the spirit of routinisation rather than revolution. But the tactics were no less vicious for their bloodlessness. For example, Hitler disposed of the war minister Werner von Blomberg by stirring up a scandal around his new wife. She was a former prostitute, the Nazi press claimed; how could a man thus compromised hold a position of such responsibility? The fact that both Hitler and Göring had served as witnesses at the wedding was conveniently omitted and Blomberg went abroad in disgrace.

Two years earlier, rumours of homosexual activities on the part of Fritsch, the head of the army, had been ignored. Now Fritsch had to go and the old charges provided the perfect means to force him out. He, like the others, had served his purpose; he had supported Hitler's regime in its early stages and helped provide it with a veneer of legitimacy by linking the new system to familiar, experienced military leaders. After four full years in power Hitler had consolidated his position and preparations for war were under way. Fritsch, Blomberg and the others had outlived their usefulness to Hitler and it was no problem to find replacements eager for their positions. Meanwhile those members of the military elite who kept their jobs fell into line with barely a murmur. It would become much more difficult to challenge Nazi rule now that not only the police but the military was firmly in hand.

Contrary to the image presented by Nazi propaganda – Germans marching in massive columns, their arms raised as one in the salute to Hitler – not all Germans fell into line. Friedrich Thimme, a trained historian and fervent German patriot who had headed the Foreign Office's division on the so-called War Guilt Question in the 1920s, railed in his private and not-so-private correspondence against Hitler and his henchmen and refused to break ties to his Jewish friends. Thimme's daughter Annelise, a teenaged schoolgirl in Berlin in the early years of the Third Reich, announced to her classmates that obviously the Nazis had lit the Reichstag fire themselves and she scoffed at nazified teachers who preached the party line in the classroom. With a group of high-spirited schoolmates, Annelise once played a trick on one of the worst offenders. One at a time the girls rode by the teacher, who was on her own bicycle, calling out 'Heil Hitler' so that the woman repeatedly had to raise her right arm in salute until she lost her balance and fell. In a small way, that youthful prank reveals the continued presence in Hitler's Germany of people who for all kinds of reasons – family ties, personal loyalties, religious and moral principles, political allegiances – remained sceptical and even critical of their government and its actions.

In early 1938, however, most Germans were not thinking about challenging Nazi rule. Looking back on his youth in
Germany, Alfons Heck could see some of the factors that made
him an enthusiastic Nazi. There was the indoctrination in school
and in the Hitler Youth, for example and the unrelenting propaganda. But there were also concrete ways that Nazism benefited
him. It promised action, rewards for his ambition, power, a
chance to be an insider and a role in something enormously successful. Heck, like many of Hitler's German supporters, was no
brainwashed automaton. He was just one of millions of 'ordinary people' who, for all kinds of ordinary reasons, endorsed and
accepted a brutal system.

4

Open Aggression: In Search of War, 1938–1939

By early 1938, Nazi rule had become a familiar routine for most Germans. For some, such as the eager young Hitler Youth member Alfons Heck, it was a comfortable yet exciting existence. Ambitious and enthusiastic, Heck could expect to realise his goal of becoming an airplane pilot. After all, was not Germany becoming richer and stronger? Its new air force beckoned him from its triumphs in Spain; his teachers and the books and newspapers he read assured him the future was his. Born in 1927, Heck could hardly remember the Nazi revolution. The normalisation of Nazi power coincided with his development of political and social awareness. It was really the only world he knew.

Born the same year as Alfons Heck, the Gypsy boy Otto Rosenberg also grew up with the Nazi system. By 1938 he knew all the miseries of the Marzahn 'lot' and had mastered some ways around them. Often hungry, he pulled beets for nearby farmers in exchange for pennies and food: Belgian buns with icing, coffee with milk. He became used to seeing the riot squad beat people with sabres and haul them off to what was known in local parlance as the 'concert-camp'. In 1938, he watched police round up the men of Marzahn and drive them away in lorries to Sachsenhausen. Still, when his mother who had arrived in Marzahn after him, was ordered to report to the police in Berlin, Rosenberg waited for her to return. Instead she was sent straight to the women's camp at Ravensbrück.

For Victor Klemperer, professor of French literature in Dresden, routinisation of Nazi rule meant an ever-tightening trap. The university dismissed Klemperer in 1935, even though he was both a convert from Judaism to Christianity and a veteran of the First World War. One insult and deprivation followed another. Klemperer was forbidden to publish. He lost borrowing privileges at the library and eventually library staff refused even to let him use the reading room. Over the years Nazi regulations robbed Klemperer of his car, his house, his driver's license, even his pets. If the years from 1933 to 1938 seemed to fly on magical wings for the young Nazi boy Heck, for the middle-aged 'non-Aryan' Klemperer they crawled by, an endless drudgery of discouragement and abuse. The years ahead would be even worse.

Beginning in early 1938, Hitler's Germany entered a third stage of development. After the euphoric phase of revolution and the consolidating period of routinisation, Hitler and his inner circle took off the gloves and began seeking war. For Hitler war was more than military conflict; it was to be a decisive step toward realising his ideas. By 1938 he had already prepared the ground by rearming, isolating target groups and appointing loyal supporters in key positions. Now, open aggression would characterise developments in Nazi Germany even before the invasion of Poland in September 1939.

Contrary to the stereotype, most Germans were not foaming at the mouth, eager for war, in 1938 and 1939. In fact, the German public as a whole, including many people who were enthusiastic about aspects of the Nazi domestic program, would greet with scepticism many of the moves that Hitler and his Nazi elite would make in this phase of open aggression. It was one thing to assert German strength and revolutionise conditions at home, but it was quite another to risk war when, for many Germans, memories of the previous war remained painfully fresh. Such uneasiness, however, was not enough to derail Hitler's plans. Instead he was able to use 1938 and 1939 to construct a unified front for the cause of race and space. He did so by resorting to such old loyalties as nationalism, patriotism and solidarity against common enemies. Even more important, he built support through success.

It is often said that nothing succeeds like success. Certainly Nazi Germany seems to confirm that saying. Every time Hitler took a risk and won, he decreased the anxiety among the German people and convinced more of them to trust him. Many feared war because they dreaded bloodshed, personal and financial loss and defeat. The wounds of world war and especially its bitter outcome in 1918 were still raw for most adults, but what they perceived to be Hitler's foreign policy triumphs in 1938–1939 did a great deal to relieve their concerns.

Events in 1938–1939 demonstrate how domestic and foreign policies were intertwined in Hitler's Germany. Foreign policy successes helped ease concerns and buy support at home. Meanwhile Hitler's regime pursued the goals of race and space on both fronts: abroad it attacked Germany's supposed enemies and took steps toward a military offensive; at home it enforced 'racial purity' and trained its people for war.

Scepticism and Success: German Annexation of Austria and the Sudetenland

The first of Hitler's string of foreign policy successes in 1938 and 1939 was the *Anschluss*, the German annexation of Austria in March 1938. The Treaty of Versailles had forbidden Austria and Germany from uniting. In 1936, in order to placate Mussolini's Italy, Hitler had issued assurances that Germany would not violate Austrian independence. Mussolini and some other Italians were worried about German designs on Austria and on territories long disputed between Austria and Italy: South Tyrol and Trieste. Like all of Hitler's promises, the pledge to respect Austrian independence was made to be broken.

In early March 1938, the Austrian chancellor Kurt von Schuschnigg announced a plebiscite to show Austria's determination to resist Nazi power. The next day, Hitler called together his military leaders to address the possibility of German occupation. It took only hours to prepare a plan; Hitler ordered German forces to cross the border into Austria on 12 March.

The plan was no work of genius. Supposedly, German tanks had to stop at commercial petrol stations to refuel on the way. Rumours abounded that one commander relied on Baedeker's guide, a popular handbook for tourists, to plot his route. Nevertheless the Germans arrived, greeted by cheering crowds. Contrary to the impression created by the Hollywood film *The Sound of Music*, most Austrians did not oppose the German invasion. In fact the *Anschluss* sparked vicious displays of anti-semitism within Austria. Austrian Gentiles, sometimes urged on by Germans but often acting on their own, seized the opportunity to assail their Jewish compatriots. They stole their property, harassed and beat them and subjected many to public rituals of humiliation. In Vienna, crowds took delight in forcing professors, artists, journalists and other prominent Austrian Jews to scrub streets with toothbrushes. Decades after the war a small statue in Vienna commemorates the 'Jew with a toothbrush' and reminds Austrians of the complicity of ordinary people from their country in the crimes of Nazism.

The other European and international powers did not try to stop the German annexation of Austria. Many foreign observers saw the event simply as Germans taking control of their own 'back yard'. Meanwhile German authorities together with local supporters moved quickly to implement the Nazi revolution in Austria. Measures against Jews, Gypsies, the disabled and others that had been implemented over five years in Germany were rushed through within months in the new Nazi lands. Members of target groups in Austria had even fewer options to help themselves than did their counterparts within the pre-1938 German borders.

Initially there were some popular misgivings about the *Anschluss* within Germany itself. Many Germans worried that this blatant defiance of the Versailles settlement could mean war. When the response instead was accolades within Austria and assent around Europe, they too welcomed this destruction of an independent nation as a legitimate expression of German strength. Once again Hitler had followed his familiar pattern: push forward hard and wait to see if anyone pushes back. If not, keep pushing.

Memoirs by Austrian Jews provide moving accounts of the impact of the *Anschluss*. In her memoir, *Still Alive*, Ruth Kluger, a young girl in Vienna in 1938, recalls the events of that year. She remembers lying in her bed hearing bands of men march by outside singing the song about 'Jewish blood' spurting from German knives. One day her mother sent her to see the film *Snow White and the Seven Dwarfs*. The girl was afraid to go; she knew Jews were not allowed in the cinema. Ridiculous, her mother insisted; no one would bother a child. They did bother, young Ruth learned. She ended up sitting next to the teenaged leader of the neighbourhood Nazi girls' club, who threatened and shamed her. Sometimes children grasped more quickly than adults how things had changed.

Emboldened by success in Austria, Hitler made his next move against Czechoslovakia, a country he had identified in 1937 as the first target of his planned expansion. He was willing to risk war; in fact he sought it and was disappointed in 1938 when it did not happen. With regard to Czechoslovakia the issue used to generate a crisis was the ethnic German minority in the Sudetenland, near the border with Germany.

In the summer of 1938, members of the ethnic German minority became increasingly vocal with complaints of mistreatment at the hands of the Czech government. Nazi agents from Germany encouraged and provoked their discontent. In response to reports that Hitler planned military action to rescue the ethnic Germans of the Sudetenland, the Czechs began to mobilise their own forces. They also appealed to the French and the British for help. Alarmed at the risk of war, representatives of the European powers agreed to meet with Czech and German negotiators to seek a resolution. At the Munich Conference in September 1938, French and British delegates decided Czechoslovakia should cede the Sudetenland to Germany. The area had a substantial ethnic

German population, they reasoned and if they made this concession to Hitler's demands, he and his supporters would be satisfied.

Decades after the Munich Conference, it and its most famous spokesman, British Prime Minister Neville Chamberlain, are still synonymous with the term 'appeasement'. The term is almost always invoked with contempt and Chamberlain is mocked for his triumphant announcement that he and his colleagues had achieved peace in their time. Some critics even suggest that the appeasers were somehow responsible for the Second World War, as if a harder line from them in 1938 would have melted Nazi aggression.

Chamberlain and the others may have shown weakness, but they wanted peace, whereas Hitler was set on war. Instead of rejoicing at his successful manoeuvre, Hitler felt cheated when he returned to Berlin with a negotiated settlement giving Germany control of territories that had belonged to Czechoslovakia. Hitler worried that the optimum moment for war might have passed him by, because Germany's enemies would now have time to prepare for confrontation. A show of force at Munich from the British and the French would not have prevented war. It would only have moved it to a timetable that Hitler himself considered preferable.

This time too there were misgivings at home. At the peak of the war scare, Protestant church leaders sponsored prayers for peace that landed a number of pastors in prison for their implied criticism of Hitler's actions. Within the army, some of the top brass worried about what seemed a slide toward a war they thought Germany could not win. There were even some tentative plans for a coup against Hitler in case it came to hostilities. All came to nothing. Instead Hitler's successful bid for the Sudetenland – although he regarded it as a failure – gave his prestige within Germany another substantial boost. In 1939, just months after the Munich Conference granted Sudetenland to Germany, German troops entered the rest of Czechoslovakia. On Hitler's orders the state was dismantled. Parts were incorporated into the German Reich and other parts were set up as a protectorate, a kind of colony. Slovakia became a semi-independent client state under the government of the antisemitic Catholic priest Josef Tiso.

Those who blame the supposed harshness of the Treaty of Versailles for the rise and expansion of Nazism might note the considerable territories the Germans had gained even before war began in 1939. By the end of 1938 Germany had already recouped most of its First World War losses. With the destruction of Czechoslovakia in 1939, Germany acquired lands it had never controlled before, but Hitler was not satisfied. His ambitions went far beyond merely revising the terms of Versailles.

Domestic Targets: The *Kristallnacht* Pogrom and Expansion of the Concentration Camp System

The year 1938 also signalled a heightened wave of aggression in racial policies. The most dramatic expression of this new stage of Nazism was the attack on Jews in Germany and Austria on the night of 9–10 November 1938. Nazi leaders called the pogrom the *Kristallnacht* (in English, the 'night of broken glass') and that name continues to be used.

In October 1938, the German government expelled more than 14,000 Jews who resided in Germany but were citizens of Poland. The order was a response to a decree issued by the Polish ministry of the interior requiring all Polish citizens living outside the country to revalidate their passports or lose the right to return. Worried that they would be stuck with these people, German authorities struck first. Transports dumped the Jews of Polish citizenship at the Germany–Poland border, where Polish authorities refused them entry. Forced to spend desperate weeks in limbo, they were finally permitted into Poland after Jews inside the country promised to give them shelter.

Meanwhile Herschel Grynszpan, a seventeen-year-old German-Polish-Jewish student in Paris, went to the German embassy and shot an official there. Grynszpan's motives are no longer completely clear. We know that his parents and sister were among those Jews thrown out of Germany, and Grynszpan's action was an expression of outrage at their treatment. Rumours of a love affair between Grynszpan and the German official also surfaced. It has been suggested that Grynszpan was trying to blackmail the consular officer in order to get the papers he needed to stay in France. In any case, for Nazi propaganda minister Goebbels, this incident provided the perfect excuse for a violent assault against Jews within Germany.

Nazi propaganda described the pogrom that followed announcement of Herschel Grynszpan's shooting of the German diplomat as a spontaneous expression of hatred of Jews on the part of the majority German population. In fact the event was the carefully prepared culmination of a period of increasing pressure on Jews in Germany. Even the date was chosen with care – 9 November, the date of Hitler's attempted putsch in 1923, was a holy day in the Nazi calendar.

Permission – and instructions – from above unleashed the hatred of storm troopers and other Nazi activists. All over Germany they torched synagogues and destroyed ritual objects associated with Judaism, such as Torah scrolls. Others joined in the attack, some driven by antisemitic fervour, others lured by the possibility of loot, still others just eager for action. Crowds smashed the windows of businesses owned by Jews; they vandalised and stole Jewish property. The attackers did not spare Jewish homes. They forced their way in, robbing, beating, raping and demolishing. Memoirs describe the clouds of feathers that surrounded Jewish residences as the aggressors slashed bedding in their quest for valuables and their lust for destruction. They burned scores of synagogues all over Germany and Austria and killed about a hundred Jews. Nazi authorities rounded up some 26,000 Jewish men and sent them to concentration camps. Those men seized in the *Kristallnacht* pogrom were the first Jews in Germany arrested simply for being Jewish.

Responses to the violence varied widely. Alfons Heck recounts how he and another boy eagerly joined a crowd singing as it stormed a synagogue. For them the pogrom was a chance to throw rocks and 'smash some stuff'. An outraged uncle caught them and dragged them away by the ears. Foreign journalists watched the event with horror. Their accounts differ considerably in the degree of popular participation they describe.

Some observed how onlookers joined the rampage and plunder, whereas others sensed disapproval from ordinary citizens. Reports of the events filled the front pages of *The Times* of London and the *New York Times*.

Certainly the German public as a whole was less enthusiastic about *Kristallnacht* than the pogrom's instigators had hoped. In this case it seemed that misgivings had less to do with fear of war or support of Jews than with a dislike of disorder. There was grumbling about the mess, the disruption and the general impropriety of such open violence. Still such uneasiness did not produce a general outcry. At most it took the form of private aid to acquaintances. Peter Gay, a young boy in Berlin in 1938, recalls how a non-Jewish friend of the family hid his father from the police for weeks during and after the pogrom. Much more commonly, misgivings prompted non-Jews simply to turn their backs on the violence.

Nazi authorities, always alert to public opinion, noticed even that low level of disapproval. It is no coincidence that *Kristallnacht* marked the last open pogrom they organised in Germany and annexed Austria. In the future they would avoid having reluctant 'Aryans' witness wide scale violence at home. It would prove easy enough to move blatant attacks further from the public eye.

As in the cases of the *Anschluss* and the Sudetenland crisis, success made *Kristallnacht* more palatable for nervous Germans. Many Jews, terrified by the open attack and acutely aware of their vulnerability, became desperate to leave Germany. So-called Aryans benefited from that desperation as they scooped up Jewish property at bargain-basement prices. No doubt many who had shaken their heads at the unruly mobs on 9 November nevertheless were willing to share in the spoils, and once they had the goods those Germans had a stake in the continuation of Nazi anti-Jewish policies.

Afterward the German government added insult to injury by requiring the Jewish community to pay for the material damage of *Kristallnacht*. It extorted an estimated $400 million from Jews for the death of the German diplomat and another $100 million for damages to property. That cynical policy no doubt furthered the false notion within Germany that the Jews were a bottomless source of wealth they did not deserve. Even the name *Kristallnacht*, chosen by Goebbels, focused on the destruction of Jewish shop windows, as if the pogrom were somehow merely about correcting economic injustices within Germany. In fact it was the synagogues, sites of Jewish religious and communal life, that were the first targets of attack.

As for Jews themselves, how did they react? Between 1933 and the outbreak of war in September 1939, approximately half of the Jews in Germany – some 300,000 people – left. Much of this exodus took place in the wake of *Kristallnacht*, from the Sudetenland and what had been Austria as well as from all over Germany. For most European Jews it took enormous perseverance and ingenuity to get out, to find somewhere to go and to figure out ways to start new lives.

Successful relocation also took luck. Many Austrian, Czech and German Jews saw the threat of Nazism and tried to move beyond its reach. Some had the resources, connections, or relatives necessary to get to Britain, Palestine, the United States, Canada or Australia. Others, often blocked from those most desirable destinations, took refuge in Cuba, the Dominican Republic, China, or Turkey. Many found their way to neighbouring European countries: France, the Netherlands and Poland. How could they know that within years, in some cases only months, they would end up in Nazi hands once again?

Open aggression in 1938 and 1939 meant expanding the network of concentration camps begun in 1933 with the creation of Dachau. The history of the camps provides a kind of microcosm of the development of Nazi persecutions. The German word for concentration camp is *Konzentrationslager*, often abbreviated as 'KZ' or *Lager*. Throughout the 1930s the SS set up new camps so as to provide regional coverage. For example, Buchenwald, built in 1937, was located near Weimar; Sachsenhausen was not far from Berlin. A camp for women inmates at Ravensbrück was started up as well. After 1935 many German municipalities set up Gypsy camps into which police forced thousands of the country's 35,000 Roma and Sinti, ostensibly in order to prevent crime.

Those camps, parallel structures within the concentration camp system, became sites of anthropological research and compulsory sterilisation as well as sources of forced labour. The anthropologists Dr Robert Ritter and Eva Justin found human subjects for their studies of Gypsies in Marzahn. One of them was Otto Rosenberg, who, as part of the project, slept overnight at Justin's home in Berlin and was served kohlrabi by her mother.

Concentration camps echoed the regime's ideological goals. Originally their founders described their purpose as re-education. In the camps, political opponents – communists, Social Democrats, liberals – and so-called antisocial elements – vagrants, Gypsies, homosexuals, Jehovah's Witnesses and others – were to be turned into 'useful' citizens. Authorities also spoke of the camps as a place to put troublemakers into 'protective custody for the restoration of law and order'. Under that guise, the Nazi government gave itself the legal right to imprison suspects without a trial. From their start the camps were brutal places with terrible conditions for inmates. Torture, beatings and deprivation were the order of the day. The move from Nazism's revolutionary phase to the consolidation of power did not mitigate the suffering of its targets. Instead that transition gave violence new forms backed by the full weight of the state and its institutions. The camps were an example. Between 1933 and 1939 the number of inmates skyrocketed, as attacks on target groups proliferated and increased in intensity.

The Nazi revolution of 1933 and 1934 brought large numbers of communists into the camps. Homosexuals and Jehovah's Witnesses followed. The Sterilisation Law of July 1933 brought a wave of arrests of supposed degenerates. Despite the Concordat with the Vatican, Nazi suspicion of the Christian churches also brought people into the camps. In violation of the agreement reached with the pope, Nazi authorities placed restrictions on Catholic priests, in particular regarding youth work. Some German priests refused to comply and more than one hundred served terms in the camps as a result.

The period of routinisation also enlarged the camps. When German courts and police tightened the enforcement of anti-

homosexual laws, they caused a jump in camp populations. At the
same time the authorities became more proactive, arresting men
and then pressuring them to reveal the names of their sexual partners, so that they could be charged as well. The Nuremberg Laws
created a whole new category of crime, *Rassenschande*, or crimes
against the blood. The 1936 Berlin Olympics meant a 'cleanup'
of vagrants, prostitutes, pickpockets and Gypsies. The result:
more people dumped into camps. In some cases police created
new camps, such as Marzahn, outside of Berlin, which was set up
especially for Gypsies. Meanwhile existing camps, among them
Dachau, continued to expand. German Jehovah's Witnesses added
to the population of the concentration camps as well. Arrests of
group members peaked in 1937 and 1938. German authorities
cooked up many reasons to be suspicious of them. Their organisation had international connections, in particular to the United
States, although the same was true of the Church of Jesus Christ
of Latter-day Saints, whose members were not generally persecuted in the Third Reich. Because Jehovah's Witnesses emphasised
the Old Testament and believed Jews had to return to the 'Holy
Land' before the world would end, their critics accused of them
of being pro-Jewish and Zionist. Their door-to-door preaching
made them an easily identifiable, unpopular, marginal minority
whom other Christians ridiculed as a cult. Mockers dubbed them
'Bible students', 'Bibleworms' and 'Bible-bees'.

Perhaps most significant at a time when Germany was preparing for war, many Jehovah's Witnesses refused to serve in
the military. Nor would they vote, give the Hitler salute, or do
anything that would imply supremacy of the nation over God.
Few in number, honest and law abiding, Jehovah's Witnesses
never posed a real threat to the stability of the Nazi German
state. Evidence suggests that at least some of their leaders tried
in 1933 to win the favour of Hitler's government by insisting
that Witnesses were loyal Germans who did not look kindly on
Jews. Nevertheless, Jehovah's Witnesses' insistence that their loyalty belonged to Jehovah alone and their firm refusal to abandon
their beliefs made them dangerous in the eyes of a regime that
tolerated no rivals for the allegiances of the German people.

Nazi authorities used their usual weapon – force – against the Jehovah's Witnesses, but with less success than they expected. Only about 20,000 Jehovah's Witnesses lived in Germany in the 1930s; approximately 10,000 of them were arrested over the years and sent to concentration camps, where they were beaten and tormented like their fellow inmates. Some were executed for refusing military service. Some of those who managed to stay out of the camps had their children taken from them, many lost their jobs, their pensions and their civil rights. Officials dragged them before special courts for refusing to enlist, to undertake air-raid watches, or to stop their preaching.

The Jehovah's Witnesses proved remarkably strong against assault. Camp authorities gave most of them the option of release if they signed a statement repudiating their beliefs. Very few did so. Instead they concentrated on building a strong network within the camps. They sang hymns, preached to the guards and continued to meet as best they could to provide psychological and emotional support to one another. They interpreted ridicule and persecution as a fulfilment of prophecy, proof that they were correct in their faith. Those who remained outside tried to keep the faith as well. When police arrested one local leader, another took his or her place. They persisted in meeting and distributing literature, even to Nazi Party headquarters. In all, between two and a half and 5,000 Jehovah's Witnesses were killed in German camps and prisons between 1933 and 1945.

One such victim was Wolfgang Kusserow. In 1942, Kusserow, a twenty-year-old Witness, was executed for refusing to perform military service. One of eleven children in his family, he assured his parents, brothers and sisters in a farewell letter, 'Our faith will be victorious'. Helene Gotthold also paid for her faith with her life. The mother of two children, Gotthold was arrested many times for continuing her Jehovah's Witness activities despite the government's ban. Condemned to death, she was beheaded in Berlin in 1944.

German authorities viewed the Jehovah's Witnesses more as an annoyance than a major threat. Nevertheless members of the group suffered terribly during the Third Reich. Their strength and resolve earned them a kind of grudging respect, even from some top Nazis. Himmler, for example, considered using them to resettle parts of the territories to be conquered by Germany. They were docile, obedient and productive, he said, perfect qualities for pioneers. Inside the camps Jehovah's Witnesses sometimes functioned as personal servants to the SS. Who else could be trusted as barbers wielding razors? Generally it seemed the Witnesses retained the respect of their fellow inmates and tried to do what they could within the camps to alleviate the sufferings of those even worse off than they were.

The third phase of Nazi development – open aggression in 1938–1939 – added to the camp network in other ways too. The annexation of Austria meant building camps there; Mauthausen is the best known. The crisis around the Sudetenland brought some German Protestant clergy into the camps, mostly for short sentences. In November 1938 arrests of Jews during the *Kristallnacht* pogrom added about 26,000 male inmates. Some died in the camps, many from being beaten; others were released in exchange for huge payments and often agreement to leave the country.

The Tightening Trap

Throughout this third phase of Nazi development – preparation for war – Hitler's approach to foreign policy was to talk peace and plan for war. His diplomats had been active during the 1930s making pacts that, like the Concordat with the Vatican and the Non-Aggression agreement with Poland, were intended to be broken. In 1935, Hitler signed the Anglo-German Naval Agreement with Britain, which he then began spending enormous amounts of money to contravene. The agreement was supposed to prevent a naval arms race by limiting the German fleet to certain percentage of the British navy. Instead it got the British to approve a German violation of the Treaty of Versailles. Meanwhile Hitler ordered construction of as many new super-battleships and aircraft carriers as he pleased, all designed to be used against Britain and the United States, on the assumption that the British would not discover the violations until it was too late. Although only two of the planned ships could be completed before the war was over, German intentions were nevertheless clearly the exact opposite of the peaceful arrangement promised by the agreement.

In May 1939 Germany signed the 'Pact of Steel' with Italy, promising friendship and mutual aid. This arrangement would lay the foundation of what would develop into the wartime alliance called the Rome–Berlin Axis. The summer of 1939 also brought nonaggression treaties with Estonia, Latvia and Denmark. The crowning achievement of this phase of preparation for war, however, came in August 1939 with the German–Soviet Non-Aggression Pact, sometimes referred to as the Hitler–Stalin Pact or the Molotov–Ribbentrop pact.

The deal had two parts. The first included public proclamations of friendship and non-aggression between the two rival powers. To a world that had seen six years of Nazi attacks on communists and the proliferation of German anti-Soviet propaganda, this was shocking enough, but the second part went much further. In a secret arrangement, Hitler's and Stalin's negotiators agreed to divide Eastern Europe between German and Soviet spheres of interest. They settled on a line through the middle of Poland as their secret boundary. Initially the Baltic States were also divided, with Estonia and Latvia going to the Soviets and Lithuania to Germany, but the Germans later traded Lithuania for more of Poland.

For Hitler the pact with the Soviet Union required some fairly dramatic reversals. In a sudden about-face he dropped his public anti-communist stance to proclaim friendship with his ideological foe Stalin. For Hitler, the gains were well worth the inconvenience. By cutting such a deal he secured the eastern border of Poland in case of war. Instead of worrying that the Soviet Union might attack invading Germans, he could rest assured that the Soviets would be busy securing their own designated sphere of interest. Germany would have a free hand in Poland, at least in the half that the secret pact reserved for German control. Even more important, given Hitler's plans, he

could wage war with the West with impunity. War with the
Soviet Union, which Hitler believed was ultimately necessary to
accomplish his mission, could wait. In the meantime, Hitler and
his henchmen spent the spring and summer of 1939 preparing
for war. They conducted a massive propaganda campaign against
Poland, accusing the Polish Government and people of terrible
violations of the rights of ethnic German minorities.

Already on 30 January 1939, Hitler had proclaimed his
vision of the war to come to the German representatives in the
Reichstag. As his speech made clear, it would be a war for race
and space. 'Europe cannot find peace until the Jewish question
has been solved', Hitler told his audience. By the end of his
remarks he had become more explicit:

> In the course of my life I have very often been a prophet and
> have usually been ridiculed for it. During the time of my
> struggle for power it was in the first instance only the Jewish
> race that received my prophecies with laughter when I said
> that I would one day take over the leadership of the State and
> with it that of the whole nation and that I would then among
> other things settle the Jewish problem. Their laughter was
> uproarious, but I think that for sometime now they have been
> laughing on the other side of their face. Today I will once
> more be a prophet: if the international Jewish financiers in
> and outside Europe should succeed in plunging the nations
> once more into a world war, then the result will not be the
> bolshevizing of the earth and thus the victory of Jewry, but the
> annihilation of the Jewish race in Europe!
>
> (Noakes and Pridham 3:1049)

Not everyone was deaf to Hitler's boastful warnings. Ever since
1933 large numbers of Germans had been leaving the country,
fearful for their own safety. Finding a place of refuge could prove
very difficult for all kinds of reasons. Thousands of German communists fled to the Soviet Union after Hitler came to power.
There some of them ran into troubles of their own with the
paranoid and repressive regime of Josef Stalin. The purges of the

1930s did not spare these newcomers; Stalin and his associates had some evicted from the Communist Party, forced into labour camps in Siberia, imprisoned and even killed. Still, to an important extent, German communism would survive the Nazi era in the Soviet Union.

Other Germans also tried to get out or found themselves refused re-entry by the Nazi government when they returned from trips abroad. Jews, liberals, pacifists, gay and lesbian activists, outspoken critics of National Socialism – all kinds of people went into exile. The writer Thomas Mann ended up in the United States as did the physicist Albert Einstein, the playwright Bertolt Brecht, the filmmaker Fritz Lang and the actress Marlene Dietrich. In fact exiles from Nazi Germany played an enormous role in building the Hollywood film industry in the 1930s and 1940s.

The United States was not the only destination for exiles. International feminist activists and long-time companions Lida Gustava-Heymann and Anita Augspurg stayed in Switzerland after a trip rather than risk imprisonment back home. In the summer of 1939 some 17,000 Jews from Germany, Austria and Poland made their way to Shanghai. Unable to get visas permitting them to enter places more culturally familiar to them, such as the United States and Britain, they seized the chance to get out of Europe even though it meant leaving behind almost everything they knew. Many of them would survive the war, including the Japanese occupation of China.

One family that left Germany for Shanghai in 1939 included seven-year-old Karin Zacharias. The Zachariases lived in a town in East Prussia not far from Königsberg (later the Russian city of Kaliningrad). Karin's father saw the writing on the wall early on with Hitler's government in Germany. Since the mid-1930s he wanted to get the family out of Europe, but his wife was not willing to go without her aging parents, who refused to leave their home. Only in 1937, after the two older people both died, could the Zachariases begin to tackle the enormous project of getting out of Germany and finding a new home. Karin's father, educated as a lawyer, needed to learn a trade in order to get exit papers, so he became a welder. The family had to jump through endless bureaucratic hoops. To facilitate the process they relocated to Berlin. Finally in 1939 they left for China, where they would remain until 1948, when they were allowed to enter the United States. Karin, daughter of an assimilated German Jewish family, spent much of her childhood and her early teenage years in Shanghai. Half a century later Karin Pardo, as she is now called, lives in Chicago and still has vivid memories of the Chinese chapter of her life. Her experience is a reminder that the Holocaust was truly a worldwide event.

Even for those who recognised the dangers of Nazi Germany it was very hard to escape. Money and occupational skills such as medical training helped but did not guarantee success. For some people, distant destinations in Africa, India and the Caribbean proved the only possibility, and conditions upon arrival could be difficult. After war broke out, many Jews were interned as enemy aliens. In 1939, American immigration authorities decided to allow only around 20,000 Germans and Austrians to immigrate to the United States. There was no separate quota for European Jews, although of course a large proportion of the Germans and Austrians who applied for entry into the United States were Jewish. Only those who had relatives in the United States willing to sponsor them would be admitted. Sponsors had to demonstrate that they had enough money to support their European relatives once they arrived, if necessary. They also had to make their way through a mountain of red tape. Many Jews in Europe spent years trying to get visas to the United States and most of them failed. It was no easier to get into Canada or Australia. In times of economic depression most people in those countries worried that immigrants would cost money and take away jobs.

In early 1939, the government of Cuba agreed to grant visas to a number of Jews desperate to get out of Europe. Between eight and nine hundred people set sail from Hamburg to Havana on board the steamship *St Louis*. Before the ship came in, Cuban authorities changed their minds about the refugees; when the *St Louis* arrived, they refused to allow the passengers to disembark. The ship remained offshore for days while representatives of the passengers tried to negotiate with the Cubans or find some alternative destination. Finally the *St Louis* left Havana. Sailing slowly up the coast of Florida, its captain radioed to officials all along the way in the United States and Canada, but no one would permit the ship to dock.

The crew had no choice but to return to Europe. Negotiations by Jewish organisations managed to get refuge for many of the passengers from the *St Louis* in Britain, France and the Netherlands. In the years ahead some of those people, like most of those forced to return to Germany, would end up dead at Nazi hands, but some also found ways to stay alive. Careful research at the U.S. Holocaust Memorial Museum has traced all but a handful of the passengers of the *St Louis*. Their stories show that foresight alone could not save a Jew from the Nazi trap. Connections, money and determination were all factors, but so, above all, was luck, or whatever one might call chance at a time when no Jews could be counted lucky.

Like Jews in Germany, people deemed handicapped also experienced the open Nazi aggression of 1938–1939. Hitler and other proponents of so-called racial purification would have to wait for the cover provided by war to implement murder on a mass scale, but by 1939 they felt confident enough to take steps in that direction. They began with the most defenceless segment of an already vulnerable group: the children.

In the winter of 1938–1939, a man named Knauer wrote to Hitler. He and his wife had a deformed baby. They wanted to have 'this creature', as he called the child, killed. Hitler seized on the request as a way to begin having children who were considered 'unworthy of living' killed. He assigned his personal physician, Dr Karl Brandt and the head of his personal staff in the Nazi Party, Philipp Bouhler, to deal with the Knauer case. Hitler instructed Brandt and Bouhler to inform the doctors involved that they could kill the child. Brandt and Bouhler were to tell the doctors that if any legal action were taken against them, it would be thrown out of court.

Hitler authorised Brandt and Bouhler to deal with similar cases in the same way. They recruited a group of officials and doctors who were positively disposed toward such ideas. The group's official title was the Reich Committee for the Scientific Registration of Serious Hereditarily- and Congenitally-based Illnesses. By August 1939 the Reich Committee required all midwives and doctors to report the existence of any children with deformities. It passed the forms on to three paediatricians. They marked each form with a plus or a minus sign to indicate whether the particular child was to die or be allowed to live. Those doctors never saw the children whose fates they decided.

Brandt, Bouhler and their committee were not confident that most of the German people would support the killing of children with deformities, so they shrouded the process in secrecy. Still they had no trouble finding enough personnel to participate in these early stages of the program. The programme to kill deformed children served Nazi planners as a kind of trial balloon, sent up to test reactions. The responses they perceived and the cooperation they received from the relevant professions indicated that it was possible to go even further in attacks on people considered handicapped.

5

Experiments in Brutality: War against Poland and the So-called Euthanasia Programme, 1939–1940

In 1939 Hitler got his war. It would not be against Czechoslovakia as he had hoped but against Poland. Still Poland was not a surprising target; along with many of Germany's leading military men, Hitler had always considered existence of an independent Polish state to be anathema and of course for Germany, Poland was the gateway to the east, where Hitler intended to find *Lebensraum* – living space – for his superior 'Aryan race'.

With the German invasion and conquest in 1939, Poland would become a laboratory for experiments in spatial expansion and racial ideology. In Poland the Germans seized control of large numbers of Slavs and Jews, those people Nazi teachings described as subhuman. In Poland, German planners began to implement schemes to recast the face of Europe. They forced millions of people to move, resettled those they deemed desirable and robbed, evicted, enslaved and eventually killed those they did not want. For two years, even before construction of the first killing centres in 1941, the German occupiers of Poland tried out various solutions to what they considered their population problems, above all their self-made 'Jewish problem'.

This first stage of the war also brought experiments of another kind – in the murder of people deemed handicapped. In 1939 and 1940 the so-called Euthanasia programme got into full swing within Germany. The word 'euthanasia' comes from the Greek for 'good death' or 'good dying'. In the Nazi case the label itself was a lie, suggesting as it did that the killings had something to do with concern for the patients' well-being. They did not. The program's initiators did not care about the suffering of their targets but asked only whether those people could contribute to the supremacy of the 'Aryan race'. As in Poland, planners and functionaries in the Euthanasia programme tested methods and developed techniques to implement the teachings of race and space. Their goals involved learning how to kill large numbers of people and then dispose of their bodies most easily. In the years ahead the lessons of this early programme against handicapped people would be applied again and again.

This chapter traces Nazi German experiments in brutality in 1939 and 1940. From the outset two principles seem to have guided German policy, both in defeated Poland and with regard to people deemed handicapped. First, Nazi leaders encouraged experimentation – even rivalry and organisational confusion – among the people who carried out their plans. Rather than easing the situation of those targeted for persecution, such chaotic conditions often increased the victims' vulnerability and exacerbated their suffering. Second, German decision makers endorsed the notion of divide and conquer. Whenever possible they stirred up dissension and hatred among those over whom they ruled in order to advance their own cause. That kind of cynical manipulation by Nazi overlords of their subject peoples added to the wartime misery too, first in Poland and later throughout Europe.

The German Invasion and Occupation of Poland

On 1 September 1939 German forces invaded Poland. German planners tried to disguise this act of aggression as a defensive measure. They dressed 150 concentration camp inmates in Polish uniforms and used them to stage a mock attack on a German radio station near the border. The corpses of those men then served as 'proof' of Polish belligerence and justification for attack. Hitler and his inner circle were not confident that the German public was ready for war. They had already spent the summer of 1939 rousing anti-Polish sentiment in Germany, using the newspapers to publicise wild accusations of Polish crimes against the ethnic German minority in Poland. Still, within Germany the initial reaction to war was cautious. When Hitler appeared on his balcony in Berlin following announcements of the attack on Poland, he expected to be greeted by throngs of zealous supporters. Instead the crowd was so small that he went back inside to avoid embarrassment.

The assault of 1 September 1939 did not take the Poles completely by surprise, because they had had plenty of opportunities to observe German sabre-rattling in the preceding months. They were, however, stunned by the rapidity of the German advance. The Germans' technological advantage enabled them to wage a blitzkrieg – a war at lightning speed. First their planes pounded the Poles from the sky. Then tanks rolled in to crush resistance and clear the way for occupying troops. With eleven cavalry brigades, a single tank division and 750 armoured vehicles, the Poles were no match for the Germans, who smashed into Poland with fifteen tank divisions and some 3,600 armoured vehicles. Jack Pomerantz, at the time a young Jewish man in the Polish town of Radzyn, recalls that he had never seen an airplane until the German attack on 1 September 1939. That day the sky was black with them.

The repercussions were enormous. France and Britain declared war on Germany, although for the time being they remained outside the fray. The Hitler–Stalin Pact of August 1939 assured the Germans of non-aggression from the Soviet Union. As the secret arrangements had anticipated, the German offensive was followed beginning on 17 September, by a Soviet advance into Polish territory from the east, up to the line previously agreed upon. By early October, the Germans had forced the Poles on their side to surrender. Meanwhile eastern Poland would remain under Soviet control until mid-1941.

In the 1939 attack Germans killed at least 70,000 Poles. German losses were much lower but still considerable, some 11,000 men. At least one million Poles were taken prisoner – many by the Germans but also a substantial number by the Soviets. Anti-Polish prejudices and a military culture that called for absolute destruction of the enemy fuelled German brutality against the Poles. The assumption that Poles were dangerous bandits, irregular combatants who attacked from concealed positions, served the Germans as justification for a massive assault on soldiers and civilians alike.

The Polish leadership fled to London to establish a government-in-exile. Members of the Polish army buried huge caches of arms rather than relinquish them to the Germans. Those weapons would provide the nucleus for the underground armies in the half decade of struggle that still lay ahead for the Poles.

From the outset, 'divide and conquer' was the German byword in Poland. The arrangement with the Soviet Union reflected that approach as did the German decision to divide its own part of conquered Poland into two parts. The western areas, known as the 'incorporated territories', were annexed by the Greater German Reich. This area included such important cities as Danzig – now called Gdansk – and Łódź, which the German leadership would later rechristen Litzmannstadt. The incorporated territories were home to ten million people, around eighty per cent of them ethnic Poles. Also living there were ethnic Germans, Jews and small numbers of other groups, including Gypsies, Czechs and Ukrainians.

The Germans called the remaining part of their Polish territory the General Government and administered it like a colony. Warsaw, Krakow and Lublin were its major cities. Under the leadership of Governor General Dr Hans Frank, a long-time associate of Hitler, the General Government became a key site of Nazi brutality. Much of the mass killing of Jews after 1941 would be done there; plans to reduce Poles to slaves of Germany also found early implementation in the General Government.

Germans, in particular Nazi Germans, are often described as hyper-efficient and organised. German rule in the territories of occupied Poland, however, contradicts that stereotype. Rather than orderly, it was chaotic, characterised by overlapping jurisdictions and competing authorities. The German military was involved as was the SS under Heinrich Himmler. Hans Frank and his administration in the General Government played an important role; so did Hermann Göring, Hitler's deputy and head of the Four-Year Plan for the German economy. Local Nazis got involved, especially in the incorporated territories, as did German police and representatives of the interior ministry. Almost every ambitious German Nazi activist, military man and bureaucrat wanted a piece of the action. So did many German women – social workers, teachers and others – who sought adventure and new career opportunities. Germans who wanted to get ahead in defeated Poland found it expedient to further Nazi goals. Whether in the incorporated territories or in the General Government, they tried to distinguish themselves from their colleagues and rivals by being more effective – that is, harsher – and more ambitious – that is, more brutal – in their treatment of the local populations.

Hitler and his inner circle had grandiose plans for Polish territories. Initially they intended to force the ethnic Poles farther east, to confine Jews to some desolate reservation and to establish an area of pure 'Aryan' settlement. Although details remained vague, implementation began immediately. On 7 September 1939, Reinhard Heydrich, head of the German Reich Security Main Office, issued an order to the special units of police and SS under his jurisdiction. It would be necessary, he instructed, to destroy the leadership class in Poland and expel all Jews from areas in German hands. In short, as he told a subordinate, the 'nobility, clergy and Jews must be killed'. Heydrich's position was in line with the views of his bosses Hitler and Himmler. They wanted to reduce the Poles to a people of slaves, to destroy their intellectuals and their sense of tradition – anything that might give them a way to organise against Germany. Accordingly they encouraged German forces to target Polish Catholic priests. In the opening months of the war, Germans shot as many as fifteen hundred priests and imprisoned countless others. They also humiliated, arrested and murdered many other prominent Poles – for example, journalists, professors and artists.

German authorities prohibited any activities that advanced the education of Poles, fostered communal ties, or promoted national feelings. They imposed curfews and seized Polish businesses. They shut down Polish newspapers and used forced labour and public hangings to make examples of Poles who defied them. Members of the SS, police and regular military, along with local collaborators, also terrorised Poles in less organised ways that included theft, beating, castration and rape.

The war in 1939 brought massive expansion of the network of concentration and labour camps. Some Poles were forced to build roads and dams in labour camps, where the terrible conditions were often deadly. Others were sent to Germany. The existing camps in Germany could not hold all of the new inmates, so German authorities also set up camps in their newly acquired territories – places such as Majdanek, near Lublin, or Plaschow, outside Krakow, depicted in Steven Spielberg's film *Schindler's List*.

Officials also introduced a whole range of measures intended to differentiate Poles and Germans, two groups that in fact were not always easy to separate in a part of Europe that had traditionally been ethnically mixed. Poles were not permitted to say 'Heil Hitler', nor could they serve Germans in shops. Laws forbade friendships between Germans and Poles and criminalised sexual relations. Nevertheless, sexual assault of Polish women by German men was common. Later in the war German military authorities would force some Polish Gentile women into brothels to serve German men and non-Germans who fought for the Reich.

Most of these measures applied to Polish Gentiles and Jews alike, but sometimes the Germans showed additional, often improvised brutality toward their numerous, new Jewish subjects. In the 1930s far more Jews lived in Poland than in Germany. Germany's half million Jews in 1933 made up less than one per cent of the population; Poland's more than three million Jews in 1939 represented approximately ten per cent.

The first phase of the war became a kind of open season against Polish Jews for storm troopers, SS, Nazi Party members and unruly soldiers. Undisciplined and often drunk, they roamed around Polish territories burning, looting and raping. The distinctive appearance of Orthodox Jewish men made them favourite targets for ridicule and violence. Rowdy Germans pulled out their beards and forced them to crawl in the street. Thugs attacked synagogues, where they desecrated ritual objects and abused the observant.

Hostage takings and demands for ransom were common. On 18 October 1939, Germans murdered one hundred Jews in a café in Łódź and forced others to pay for their lives. Similar incidents occurred in many cities and towns.

Nazi racial policy had two sides: attack on people deemed undesirable and advancement of those considered 'Aryan'. In 1939 and 1940 the second part of that scheme included locating ethnic Germans, people living outside Germany who identified themselves culturally as Germans (but not as Jews). In 1939 German experts estimated there to be about 700,000 ethnic Germans in Poland alone.

German forces used the ethnic Germans to increase the terror of the early months of the war. Some ethnic Germans were killed by their Polish neighbours for helping the invading Germans. The numbers are unclear; respectable estimates range from 2,000 to 5,000 such casualties, but official German reports claimed that vengeful Poles had slaughtered 58,000 ethnic Germans in early September 1939. That charge served to whip up hatred against Poles within Germany and also helped the SS form ethnic Germans into vigilante groups that attacked Poles and stole their property.

Many German officials who flocked into the newly conquered Polish territories busied themselves drawing up lists of people who should count as ethnic Germans. They organised programmes to relocate them to the most desirable areas and evict the Poles who had been living there.

Plans for resettlement went even further. In October and November 1939 German diplomats worked out deals with Estonia, Latvia and the Soviet Union so that ethnic Germans in those parts of Europe would also be brought 'home into the Reich'. The idea was to move those ethnic Germans out of the Baltic states and eastern Poland into the newly incorporated territories. Of course, moving ethnic Germans in meant moving other people out.

By 1940 some 200,000 ethnic Germans who had signed up for resettlement needed homes. That year German police forced 325,000 Poles to leave the incorporated territories for the General Government. Often they were given only hours to get out, with instructions to leave their houses swept and the keys in the cupboard for the new inhabitants. Meanwhile, in the General Government nothing awaited the deportees but misery.

In late 1939 and 1940 German police evicted tens of thousands of Polish Jews from their homes and squeezed them into ghettos in the cities. The most desirable residences and businesses went to ethnic Germans or Germans from the Reich. Poor properties were allotted to Polish Gentiles.

Some German officials took their own initiatives against people whom Nazi ideology deemed inferior. By doing so they hoped to catch the attention of their bosses and advance their careers. For example, in the fall of 1939, Adolf Eichmann (1906–1962), an ambitious bureaucrat in Heydrich's Reich Security Main Office, began to organise transports of Jews to the General Government – from Vienna, from Silesia in the incorporated territories and from parts of the former Czechoslovakia.

After the war, when he was tried in Israel for his role in the Holocaust, Eichmann would insist that he had never been an anti-Semite. It does seem that in Eichmann's case, careerism was a more powerful motivation than antisemitism. In any case Eichmann played a central role organising forced emigration of Austrian Jews in 1938 and of Czech Jews a year later. Throughout 1942 and 1943 he would be instrumental in arranging transportation of Jews from all over Europe to killing centres. He also coordinated deportation of Hungarian Jews to Auschwitz in 1944. In 1962 Adolf Eichmann was hanged in Israel.

Eichmann, trained as an expert in Jewish affairs, had no formal authorisation for his 1939 project. Nor had he made any arrangements for the Jews when they arrived in the General Government. Instead his men simply dumped their prisoners off at a place called Nisko, near the city of Lublin and told them to get lost. Most of the Jews fled into the woods and the Germans shot those who returned.

As the Nisko incident illustrates, competition among German authorities often made the situation of the people they targeted worse. Sometimes, however, the resulting disorganisation also undermined the Germans' ability to achieve their goals. By early 1941, top Nazis had to stop expelling Poles into the General Government, because the situation had become too unstable. Hans Frank announced he could not take any more Poles in his area. Göring agreed that it was economically unwise to keep up the transports. Neither man was motivated by humanitarianism. Both were interested above all in expanding their own power and during 1941 both would be instrumental in moving German policy from the confused resettlements and expulsions of 1939 and 1940 to the so-called Final Solution of the Jewish Question: annihilation.

All of the German schemes in Poland relied on the notion of divide and conquer. Privileging ethnic Germans turned their neighbours against them. Dangling promises of Jewish property in front of Gentile Poles gave them a stake in attacks on Jews and encouraged them to betray Jews to the Germans. SS leader Himmler explicitly encouraged his men to do all they could to turn ethnic groups within Poland against one another. It was a good idea to recruit local policemen and mayors from minority groups, he suggested. That way the majority's anger would be diverted from the Germans onto those petty officials. Accordingly Germans in the General Government often used Ukrainians and Belorussians against ethnic Poles and Jews. In many cases German authorities relied on local Polish Gentiles to point out who was Jewish.

Some people spoke out against German atrocities in Poland. Shocked by the slaughter of Polish Catholic priests, Roman Catholic leaders in Germany appealed to the Vatican. Perhaps Hitler would listen to the pope, they reasoned. Polish clergymen also begged the pope to take action, but Pope Pius XII remained silent. His reasons are unclear. He may have believed that a strict policy of neutrality was the most powerful position the Vatican could take. Perhaps he feared reprisals against Catholics within Germany, or against the Vatican itself. A staunch opponent of communism, he may have thought that Nazi Germany – even given its excesses – was still preferable to Soviet domination of Europe. The anti-communist argument, however, rings hollow for 1939, when Nazi Germany and the Soviet Union worked in tandem to dismember Poland, and both powers singled out Polish Catholic clergy for abuse. In any case, the pope's silence in the fall of 1939 – when the victims of German aggression were priests in his own Church – would make it hard for him to speak out later in the face of crimes against Jews.

Some members of the German army protested the brutality around them. The best known case involved General Johannes Blaskowitz, commander of a military region in occupied Poland. In early 1940 Blaskowitz sent a long memorandum directly to Hitler. It provided specific examples of German crimes against civilians. For example, Blaskowitz described how a drunken German policeman beat a Polish man to death and forced a woman who may have been his wife to bury the body while scores of Germans and Poles looked on. Blaskowitz also told about some German soldiers who raped a teenaged Jewish girl in a cemetery. His account included many other cases of viciousness on the part of German police and SS men.

Such behaviour was counterproductive, Blaskowitz warned. It would lead to demoralisation and a breakdown in discipline among the German forces. It would stir up bad press abroad, he wrote, and alienate even those elements of the population that might otherwise have been sympathetic to the Germans. According to Blaskowitz, German abuses would drive Polish Jews and Gentiles together. Polish Gentiles were particularly worried by German brutality toward the Jews, Blaskowitz reported, because they feared that anything done to Jews would eventually be done to them too.

Hitler dismissed Blaskowitz's memorandum as childish and naive. One could not 'win a war with Salvation Army tactics', he allegedly responded. One might expect that Blaskowitz was shot or imprisoned for daring to send his report, but he was not. Instead he was merely transferred out of Poland. Others were happy to take over his powerful position there.

Over time such protests ceased. Other military men who felt as Blaskowitz did in the fall of 1939 probably got used to conditions or forgot their misgivings in the face of Germany's dramatic military triumphs. Meanwhile, those who showed they were willing or even eager to fight a war of atrocity found themselves favoured for promotions. By consistently rewarding behaviour that furthered the goals of race and space, the Nazi leadership made sure that it always had a supply of ambitious, loyal individuals at every level of the hierarchy. As the case of Blaskowitz indicates, Nazi Germany did not need unanimity in order to function. The Third Reich was not merely the work of 'true believers' – fanatics who blindly endorsed every detail of Hitler's ideology. It also built on the efforts of critical Nazis and even opponents of Nazism, people who grumbled about some of its excesses even while they applied their energies and abilities to ensuring its stability. Not mass brainwashing but the participation of ordinary people of all kinds enabled the Nazi system to operate as it did.

Ghettoisation of Polish Jews

At first German decision makers were not sure what to do with the many Jews who fell into their hands in 1939. Not until 1941 would they cross the line to total mass murder as the 'solution' to the 'Jewish problem'. From the outset, however, they did all they could to isolate Polish Jews from the rest of the population. They targeted Jews in particular ways in order to make them so vulnerable and contemptible that non-Jews would lose any sympathy for them and would worry only about how to avoid being treated that badly themselves.

Ghettoisation, the measure that German authorities developed in late 1939 and early 1940, was a logical extension of the approach of divide and conquer. All over Polish territories German officials forced Jews out of their homes, in villages, small towns and cities, into designated urban areas called ghettos. There the Jews were to be concentrated and isolated. Meanwhile German authorities seized Jewish property to dispose of as they saw fit. In some cases eager non-Jewish neighbours rushed in before them to pick up the spoils. The Germans also forced many Jews in the ghettos to work for them producing supplies for the war.

German planners always considered ghettoisation a temporary measure, a sort of holding pattern until subsequent steps could be taken. But what were those steps to be? In 1939 and 1940 some Nazi decision makers were still talking about a Jewish reservation in the east, near Lublin. Officials in the German Foreign Office would propose another scheme, the Madagascar Plan, to ship all of Europe's Jews to that island. Others floated different ideas such as using the Jews in the ghettos as enslaved labour or allowing them to die of starvation and disease there. The Nazi leadership encouraged every plan as long as it aimed to destroy Jewish life in Europe.

Between 1939 and 1941, during this phase of experimentation and uncertainty with regard to German policy toward the Jews, over half a million Polish Jews died in ghettos and labour camps. Many starved to death; many also died of diseases brought on by the crowding and terrible sanitary conditions. Police, guards and overseers shot and beat others to death – for trying to escape; for stealing, as if the Germans themselves were not thieves on the largest conceivable scale; for failing to work to the level demanded; or simply for sport. The ghettos were not yet a formal programme of annihilation, but they proved deadly enough for hundreds of thousands of Polish Jews of all ages.

In 1940 a visitor to the Warsaw ghetto offered the following description of living conditions there:

On the streets children are crying in vain, children who are dying of hunger. They howl, beg, sing, moan, shiver with cold, without underwear, without clothing, without shoes, in rags, sacks, flannel which are bound in strips round the emaciated skeletons, children swollen with hunger, disfigured, half conscious, already completely grown-up at the age of five, gloomy and weary of life. They are like old people and are only conscious of one thing: 'I'm cold'. 'I'm hungry'.

(Noakes and Pridham 3:1067)

Starvation and deprivation in the ghettos destroyed Jewish lives and at the same time undermined the possibilities for Jewish solidarity. Ghettoisation broke up established communities and forced into close contact people who often had little in common. In the ghettos, wealthy, educated and acculturated Jews competed for scraps of food with Jews who had grown up in poverty.

The German government-run leisure organisation Strength Through Joy organised bus tours to the ghettos so that members of the supposed master race could see the degeneracy of their alleged inferiors. No matter that the Germans themselves had created the filth and desperation evident there. That squalor was offered as proof that Nazi theories of race and space held true.

One of the largest ghettos was established in Łódź in the incorporated territory in the winter of 1939. By April 1940 it had been sealed off completely from the rest of the city. The Łódź ghetto lasted in part at least until August 1944, when the Jews remaining there were shipped to Auschwitz. Although every ghetto was different, Łódź illustrates some general conditions.

In Łódź, as elsewhere, German authorities had varying opinions about the nature of the ghetto. Was it primarily for forced labour? Was it to be self-supporting? If so, how, when it was allocated no resources? To what extent was it to be self-administered? All of this uncertainty added to the misery of those imprisoned within the poorest parts of the city.

The ghetto was disastrously overcrowded. In Łódź, an average of seven people occupied a single room – that is, in 1940 an estimated 230,000 people were crammed into some 30,000 apartments, most of them one room only. Only about 725 of those lodgings had running water. Many had electricity, but it did little good; police forbade those in the ghetto from using their lights most of the time.

Łódź was one of the most isolated of all of the ghettos. A kind of no one's land surrounded it, so smuggling anything in or out was almost impossible. Because it was in an industrialised region, there was no forest nearby to which the ghetto Jews could escape. The city of Łódź itself was slated to be 'Germanised' – that is, German planners intended to remove ethnic Poles, Jews and others from the area and replace them with Germans from the Reich and ethnic Germans from elsewhere in Europe. As a result, previous contacts in the city were of little help to Jews in the Łódź ghetto.

Food was extremely scarce – potato peels became a prized item. Lice and rats thrived; such diseases as typhus and tuberculosis ran rampant. Nevertheless hard work was required of everyone in the ghetto who wanted a chance to stay alive. By 1943 ghetto workshops were churning out uniforms, boots, underwear and bed linen for the German military; ghetto workers produced goods of metal, wood, leather, fur, down and paper and even electrical and telecommunication devices. Children as young as eight slaved away for pathetically small rations of food.

Under these conditions it is no surprise that people died in terrible numbers. In 1940, some 6,000 Jews died in the Łódź ghetto. By the following year the number had almost doubled, to 11,000. In 1942 there would be 18,000 dead. Of course, by the end of 1941 the primary cause of Jewish death would no longer be starvation and illness in the ghettos but murder in the new killing centres.

German racial experts came to think of the ghettos as repositories for people they considered human trash. Beginning in 1941 they dumped Jews from all over Europe – Luxembourg, Germany, Austria, Czechoslovakia – in Łódź. German officials also deported some 5,000 European Gypsies to the Łódź ghetto, where they inhabited a specially designated area and, like the Jews, suffered beatings, starvation and disease. In December

1941 and January 1942 those Gypsies still in Łódź were gassed at Chelmno. It is said that no Roma survived the Łódź ghetto. Nazi authorities also sent Gypsies to Jewish ghettos in other cities, for example, Warsaw, Lublin and Bialystok.

German officials saved themselves work by setting up Jewish Councils to administer aspects of the daily lives of the ghettos. They appointed recognised Jewish leaders – prominent local people, businessmen, teachers, lawyers – to these boards and assigned them the task of carrying out German orders within the ghetto. In each ghetto the Jewish Council also distributed scarce resources, organised social life, set up charities and tried to find ways to maintain some kind of human community. The autonomy of the Jewish Council, often referred to by the German word *Judenrat*, was more apparent than real. It could not escape German goals and priorities. In cases when members of the councils refused to cooperate, German officials dismissed them or had them shot and then replaced them with more compliant men. In Łódź, for example, the Germans had some trouble recruiting twenty-four members because the first Council of Jewish Elders set up had been summoned by the Gestapo and never seen again.

The Jewish Councils have often been criticised and some people have suggested that the Jewish leadership in Eastern Europe formed part of the machinery of destruction. Hannah Arendt, a political philosopher and refugee from Nazi Germany, was accused of taking that stance in her famous study *Eichmann in Jerusalem*. Arendt drew attention to what she considered the complicity, even collaboration, of the Jewish leadership with the Germans. Publication of her book in the early 1960s sparked a heated controversy.

Instead of viewing the Jewish leaders, especially those in the Jewish Councils, primarily as agents of Nazi destruction, it is more accurate to see them as caught between conflicting sets of demands. Above them loomed German orders; below them spread the ever more desperate needs of the Jews of Eastern Europe. Members of the Jewish Councils had to respond to German demands for funds, goods, information, and a labour force. If they refused or failed to do so, German officials would come and take whatever they wanted anyway. On the other hand, the Jewish Councils tried to help their people, to maintain order, to save lives and to feed, clothe and doctor the Jews in the ghettos.

It was impossible to reconcile these two sets of goals in a situation where the German priority was destruction of the Jews. In the conditions that the victorious Germans created in Poland, however, the two tasks of the Jewish Councils could not be separated either. Attempts by Jewish leaders to accomplish both in some way led to hostility on the part of their own people; in many cases it also pushed them to behave in ways counter to their own principles. Once again we can see the familiar notion of divide and conquer at work.

The tasks the Germans set the Jewish Councils were straightforward. They were to make lists of the people and property in their ghettos and, as required, turn over the money, things, or people demanded. The tasks the Jewish Councils set themselves were more ambitious. They hoped to maintain order and sustain life in the ghettos. They intended to mediate with the Germans, to reason and plead on behalf of the Jews as a whole and they tried to maintain productivity, to make the ghettos valuable to the German war effort so that Germans would want to keep Jews alive.

Critics of the Jewish Councils often imply an additional task – the councils should have warned their people. Is this charge justified? Could and should the Jewish Councils have done more to warn Jews in the ghettos of German intentions or to rouse resistance? The case of the ghetto in Lublin illustrates the complexity of this issue. In 1939 there were 38,000 Jews in Lublin, twenty-one per cent of the city's population. It was one of the oldest Jewish communities in Poland. After the German invasion in September, Jewish refugees flooded into the area. The Germans set up a ghetto and a Jewish Council, one of whose most prominent members was a lawyer named Mark Alten.

Alten believed that the terror of late 1939 was a temporary, local aberration. Things would get better once German power was centralised and control established, he assumed. Alten worked hard to cultivate contacts with Germans and used his influence to plead for exceptions, to urge a stop to arbitrary violence. More than once he was arrested for his efforts.

In the end everything Alten did was futile. In 1942 almost all the Jews of Lublin were murdered, just like their counterparts all over Poland. Alten has been accused of ingratiating himself with the Nazis, the very people who would seek to kill every Jew alive. There is no doubt that he misread the situation, although his misjudgement came out of predictable, human tendencies. He looked to the past as people do when seeking guidance for the present. He saw persecutions of Jews, pogroms and isolation. From that history he took the lesson that this attack too would pass, if the Jews could just hold on. Alten was wrong, but can he be faulted for failing to anticipate something that had never happened before? Can the Jewish Councils be blamed for not realising in 1939 or 1940 what even top Nazis did not grasp until sometime in mid-1941, that this time the goal would be annihilation of every Jew in Europe? To decent people such a thing would long be unimaginable.

The Jewish Councils are sometimes charged with having handed Jews over to their deaths. There is no denying that German officials used the Jewish Councils to their own ends; they had been created for that purpose. Beginning in late 1941, the councils prepared lists for transports out of the ghettos – to killing centres. Often they used their own police forces to help round up those slated for destruction. Not surprisingly, they generally sent first those people in the ghetto they viewed as least useful: the sick, old, very young and weak. Outsiders such as Gypsies could also expect to be on the early transports. Nevertheless Jewish leaders varied considerably in their responses. Sometimes they even managed at least temporarily to thwart Nazi designs.

Several examples give an idea of the kinds of activities possible among the councils. By 1940 the Jewish Council in Lublin was dealing not only with the ghetto in that city but with about fifty work camps. Under the crowded and desperate conditions, food, medicine and doctors were all woefully inadequate. Overwhelmed, the Jewish Council resorted in some cases to bringing in auxiliary police recruited from local ethnic Germans to keep order. Known for their viciousness toward Jews, those police contributed to the hatred that many Jews felt for the Jewish Council. Eventually the Lublin Council formed its own Jewish Order Police. To inhabitants of the ghetto, those enforcers, whether Jewish or not, were detested as the most visible representatives of German authority. In Warsaw the head of the Jewish police, Jozef Szerynski, was a convert to Christianity who had been trained in the Polish police force. He was indifferent and even hostile to Jewish traditions. Most of the population of the ghetto regarded him and his seventeen hundred policemen as tyrannical. The requirement to pay a special police tax roused particular bitterness. In Riga, in contrast, the Jewish police were recruited from among the Zionist youth. They included some of the best of Jewish society. In the ghetto they were widely respected and viewed as helpers.

Some Jewish Councils were involved in resistance activities. For example, in the summer of 1941, during a search on a train, German police discovered copies of a Jewish underground newspaper. The courier was a Polish Gentile woman who was carrying addresses, including some linked to the Jewish ghetto in Piotrków Trybunalski in the incorporated territories. The Gestapo found that the Jewish underground there was connected to the heads of the Jewish Council. They had the chairman and almost all of the community leaders arrested and tortured. In September they were sent to Auschwitz.

Critics of the Jewish Councils note that some Jewish leaders enriched themselves and relished the taste of power that their positions in the ghetto gave them. Here too the record is mixed. One can find cases of Jewish leaders who suffered from delusions of grandeur. Moishe Merin, the thirty-year-old head of the Central Council of Elders for Eastern Upper Silesia, fancied himself a kind of dictator of the European Jews. Chaim Rumkowski, head of the Jewish Council in Łódź, was even more blatant. He had money and stamps printed bearing his image; he encouraged a kind of cult of personality around himself. Still, both men tried to save the Jews in 'their ghettos', not merely to expand their own power. Jewish leaders came to recognise their powerlessness too. In 1943 Merin would address the remaining survivors of his jurisdiction with the following words: 'I stand in a cage before a hungry and angry tiger. I stuff his mouth with meat, the flesh of my brothers and sisters, to keep him in his cage lest he break loose and tear us all to bits' (Hilberg, 197).

For most Jewish elders, leadership was a burden, not a reward. At first they were not paid but served in the tradition of volunteer community leadership. By 1940 they received some pay and although it was meagre, like that of the Jewish police, it still sparked resentment in a time of such terrible want. Most Jewish leaders worked hard and suffered a great deal. Some, like Adam Czerniaków in Warsaw, saw no way out of their desperate situation but suicide. Few withstood the temptation to try to use their positions to save themselves and those close to them. Nevertheless in the end their thankless task guaranteed nothing. Jacob Gens spent years as head of the Jewish Council in Vilna, doing all he could to increase the productivity of the ghetto. He was shot anyway by the Germans in 1943 when they liquidated the ghetto. Rumkowski, for all his pomp, ended up in a transport from Łódź ghetto to a killing centre. He too died with his people; rumour had it they killed him themselves.

Hell, according to the French philosopher Jean-Paul Sartre, is a self-service cafeteria – the worst suffering, in other words, is that which you inflict on yourself. Nazi planners seem to have understood that concept instinctively. By forcing Jewish leaders to involve themselves in decisions about the fate of people in the ghettos they both lightened their own sense of responsibility and increased the suffering within the Jewish community. Powerless as they were, the Jewish Councils had painfully few options. In a lose-lose situation where the options were destruction or destruction – death or death – there could be few, if any, right decisions.

Particular Features of the Polish Situation

Poland occupies a particular place in the history of the Holocaust. Half of the Jews murdered during the Nazi era were Polish and much of the actual killing occurred in territories taken from Poland. The killing centres built after 1941 were concentrated there, although in the case of Auschwitz, the camp was in the part of Poland that was incorporated into the German Reich and most of the Polish locals were forcibly removed from the surrounding area. Of course there were also significant sites of slaughter elsewhere; for example, the killing fields in Transnistria, where many Romanian Jews were killed and the shooting pits in Lithuania and Ukraine. There is also evidence that German planners intended to build a killing centre near Minsk in Belorussia but decided against it. Nevertheless, the significance of Poland demands a special look at relations between Polish Gentiles and Jews.

The topic remains emotional. The most common interpretations can be categorised into three main groups. One idea might be called the 'Poles as arch-antisemites' theory. Some observers argue that Polish Gentiles in the early decades of the twentieth century were raised on antisemitism. According to this view, Polish Christians were even more hostile to Jews than were Nazi Germans and Polish antisemitism was an essential factor in the Holocaust. The fact that many Polish Gentiles benefited materially from German attacks on Jews might seem to support this view. Although this interpretation may be emotionally satisfying in some ways, however, it oversimplifies the past and neglects in a cruel way the terrible situation of all Poles under Nazi rule.

At the other end of the scale is a position one might label 'all Poles were victims of the Holocaust'. Some proponents of this view maintain that almost six million Poles died in the war – a number probably at least 1.5 million too high – and they sometimes fail to mention that three million of the Polish dead were Jewish. They argue that Polish Gentiles had no real choice in how they behaved under German rule and did all they could for their Jewish neighbours under circumstances in which they too were victims. Scholars who take the stance that all Poles were victims may concede some uniqueness to the Jewish experience but consider it wrong for Jews to claim the Holocaust as their own. Some criticise the scholarship of Jewish historians as a kind of special pleading; some blame Jews themselves for the fact that Polish Christians did not do more to help them. Had the Jews not rejected assimilation into mainstream Polish society, they suggest? Were they not richer than their Christian compatriots? Did they not tend to be pro-communist? Studies written from this perspective have done important work to draw attention to the suffering of Polish Gentiles during the Second World War. They sometimes do so, however, by downplaying Jewish victimisation or even reproducing antisemitic ideas.

A third alternative can be called the 'unequal victims' theory. According to this view, Nazi Germany attacked Polish Gentiles and Polish Jews, but in different ways and to different extents. Here too the numbers used are instructive. For some time, it was assumed that approximately equal numbers of Polish Christians and Jews were killed during the war. In the case of non-Jewish Poles, the estimate of three million, now widely believed to be too high, includes many people killed by the Soviets as well as by the Germans. That number – three million – computes to over ten per cent of Polish Gentiles, a terrible toll. It amounts to close to ninety per cent of Polish Jews, a total catastrophe. The 'unequal victims' approach has validity, but as the label itself suggests, it all too easily disintegrates into a kind of competition in suffering or a numbers game in which human agony is quantified in ways that do not really make moral sense.

These debates intensified with the publication of a book called *Neighbours* by Jan Gross. In graphic detail, Gross recounts how on one day in July 1941, half of the residents of the Polish town of Jedwabne murdered most of the other half. In Jedwabne, according to Gross's account, Poles, not Germans, initiated and carried out the slaughter of hundreds of local Jews. Gross's study, however, is not simply one more accusation of some kind of intrinsic, uniquely Polish antisemitism. Instead he shows the complex interplay of forces in a region first terrorised by Soviet rule between

1939 and 1941, then overrun by the Germans. Poles accused Jews of collaborating with the Soviet oppressors, but in fact it was often precisely those Polish Gentiles most deeply implicated in Soviet crimes who were quickest to take the lead in attacks on Jews – attacks that would serve both to deflect the anger of their neighbours and to curry favour with the new German occupiers.

Gross's analysis and the best of the controversy it has sparked caution against generalising and emphasise instead the wide range of actions and experiences on the part of Poles during the Second World War. Some collaborated with the Soviets, some with the Germans; some helped their Jewish compatriots, often at great risk to themselves. The fates of Polish Christians and Polish Jews under Nazi occupation were linked in complicated ways that we cannot understand if we study those groups of people in isolation from each other.

As a whole Polish Gentiles did not obstruct Nazi plans to isolate, expropriate and eventually annihilate the Jews. What factors might help understand the Polish situation? One important point involves chronology. Poland came under German domination very early – in 1939 – and remained, at least in part, in German hands until early 1945. Unlike the Italians, who began to contend with German occupation only in 1943, the Poles were broken down by years of abuse and persecution.

A second factor was ideological. Nazi racial theory considered Poles, like all Slavic people, to be *Untermenschen* – 'subhuman'. Polish Gentiles occupied a higher position on the ladder of Nazi racial theory than did Jews, but they nevertheless counted in German eyes as inferiors, worthy at most to serve their 'Aryan' masters as slaves. Hitler's Germans considered the northern Europeans over whom they would come to rule – the Danes, Norwegians and Dutch – to be racially related. Accordingly they tried to preserve what they considered their valuable 'Nordic blood' and to co-opt them into their system of world domination, but they had no such intentions for the Poles, whose lives they regarded as worthless.

Demography – ethnic division within Poland – was a third factor that shaped the Polish situation. Many of the inhabitants of Poland in 1939 were not ethnic Poles. The area seized by the Soviets in 1939 and held until 1941 was particularly mixed. Its twelve million inhabitants included only about 4.7 million ethnic Poles. The rest were Ukrainians, Belorussians, Russians, Jews and others. Relations among these groups were not always harmonious and the German invaders would prove adept at turning ethnic groups against one another to further their own ends.

The 1939 division of Poland between Nazi Germany and the Soviet Union seemed to have deepened hostilities between Polish Gentiles and Jews and exacerbated Polish antisemitism. It is unlikely that either Hitler or Stalin foresaw that outcome when the pact was signed in August 1939, but both stood to gain from anything that helped them divide and rule the Poles.

Both the Soviet Union and Germany were traditional enemies of Poland. Many Soviet leaders, like Hitler, opposed the existence of an independent Polish state. So when Soviet forces took over eastern Poland in 1939, they sent many prominent Poles to forced labour in Siberia. Moreover, in the decades since the Bolshevik Revolution, the Soviet Union had developed a reputation for attacking Christianity and the churches. No wonder then that many Poles, especially the wealthy, staunchly nationalist, or devoutly Catholic, considered Soviet rule the worst tragedy that could befall them. In the fall of 1939 some fled to the parts of Poland under German control.

Polish Gentiles would find little to choose between Soviet and German rule. Policies of resettlement and Germanisation meant that hundreds of thousands of ethnic Poles were forced out of the incorporated territories. Meanwhile life in the General Government became increasingly untenable as the Germans targeted Poles for impoverishment and forced labour. Still, at least initially, many Polish Gentiles considered their chances better with the Germans than with the Soviets.

In 1939 Polish Jews, in contrast to their Gentile neighbours, tended to regard Soviet rule as a lesser evil than Nazi German domination. At least in theory antisemitism did not exist under communism. Even in practice, Jews had possibilities to make lives for themselves in the Soviet Union, including as officers in the military. Nazi Germany offered no such option. So while some Polish Christians fled west to the Germans, many Polish Jews, like the young Jack Pomerantz, took their chances by running east.

Suspicious Polish Gentiles interpreted as a betrayal the tendency of some Polish Jews to cast their lot with the Soviets. Antisemites had long accused Jews of being communists; here they could claim to have found proof. Some Christians had always charged Jews with trying to destroy Christianity; now they could say they had evidence of an atheist conspiracy. We tend to assume that shared hardships draw people together. Often, however, quite the opposite occurs. In the early stages of the Second World War, the tribulations faced by all Poles tended to drive wedges between Christians and Jews.

Polish Jews who welcomed the Soviets in 1939 would be disappointed. Their new rulers had no intention of protecting them. Instead they shut down Jewish community institutions, banned organised activities and confiscated private assets from Jews as well as non-Jews. In some cases, they evacuated Jews to the interior of the Soviet Union and to distant regions as labourers. Soviet authorities required all young men in the areas under their control to enlist in the Red Army. Some Poles – Jewish and Gentile – chose that option. Others went west rather than risk being stranded in the Soviet Union and separated from Poland and their families forever. In 1939 they could not know that, within two years, for a Jew to be trapped anywhere in Poland would amount to a death sentence. At least in the Soviet Union Jews could keep moving east. From Poland there would be no place to go.

Some scholars suggest that Polish antisemitism was not primarily religious or racial but economic – that is, Polish Christians' hatred of Jews was fuelled by material resentments, often based on their own deprivation and fantasies of Jewish wealth. In this view it was not greed but pauperisation that led to Polish Gentiles taking advantage of German aggression to grab Jewish property. Certainly the poverty of many Poles played into the hands of the Germans. In retrospect one is struck by the pathetically small stakes that induced some Gentiles in Poland to betray Jews to the

Germans or even kill them themselves. Life seems to have been worth very little. For example, in one Polish town during the war Germans promised a kilogram of salt to anyone who brought in the head of a Jew. Local Ukrainians fanned out through the nearby forests and returned clasping severed heads. In other cases, bags of sugar served as a reward. Sometimes just the promise of whatever possessions the Jews carried with them sufficed.

Discussion of the role that greed played in the Holocaust draws our attention to the 'banality of evil'. Hannah Arendt first used that phrase in her book *Eichmann in Jerusalem*. Most of the people involved in mass killing – as perpetrators, onlookers and beneficiaries – were not crazed maniacs but ordinary people with familiar motivations. There were Polish peasants who deplored German brutality but willingly took the property of Jews forced into ghettos. There were ethnic German families who moved into homes from which the Polish owners had been evicted and eagerly accepted the booty for themselves. Such people did not necessarily initiate destruction, but they profited from it and developed a stake in its continuation.

Nevertheless one can also find many accounts that show Poles who risked their lives for others, including Jews. Yad Vashem, the Holocaust memorial and archive in Israel, honours Gentiles who rescued Jews from the Holocaust as 'the righteous among nations'. One of the criteria for being recognised as one of the righteous is that the person received no monetary benefit for what she or he did. Of all the countries of Europe, Poland has the greatest number of Gentiles recognised for heroism toward Jews – as well as the largest number of Jews killed in the Holocaust.

An important example of Polish rescue efforts is the organisation known as *Zegota*. Its network of operatives provided aid, food and medication to Jews all over Poland. *Zegota* also produced scores of forged documents. Its work is credited with saving the lives of 40,000 to 50,000 Jews.

War did not end in Poland with the German defeat of the Polish army in 1939. Instead many Poles fought on in the underground army. There were actually two underground armies, one nationalist, the other communist. The Polish nationalist army, know as the Home Army, or AK, maintained links to the Polish government-in-exile in London. Its leaders were pre-war Polish officers and it was quite well organised and equipped. For the most part the Home Army was not particularly sympathetic to the sufferings of Polish Jews. Some of its officers were themselves antisemitic and in any case their priorities lay elsewhere. They generally refused to shelter Jews or to arm them, although there were exceptions, for example, in Warsaw where the Home Army passed some revolvers to the Jewish underground. In some cases members of the Home Army even participated in killing Jews themselves in the forests. Nevertheless the Home Army did devote considerable attention to learning about what was happening to the Jews in Poland. Its intelligence assumed that any methods applied to Jews would later be used against Polish Gentiles.

Generally the communist underground army was more open to Polish Jews, at least to those who wished to join its ranks. However, it was rather weak and disorganised in many places and had little time for people ill equipped to take part in fighting: children, elderly people and the unarmed. In some places Jews would form their own underground fighting organisations. At least one of those, the Bielski partisans in western Belorussia, did accept older people, women and children. Led by the dynamic Tuvia Bielski, that forest community combined fighting and rescue activities. By 1944 it included more than twelve hundred Jews. Nechama Tec describes its efforts in her aptly titled book *Defiance*.

In his book *Anton the Dove Fancier*, Bernard Gotfryd recounts a story that shows how the lives of Polish Jews and Gentiles were intertwined. When the war began Bernard was a young Jewish boy living in the Polish city of Radom. His neighbour Anton was a Polish Christian who raised and trained pigeons. Anton was a rough man. He drank, threatened to cook his beloved birds and neglected and scolded his wife. One day German officials requisitioned Anton's pigeons for the Reich. Instead of turning them over to the enemy, Anton killed every one of them. He was arrested for disobedience and sent to a camp.

Later during the war Bernard himself ended up in the concentration camp of Majdanek. There he saw Anton, now wearing the uniform of a kapo. A kapo was a prisoner whom the Germans had elevated to a position of authority over other prisoners. Many kapos were known for their extreme brutality. Anton recognised Bernard and gave him some warm clothes and extra bread. Later he provided Bernard with water, cigarettes to barter and advice. Somehow Bernard Gotfryd lived through the war. While he was still in a camp he learned that Anton had been killed by his fellow prisoners in revenge for his cruelty. Gotfryd returned to Radom, where he saw Anton's wife. She told him that she too had been born Jewish. As a child she had been orphaned and taken in by Anton's mother. Anton had never known about her origins. Now she planned to leave for Palestine.

This case shows the danger of assuming clear-cut categories when studying a situation as complicated as that in Poland during the war. As Anton demonstrated, the same person could be a resistance figure, a perpetrator of brutality, a hero and a victim of Nazi aggression. As his wife's experience suggests, even the line between 'Christian' and 'Jew' could be blurred. There is little that is simple about Polish–Jewish relations during the Nazi era.

Murder of the Disabled

Hitler's Germany first crossed the line from persecution to mass murder not with Jews but with people considered handicapped. The year 1939 would see initiation of a programme to murder people defined as 'lives unworthy of living'. Here, too, experimentation would characterise the early stages of implementation and the outbreak of war provided both cover and justification for the killers.

The idea of 'purging' the population of elements considered undesirable predated Nazi rule and was not exclusive to Germany. Such notions, however, got a big boost with Nazi ideology and its idea that the 'collective good' – at least the well-being of those judged superior – overrode the good of the individual. Nazi plan-

ners measured the value of a human life by its contribution to the
national community, not by some inherent worth.

Even before the war began in 1939 Hitler had authorised
Dr Karl Brandt and Philipp Bouhler to organise a children's
'euthanasia' programme. Under this scheme children selected
for killing were sent to special clinics where medical personnel
starved them to death or gave them lethal injections. Doctors and
research scientists also used some children for experiments that
they hoped would advance their own careers.

In the summer of 1939, Hitler instructed another physician, Dr Leonardo Conti, to organise a similar programme for
adults. Conti, the Reich Doctors' leader and state secretary in
the interior ministry responsible for health matters, set up a huge
administrative machinery that involved doctors, professors, social
workers, nurses and other healthcare professionals. Their main
target would be institutionalised adults with mental illnesses and
disabilities. Codenamed 'T-4' for the address of its headquarters
in Berlin, Tiergartenstrasse 4, the programme was operating
by October 1939.

Conti's people developed a target number by using the following formula. Of every 1,000 people in the German Reich,
they estimated, ten needed psychiatric treatment. Five of those
were institutionalised. One of those five was assumed to qual-
ify for what was euphemistically called euthanasia. In fact, it
was murder. That formula – 1000:10:5:1 – yielded between
sixty-five and 75,000 target cases in Germany. Conti's committee prepared forms to be sent to all mental institutions.
The form was short and asked such questions as whether the
patient received regular visitors or had any 'non-Aryan' blood.
Obviously the criteria for selection had little to do with the
actual health of the person in question. Teams of medical
evaluators examined the forms. They marked with a red plus
sign those people to be killed; they used a blue minus sign
to specify who was to be left alive. Some doctors refused to
participate. For example, the director of one asylum declined
with the explanation that he was 'too gentle' for such work.
He and others like him did not suffer any consequences. It was

no problem to find enough ambitious professionals to keep the programme running smoothly.

The T-4 experts experimented with various methods of killing. They used injections and poison in the early months but soon sought quicker means. By January 1940 they had conducted the first successful gassing, at an asylum not far from Berlin. Some of the earliest gassings were carried out at Grafeneck, a former palace in Württemberg that had been made into a hospital for physically handicapped people. State authorities moved the patients out and took over the building, which they revamped as a killing centre.

An employee at the killing centre of Hadamar, in Hesse, described viewing a gassing there. He 'looked through the peephole in the side wall', he remembered:

> Through it I saw 40–45 men who were pressed together in the next room and were now slowly dying. Some lay on the ground, others had slumped down, many had their mouths open as if they could not get any more air. The form of death was so painful that one cannot talk of a humane killing, especially since many of the dead men may have had moments of clarity. I watched the process for about 2–3 minutes and then left because I could no longer bear to look and felt sick.
>
> (Noakes and Pridham 3:1027)

Meanwhile, other initiatives began against the mentally ill in Poland. Already on 29 September 1939, Germans began shooting Polish mental patients in the district of Bromberg (the Polish name is Bydgoszcz). By 1 November they had murdered almost 4,000 people this way. Elsewhere in territories conquered from Poland, SS execution squads murdered residents of mental institutions in order to empty out buildings for their own purposes. Sometimes they responded to requests from bureaucrats in the resettlement offices who needed beds for ethnic Germans being brought into an area. One SS special commando used a van labelled 'Kaiser's Coffee' as a mobile killing unit. Carbon monoxide gas was fed from a container in the cab into the back of the van to asphyxiate the passengers. During December 1939 and January 1940 the SS special commando murdered hundreds of patients from Polish asylums in that van.

Worried about possible repercussions for their activity, the organisers of the T-4 programme approached Hitler for formal authorisation that would serve to cover them should objections be raised. After all, even in Nazi Germany, murder was against the law. Sometime in October 1939 T-4 officials persuaded Hitler to sign a short statement that was typed on his personal notepaper rather than as an official document. The statement read:

> Reich leader Bouhler and Dr Brandt are charged with responsibility to extend the powers of specific doctors in such a way that, after the most careful assessment of their condition, those suffering from illnesses deemed to be incurable may be granted a mercy death
>
> (Noakes and Pridham, 3:1021)

It is significant that Hitler backdated this note to 1 September 1939, the day of the German invasion of Poland. Presumably he did so in order to link the decision to begin killing people deemed handicapped with the demands of war. In fact the murders were not a response to the exigencies of war; they were an expression of the ideology of race and space. The upheaval of wartime, however, provided the opportunity to carry out such plans with reduced public scrutiny. At the same time war increased Hitler's ability to appeal to the German nation to support his cause.

The programme's organisers tried to keep the killings secret, but total concealment was impossible. There were simply too many people involved and too many ways for information to leak out. Staff at hospitals and asylums saw patients taken away for killing. Family members received letters that announced the deaths of their loved ones. In some cases officials made errors; for example, they wrote that someone had died of appendicitis when the person's appendix had been removed years earlier; they listed another cause of death as spinal disease, but the relatives had just seen the man and he had been in perfect health. The patients themselves in some cases figured out what was going on and pleaded for their lives.

News also circulated in the German communities near the killing centres and beyond. Employees of such places sometimes frequented local bars, where they spouted off about what they had seen. The stench of bodies burning in crematoria drifted beyond fences and walls that enclosed the sites of killing. Even small children playing teased one another about being taken away in the buses with the darkened windows if they acted 'retarded'.

News of the killings of handicapped people upset many Germans. Relatives of some of those murdered launched protests of various kinds. Some wrote directly to Hitler to express their disapproval. Some shared details with their pastors or priests. Probably the ease with which the programme got started had convinced Hitler that the public would be indifferent. Perhaps most people were, but those opposed made their views known.

Church leaders in both the Catholic and the Protestant churches in Germany learned about the killings in direct ways: many asylums were run by the churches. Most of those institutions and their personnel cooperated with the programme, although there were exceptions. Nevertheless, it was from church circles that the most concerted protests to the killings would emerge. Some local Protestant and Catholic clergy made public calls to respect the sanctity of human life. In December 1940, Pope Pius XII issued a statement, quoted in the Vatican's newspaper, *L'Osservatore Romano,* that denounced 'killing of an innocent person because of mental or physical defects'. The most pointed protest did not come until the summer of 1941. By then 70–80,000 people had been killed in the programme in Germany alone. The number of Polish disabled people murdered is unknown, but in all it is estimated that by 1945 the Germans murdered some 275,000 people they deemed handicapped from all over Europe.

In August 1941 the Catholic bishop of Münster, Cardinal August Count von Galen, decided to take a stand against the killings. He preached a sermon in which he made it clear that he knew exactly what was going on and considered it a crime against humanity. Galen quoted the German Penal Code's prohibition against murder and warned the government that its policies would backfire. He told of a German soldier whose father had been institutionalised for some mental disturbance. As the younger man went off to defend his nation, his father in Germany was being killed by his German national comrades. Whose life would be safe in such a society? Galen asked his parishioners. Galen's sermon was duplicated and circulated all over Germany and even abroad by sympathetic elements within the Christian churches. Nazi leaders were furious, but they dared not take action against Galen. He was too well known and too popular. In wartime the government could not risk alienating its own population, so Galen kept his post.

Late in August 1941 Hitler gave an order to halt the 'Euthanasia Programme'. That order was little more than a ploy. It is now known that the killings did not stop – nor did Hitler intend them to. The major gassing operations ended, the killing programme was decentralised into hospitals and the secrecy surrounding T-4 was increased. Meanwhile, the priorities of the German leadership had shifted to Eastern Europe, after invasion of the Soviet Union in June 1941 and the accompanying massacres of the Jews.

It is not clear to what extent Hitler's order to halt was a response to protests such as Bishop von Galen's sermon. Certainly the stepped-up efforts at concealment were intended to placate the public. German authorities always had an eye to morale in the military and at home. During wartime the last thing soldiers and their families needed was the worry that men would be killed by their own government if they were injured. Nevertheless, the killing of disabled people continued until the end of the war and even after. The last victim of the 'euthanasia' programme was a four-year-old boy, murdered in a Bavarian hospital on 29 May 1945.

48. Jews kayaking in Poland in the 1930s. In the middle of the rear kayak, holding a child, is Tsvi Majranc. Mr Majranc died of dysentery in the Łódź ghetto. His son Nechemia survived the Holocaust as did Nechemia's wife, Shifra Horowitz. For most of the war, Shifra passed as a Gentile Pole, working as a courier for the Polish underground and hiding her husband in their flat. They left Poland in 1945, spent two years in Italy and then immigrated to the United States in 1947.

49. German Jewish soldiers celebrating Hanukkah in the field during the First World War. In 1916, the same year that this photograph was taken, German military authorities carried out a survey of Jewish contributions to the war effort. Data showing that Jews had served and sacrificed at least proportional to their numbers was not released. Antisemites spread the lie that the outcome had been suppressed because it made the Jews look so bad it would spark violence.

50. The Jewish proprietor of a kosher butcher shop in Danzig (Gdansk) stands behind the counter with his son. The photograph was taken sometime in the 1930s.

51. Children at the *Israelitische Volkschule* (Jewish elementary school) in Essen, Germany, dressed up in Purim costumes. Standing at left is their teacher, Fritz Kaiser. In the front row, fourth from the left, is Heinz (Henry) Straus. The photograph dates from 1935, 1936 or 1937. Restrictions on Jewish children's attendance at German public schools led schools like this one to expand and serve secular as well as religious Jews. In November 1938, Heinz Straus witnessed burning of the Essen synagogue and youth centre. The next day, his father was arrested and sent to Dachau concentration camp. Following his release several weeks later, the family obtained American visas and, in April 1939, departed for the United States.

52. Members of the German boxing club 'Sparta' in 1929, after winning the North German championship. Third from the right is Johann Trollmann, a Gypsy from Hanover. In June 1933, Trollmann won the new middle-weight championship (three months earlier, the title had been taken away from the Jewish boxer, Erich Seelig) but the boxing league withdrew the title. Trollmann was drafted into the German Army in 1939; in 1942, he was arrested, beaten by police and sent to Neuengamme concentration camp. SS camp personnel sometimes forced the starving Trollmann to box with them. He was shot and killed in 1943.

53. A man cares for the family mule beside wagons in a Gypsy encampment in the Dutch city of Haarlem. This photograph was taken in late 1940 as part of the German occupation authorities' efforts to register the Gypsies in Holland. Many but by no means all Roma and Sinti in Europe lived an itinerant lifestyle.

54. A scene from around 1929 in the Eldorado, a nightclub frequented by the Berlin homosexual community. The balloon displays the nightclub's name and its address (15 Motzstrasse). During the Weimar Republic, Berlin developed a vibrant gay scene that many German conservatives and moral crusaders detested. Attacking homosexuals was one way that the Nazi regime sought to curry favour with certain elements in the German population.

55. A lecture slide used during the 1930s at the national eugenics institute in Berlin. Institute scientists had examined these brothers to render an 'expert opinion on racial origin'. A notation on the slide card reads: 'phenotype [physical appearance] suspicion of Jewish descent'. Although German 'race experts' made much of such displays of scientific rigour, under German law after 1935, it was the religion of one's grandparents, not one's appearance or biological make-up, that determined whether one counted as a Jew or an 'Aryan'.

56. These portraits of the offspring of a union between an African woman (upper left) and a white man (not pictured) come from a set of slides illustrating a 1934 lecture on race and heredity by a researcher at the SS Race and Settlement office. The heading reads, 'Bastards between Hottentots and Whites'.

57. This 1936 image comes from a filmstrip of the Reich Propaganda office titled, 'The Terrible Legacy of an Alcoholic Woman'. It claims that within eighty-three years, one such woman produced 894 descendants, 50 per cent of whom were 'asocial', including 40 paupers, 67 habitual criminals, 7 murderers, 181 prostitutes and 142 beggars. Taken together, these 'deviants' allegedly cost the state 5 million Reich Marks.

Baſtarde zwiſchen Hottentotten und Weißen
(links oben Hottentottin)
Aus „Siemens, Vererbungslehre"

Schulß, Lichtbilder-Vorträge.   Vortrag II, Karte 5.

Das furchtbare Erbe einer Trinkerin
In 83 Jahren   894 Nachkommen
40 Armenhäusler 67 Schwerverbrecher 7 Mörder 181 Dirnen 142 Bettler
437 (cd. 50%) waren aſozial u. verurſachten 5 Millionen RM Koſten

58. A 1941 poster titled 'The Jewish Conspiracy'. It presented both Josef Stalin and Winston Churchill as Jews, although neither man was Jewish and falsely claimed that 406 out of 503 members of the Soviet government were Jews and that the British House of Commons held 19 'full Jews' and 90 'half Jews'. The text at the bottom reads as follows: 'To destroy Bolshevism means to stamp out completely the Jewish conspiracy against the German people. Germany has only one motto: VICTORY!'

59. A 1933 poster depicting the Nazi view of Freemasonry and its purported links to a Jewish world conspiracy. The temple, apron, square and compass are all Masonic symbols. The text reads: 'Jews–Freemasonry. World Politics–World Revolution. Freemasonry is an international organisation beholden to Jewry with the political goal of establishing Jewish domination through worldwide revolution'.

60. Adolf Hitler and Heinrich Himmler review SS troops during Reich Party Day ceremonies in September 1938. As Reich leader of the SS, Himmler became the second most powerful man in Germany.

61. Hermann Göring delivers a speech at the District Party Day rally in Weimar in April 1931. Notice Hitler standing beside the car.

62. By catching Joseph Goebbels off guard, renowned photographer Alfred Eisenstaedt captured something of the propaganda minister's sinister character. Of this image Eisenstaedt said, 'This picture could be titled "From Goebbels with Love".'

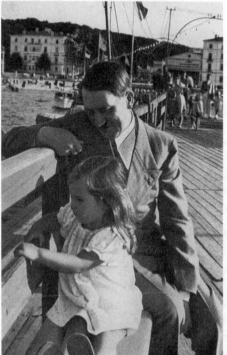

63. Hitler on holiday, pictured here with Helga, the daughter of Joseph and Magda Goebbels. In April 1945, Helga Goebbels, together with her brothers and sisters, was killed at her parents' orders before Joseph and Magda committed suicide in the bunker with Hitler.

64. Members of the League of German Girls
(*Bund Deutscher Mädel, or BDM*) take children
from large families for an airing in the park
while the mothers of the infants are busy
elsewhere. Founded in the late 1920s, the
League of German Girls was intended as the
female complement to the Hitler Youth. Its
activities aimed to prepare young 'Aryans'
ideologically, socially and physically to serve
the Reich as mothers.

65. The German artist John Heartfield
created this photomontage in response to
the Reichstag fire in February 1933. The
text, entitled 'The Gallows Greeting', reads:
'He raises his arm for the "Heil Hitler",
Göring, Prussia's General Policeman. His
arm is like a gallows, the gallows like his arm,
which blackened by fire and flecked with
blood, stretches itself across Germany. But
the judgement is coming that will hang this
gallows-face on the highest gallows'.

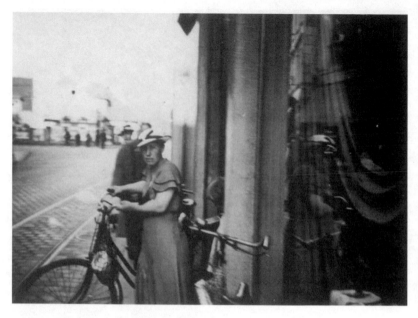

66. This snapshot shows a woman emerging from a Jewish-owned business in violation of the April 1933 boycott. Such photographs, circulated and displayed, were used to denounce individuals and intimidate members of the German public into compliance with anti-Jewish measures.

67. Heinrich Himmler (centre), Reichsführer SS, at the entrance to the Dachau concentration camp during a 1936 inspection. With him are his chief of staff, Karl Wolff (on the left) and Rudolf Hess, Hitler's deputy. By mid-1936, Himmler had used his position as head of the SS and Gestapo to win control of the political and criminal police throughout all of Germany.

68. Johannes Steyer, a German Jehovah's Witness, spent ten years in Nazi concentration camps, prisons and forced labour units. During the 1970s he painted a series of watercolours depicting his persecution under the Third Reich. In this drawing, Steyer depicts himself being threatened by a storm trooper who says, 'I'll have you arrested'.

69. In this scene, Steyer, preaching under surveillance, is told: 'We do not want Jehovah God's Kingdom! We have our church and our Führer!'

70. Himmler speaks to an inmate at Dachau in 1936, during an SS inspection of the camp. Opened with much fanfare in March 1933, Dachau was the first official concentration camp set up in Nazi Germany. Located near Munich, it remained an important site of detention, torture and death until April 1945.

71. 'Kauft Gasmasken' (Buy Gas Masks), an etching from 1934 or 1936 by Lea Grundig. A German artist of Jewish origin, Grundig, née Langer, created many drawings that depicted Nazi repression. After Hitler came to power, Grundig, a communist, was prohibited from producing art. She was arrested in 1936 and again in 1938 and spent nearly two years in the Gestapo prison in Dresden. Somehow, between 1933 and 1939, when she immigrated to Palestine, Grundig worked on numerous subversive cycles, including *Women's Life*, *Under the Swastika* and *War Threatens!* Grundig returned to Dresden in 1949 and remained active in art and politics in East Germany until her death in 1977.

72. A member of the Reich Department of Health, Racial Hygiene and Population Biology visits a Roma family in Vienna sometime in 1938 or 1939 to gather data. Such information was used to monitor Gypsies; for scholars it also provided material for publications and career advancement. After the annexation of Austria in early 1938, measures against Jews and Gypsies that had been introduced over a period of years inside Germany were implemented practically overnight, leaving members of those groups very little chance to develop strategies to escape or evade persecution.

73. A Jewish woman, expelled from Germany in October 1938, washes clothes in the Zbaszyn refugee camp in Poland. In autumn 1938, German authorities expelled some 14,000 Jews living in Germany who held Polish citizenship or were deemed stateless. Polish officials refused to allow them to enter Poland and they remained in limbo for weeks. Later Jewish relief workers organised a refugee camp inside Poland that operated until the summer of 1939.

74. On 10 November 1938, the morning after the *Kristallnacht* pogrom, local residents watch as the synagogue in Ober Ramstadt, Hesse is destroyed by fire. The fire department prevented the blaze from spreading to a nearby home but did not try to limit damage to the synagogue.

75. Georg Schmidt, a young man from an anti-Nazi family, took a series of photographs of the burning synagogue. Police confiscated the film from his home later that day, developed it and kept the prints and negatives in city hall. There they were found after the war by a German policeman whose son-in-law came across them decades later and donated them to the city archive.

76. In November 1938, a few hours before setting fire to the synagogue in Baden-Baden, police rounded up sixty Jewish men and marched them through town. SS men yelled to the onlookers, 'Here are the Jews. Do to them what you will!' No one raised a hand against them. At the synagogue, the Jewish men were forced to sit and listen while a Jewish teacher read selections from Hitler's *Mein Kampf* at the lectern. Afterward the Jews had to practice the *Horst Wessel Song* until they knew it perfectly. Police later sent forty of the men to Dachau.

77. An official visit by Hitler to the Sachsenhausen concentration camp around 1938. Some 6,000 of the German Jewish men arrested in the wake of the *Kristallnacht* pogrom were sent to Sachsenhausen, located not far from Berlin.

78. Prisoners of Sachsenhausen at forced labour. Thousands of German Jewish men were sent there in 1938 and 1939, followed by Poles beginning in 1939 and Soviet POWs in 1941. Also in 1941, authorities at the camp began selecting out prisoners too sick or exhausted to work and sending them to be gassed through a programme known as 14f13.

79. A carnival parade in February 1939 in the south German town of Neustadt mocks Jews. The float features a burning synagogue; the man in front represents Moses with the Ten Commandments. Note the large false noses on some of the men.

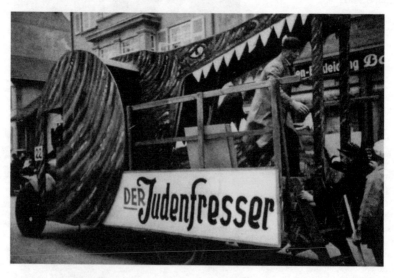

80. A float in the Shrove Tuesday parade in the German Catholic town of Singen am Hohentwiel in February 1939 features members of the local jesters club feeding 'Jews' – men wearing paper noses – to the 'Jew Devourer', a voracious monster.

81. Nurses assist a group of children from the Catholic institution for the disabled in Ecksberg as they board a bus that will transport them to a killing facility. In 1940, the Ecksberg healthcare facility held sixty patients, all of them women or children. The Nazi programme of killing of people deemed handicapped began in August 1939 with the murder of disabled infants and toddlers. Health care workers killed at least 5,000 children by administering lethal doses of medication or through starvation. This photograph was taken in 1939 or 1940.

82. Hajj Amin al-Husayni, the Grand Mufti of Jerusalem, poses with German officials at a reception in Berlin, 1941-1943. Hajj Amin al-Husayni was a prominent Arab political and religious leader and an opponent of Jewish settlement in Palestine. During 1941 he met with both Mussolini and Hitler and in 1943, he helped recruit thousands of Bosnian Muslims in Croatia to serve in Waffen-SS units. After the war, al-Husayni was arrested in France but managed to escape to Egypt. Although there was ample evidence to try him as a war criminal, the Allies made no effort to do so.

83. Poles seized during the 'pacification' of Bydgoszcz (Bromberg) in September 1939 are lined up against a fence before being shot by men of the German 6th Motorized Police Battalion. On 3 September 1939, ethnic Germans in Bydgoszcz staged an uprising against the local Polish garrison. It was put down the next day, just before German units arrived in the city on 5 September. During the following week, German troops, assisted by military field police and Einsatzgruppe IV, executed at least 500 Polish civilians and arrested over 1,000 more.

84. In late 1939, SS personnel lead Polish women from the Pawiak and Mokotow prisons in nearby Warsaw into the forest to be killed. Members of the Polish underground sent this photograph to the Polish government-in-exile in London to illustrate German terror in occupied Poland.

85. The execution of Piotr Sosnowski, a Roman Catholic priest, by Germans and local ethnic German militia in October 1939 near Bydgoszcz (Bromberg). Forty-five Poles, among them Father Sosnowski, were forced to dig a grave in the forest and then were shot into it.

86. A postcard showing the entrance to the Łódź ghetto in 1940 or 1941. Before the war, Łódź was home to the second largest Jewish community in Poland (after Warsaw). When the ghetto was established in early 1940, it isolated 160,000 Jews – one-third the population of Łódź – into a small area. An estimated twenty per cent of the ghetto's population died of starvation and disease.

87. Rabbi David Lifszyc (left) and another man pose in front of a cabinet full of Torah scrolls that were smuggled out of the Polish city of Suwalki. This photograph was taken in 1940. David Lifszyc (later Lifshitz) served as rabbi of Suwalki from 1935 through 1939. After the Germans occupied Suwalki in 1939, Rabbi Lifszyc and other community leaders hid the town's Torah scrolls fearing possible confiscation. Later that year, Rabbi Lifszyc and his family went to live near Kovno, but when the Soviets occupied Lithuania, they began trying to get out of Europe. Eventually they managed to obtain the necessary visas and tickets to travel across the USSR and, in May 1941, set sail from Japan to San Francisco.

88. Norbert Swislocki (standing) and his parents Abraham and Masza celebrate Passover with other refugees in April 1940 in Vilna. Born in Warsaw, Norbert Swislocki was three years old when the war began. His father was called up for service in the Polish army and the family's home was destroyed in the bombing of Warsaw. The family managed to get to Vilna, where they lived for a year before obtaining visas for Curaçao and the Soviet and Japanese transit visas necessary to begin the journey. They made it to Japan but, before they could continue the trip, were deported to Shanghai where they survived the war. In 1947 the Swislockis moved to the United States.

89. Women prisoners gather by the barbed wire fence surrounding a North African internment camp. After signing the armistice agreement with Hitler in 1940, Vichy French authorities sent foreigners, including Jews, who had volunteered for and fought in the French army against Germany and foreign Jewish refugees to work camps in Algeria and Morocco. An estimated 4,000 Jewish refugees were also sent to do forced labour on the pan-Saharan railroad line. This photograph was taken between October 1941 and February 1943.

90. Prisoners gather outside their barracks in a North African internment camp, probably El Ayachi. Among them was Hans Landesberg, a Viennese doctor who had fought with the International Brigade in the Spanish Civil War. Interned in France in 1939, he was sent in 1941 to a camp in Algeria. Through a friend, he managed to get out to Morocco, where he hoped to obtain an immigration visa for the United States. However, Moroccan police only allowed refugees to remain at large for fourteen days, so he was again incarcerated, this time for a year and a half. In early 1943, he received an American visa and moved to New York.

91. Two German Jewish refugee women stand behind the counter of the Elite Provision Store (delicatessen) in Shanghai in 1939 or 1940. Pictured on the left is the owner, Gerda Harpuder; on the right is her cousin Kate Benjamin. The Harpuders managed to leave their home in Berlin for Shanghai in March 1939. They sold the belongings they had transported to Shanghai and used the proceeds to open a delicatessen. In 1943, they relocated into the newly formed Hongkew ghetto. Gerda's husband Hans Harpuder became sick and died in Shanghai in 1945, shortly after VJ Day. The rest of the family immigrated to the United States in 1947.

92. Joseph Fiszman poses with four Chinese children in a store in Shanghai. Born in 1918 in Poland, Joseph Fiszman was a Yiddish writer. Together with his father Jankiel, he managed to flee Warsaw in December 1939 for Vilna. There they obtained visas for Curaçao and, thanks to the efforts of the Japanese diplomat Sugihara, for Japan. While in Japan, they bought strings of pearls for the women of their family, Jankiel's wife Gale and Joseph's sister Ursula, hoping to be reunited with them soon. Instead father and son were deported to Shanghai, where they survived the war. Mother and daughter were imprisoned in the Warsaw ghetto and killed in Trawniki.

93. A Polish Gentile woman and two Polish Jewish men are forced to walk together, probably to an execution site, sometime in the 1940s. The sign around the woman's neck reads, 'For selling merchandise to Jews'. German policies and practices in occupied Poland targeted Jewish and Christian Poles but deliberately tried to prevent and break down ties of solidarity between them.

94. A public execution with onlookers in occupied Poland. This photograph reveals the proximity and interaction of people we might categorise as 'perpetrators, victims and bystanders' of the Holocaust.

Left: 95. A German soldier searches a Gypsy in Poland, probably in 1940. Attacks on Gypsies outside Germany were less organised and systematic than those inside the country, but Germans still singled Roma and Sinti out for harassment and persecution and often included them in the mass killings of Jews carried out by the *Einsatzgruppen* that started in mid-1941.

Below: 97. A Jewish soldier in the Dutch army poses astride his motorcycle. Pictured is Leo Krell, who was born in Poland but moved to Holland as a baby. With his wife Emmy, Leo lived in The Hague where he worked as a furrier and she as a seamstress. Their son Robert was born in 1940. In 1942, they went into hiding, Robert with a Dutch couple, Leo in the attic of his business partner and Emmy in Rijswijk where she lived on false papers. After the war the family was reunited and immigrated to Canada in 1951.

Below left: 96. A German soldier stands guard in front of a castle. Pictured is Kurt Winterstein, one of Hitler's personal drivers. When Nazi authorities found out that his mother was Gypsy, they took him out of the army and sterilised him.

98. The ruins of Rotterdam after its bombing by the German air force on 14 May 1940. The bombing attack destroyed the old city core and killed hundreds of civilians in a deliberate move intended to terrorise the Dutch into surrender.

99. French colonial troops and their German captors in an unidentified POW camp. During 1939–40, the French recruited 100,000 soldiers from French West Africa. Among them were 63,000 *Tirailleurs Sénégalais* who fought in the front lines against the *Wehrmacht* in 1940. Separated from the white French soldiers taken POW, they were targeted for abuse and neglect. It is estimated that at least 3,000 of the *Tirailleurs Sénégalais* were captured and killed in May–June 1940 alone. In all, the Germans killed about 10,000 French black soldiers.

100. A Gypsy woman with a group of children in the Rivesaltes internment camp in 1942.
Located in the French Pyrenees Mountains, Rivesaltes was used in the late 1930s for refugees from
the Spanish Civil War. In 1941 and 1942, thousands of Gypsies and foreign-born Jews rounded up
in France were interned there.

101. A Serbian gendarme, serving the puppet government of Serbia/Yugoslavia under German
military administration, escorts a group of Gypsies to their execution. Only Poland and the
western parts of the Soviet Union were more drastically affected by the deaths and destruction of
war than Yugoslavia. There the Germans, their allies and local collaborators sharpened their tools of
divide and rule amidst a ruthless occupation, a brutal civil war and endless massacres that regularly
included Gypsies and Jews among their many and diverse victims.

102. A young girl wearing a Jewish badge in 1941 in the Loborgrad concentration camp in Croatia. Between 1941 and 1945, Germans and the Croatian Ustasha killed an estimated 32,000 Jews from Croatia, more than 20,000 of them in the Jasenovac complex of camps alone.

103. The body of a Jewish doctor hangs on an electric pole in front of a bank in Sabac, Yugoslavia, in August 1941. The building has been painted with antisemitic graffiti showing a rich banker, presumably a Jew, holding a money bag in one hand and in the other pulling the strings behind Franklin Roosevelt, Winston Churchill and Josef Stalin.

104. Germans pose near the bodies of recently murdered Serbian civilians in 1941 in Yugoslavia. Many German soldiers took photographs like this one and sent them home to their families. In Yugoslavia members of the regular military, not special SS units, were responsible for the massive death toll, which included many Serbs.

105. German troops stand at the edge of a trench used as a mass grave for the bodies of Jews and Gypsies killed by the 750th Infantry Regiment in October 1941 in the Macva region of Yugoslavia. A German soldier sent this photograph to a woman friend in spring 1945.

106. Germans shoot a group of Poles in Lithuania in 1941 or 1942 as Lithuanian auxiliaries and others, including a young man taking a photograph, look on. Open-air killings like this were common; there was little attempt to maintain secrecy, nor was it possible to conceal such killings from onlookers.

107. A column of Soviet POWs moving toward a German internment camp near Kharkov. Most Soviet POWs were held in facilities administered by the German military, not in camps run by the SS. Many of them provided nothing whatsoever by way of shelter or food. The murderous brutality toward Soviet POWs was in marked contrast to German treatment of British and French POWs (of the white men among them, that is).

108. Soviet POWs in the *Sonderlager* (special camp) at Sachsenhausen. Beginning in 1941, some 18,000 Soviet POWs were sent to Sachsenhausen, where Germans shot an estimated 13,000 of them. Soviet forces liberated Sachsenhausen in April 1945 and soon thereafter, a Soviet investigation commission convened at the site to collect evidence of SS crimes. The resulting trial, held in 1947 in Berlin, charged and convicted sixteen former guards.

109. A column of Soviet POWs heading toward the rear and internment. This photograph was taken in September 1941.

110. A man filling a bucket from a standpipe in the Lublin ghetto. The Lublin ghetto was established in early 1941, and mass transports of Jews from the ghetto to the killing centre of Belzec started a year later. Within one month, 30,000 Jews had been murdered there or in nearby forests.

111. Wearing his prayer shawl and phylacteries, Shmuel Grosman recites the morning prayer service in his bed in the Łódz′ ghetto. Grosman died in the ghetto at the age of sixty. His son Mendel took this picture in 1941 or 1942. Born in 1913, Mendel Grosman studied painting before devoting himself to photography. Forced into the ghetto, he was assigned by the Jewish council to take pictures. Grosman also took thousands of illegal photos documenting Jewish life and death in the ghetto. He was shot by a guard on a death march in April 1945.

112. A woman selected for 'deportation' communicates with her son through the fence of the central prison in the Łódz´ ghetto. In September 1942, along with fifteen thousand other Jews deemed unsuitable for work – children, the elderly and the infirm – she was sent to the killing centre at Chelmno to be gassed.

113. A young Jewish woman in the Łódz´ ghetto writes a last letter before being transported to the killing centre at Chelmno. Such letters, written on scraps of paper, cloth, wood or anything else available, were thrown out windows, stuffed through cracks in wooden freight cars, or scattered along roadsides in a final attempt to make contact with the world of the still-living.

114. In late June 1941, the Romanian city of Iasi was the site of a major pogrom. Some 5,000 Jews were rounded up, with nearly half of them being shot or beaten to death. The rest were boarded onto freight cars that were nailed shut. Hundreds died of heat exhaustion, suffocation, dehydration and suicide during a journey that followed a circuitous route. While stopped on 1 July, some of the cars were opened to remove the dead. Because the surviving Jews were too weak to do the work, local Gypsies were brought in to unload the bodies.

115. A group of Roma, awaiting instructions from their German captors, sits in an open area near the fence at Belzec in late 1941 or 1942. Gypsies were murdered in all of the killing centres used for annihilating Jews.

116. Bogumila Babinska (Jasiuk). Babinska worked for the Polish underground during the war. Arrested in 1941, she was sent to Ravensbrück. In 1942, German doctors selected Babinska as one of the 'rabbits' (guinea pigs) for medical experimentation. They experimented on her twice, cutting into the muscles and bones of her leg. Babinska and a group of friends were instrumental in informing the Polish government-in-exile in London and the Red Cross about the existence of the experiments, through invisible messages they wrote in urine to their families. This photograph was part of that effort of documentation. Babinska survived the war.

117. Christmas card given to Jadwiga Hassa in December 1942 by a fellow inmate of Ravensbrück concentration camp. The rabbit is a reference to their common experience as victims of medical experimentation. The Polish text reads: 'Dear Jadzienko Bunny, For Christmas I wish that baby Jesus will grant you health and hope and that you will get back home'. Jadwiga Dzido (later Hassa) was arrested in 1941 for assisting the underground and sent to Ravensbrück. Selected for medical experimentation, she was subjected to injections of highly potent bacteria and incisions into her leg that left her permanently scarred. She survived the war and presented evidence in 1946 at the Nuremberg Medical Case trial.

118. Dr Bigula Vajs, a Jewish member of the resistance, attending to a sick child in Yugoslavia during the war. From Yugoslavia to Belorussia, North Africa and France, Jews were active in all the resistance movements that would accept them (and, with concealed identities, in some that would not), in numbers often vastly disproportional to the size of their populations.

119. Dutch-Jewish children brought into hiding by the Dutch underground. This photograph comes from Hilde Jacobsthal Goldberg, who worked at a childcare centre in the Joodsche Schouwburg in Amsterdam. Jacobsthal was born in Germany and moved to Holland with her family to escape Nazi persecution. In 1943 Jacobsthal made her way to Belgium where she worked for the underground as a nurse and ambulance driver.

Above left: 120. In August 1942 Bronia Szyr (later Brenda Senders) escaped from the ghetto in Sarny, a town in eastern Poland. She joined a Russian partisan group and spent the rest of the war fighting the Germans. This photograph was taken in 1944 in Ukraine.

Above: 121. Stjepan Filipovic, commander of a partisan detachment, calls on the people of Serbia to fight, just before his execution in May 1942. Such shows of defiance often had a profound impact on those who saw them. Partisans, led by Tito, succeeded in liberating Yugoslavia from the Germans themselves, a remarkable accomplishment.

Left: 122. Sara Ginaite, a partisan fighter from Kovno, at the liberation of Vilna in August 1944. A Red Army major took the photograph and published it in the Soviet Union. He was surprised to see a Jewish woman standing guard. Ginaite remained in Lithuania after the war, where she made a successful career as an economist. She moved to Canada in the 1980s.

Above left: 123. Georges Herz leads a pair of oxen on the grounds of the Chateau La Hille. In the year preceding the outbreak of war, over 200 Jewish children from Germany and Austria found refuge in Belgium, through a rescue effort organised by the *Comité d'Assistance aux Enfants Refugees Juifs*. In 1940, the *Secours Suiss aux Enfants*, an agency of the Swiss Red Cross, moved the children to a more secluded site, the abandoned Chateau de La Hille, not far from the Spanish border.

Above right: 124. Cousins Henia Wisgardisky (right) and Bluma Berk. This photograph was taken in July 1943, a few months before Henia's mother smuggled the two girls out of the Kovno ghetto. Hidden by Lithuanian families, both children survived the war. Reunited after the war, the family immigrated to Palestine and later to Canada.

125. A sick child in a crib in the Kovno ghetto hospital, covered by a blanket with a Star of David. The Ghetto's Jewish council established medical clinics, an old age home and an orphanage. Because the survival of the ghetto depended on the community's ability to work, medical workers' first priority was keeping residents fit for labour. As labourers, children and the elderly had little or no value to the Germans. In July 1942, SS Sergeant Helmut Rauca ordered that all pregnancies in the ghetto be terminated and pregnant women be shot. Ghetto obstetricians performed abortions to save women's lives and hospital workers hid some orphans to try to protect them from death.

126. Pictured are Avram (five years) and Emanuel Rosenthal (two years). Emanuel was born in the Kovno ghetto. Approximately 10,000 children and youths moved into the Kovno ghetto in August 1941. Within a few months, almost half of them had been killed. During the two days of the March 1944 'Children's Action', Germans and Ukrainian auxiliaries went from house to house rounding up children below the age of twelve. They shot many of their 1,300 victims at the Ninth Fort and sent the rest to Auschwitz to be gassed. The children shown here were among those killed.

127. Drawing made in December 1943 by Anatoli Garnik depicting exhumation and burning of corpses at the Ninth Fort, near Kovno. Garnik was a Jewish Soviet POW forced to work for the Germans, digging up and burning bodies. On Christmas Eve 1943, Garnik and the other members of the Sonderkommando escaped. Earlier Garnik arranged to have this drawing forwarded to Soviet journalists. The picture reached its destination and Garnik returned to his unit, only to be shot after being falsely accused of having collaborated with the Germans.

128. Willem Arondeus (left) and friends dancing at a garden party. During the war, Arondeus led a Dutch gay resistance group that bombed the Amsterdam Population Registry offices in an effort to destroy government records on Jews and others hunted by the Germans. Arondeus was executed in 1943.

129. A group of Jewish women and children standing by the road see their fathers, husbands and sons as they are driven away from the deportation assembly point in Ioannina, Greece. This photograph was taken on 24 March 1944.

130. A group of Jewish women and children who have been assembled for transport in March 1944 from Ioannina, Greece, prepare to board a truck. Most of the Greek Jews rounded up in 1944 were sent to Auschwitz and killed.

131. Women, children and elderly await a train while behind them a van filled with trunks and suitcases is unloaded. German forces occupied Hungary in March 1944 and the following month, Hungarian authorities, working with the Germans, ordered all Jews outside Budapest to concentrate in certain cities. Within two months, some 440,000 Jews had been transported, most of them to Auschwitz. In all, 500,000 Hungarian Jews died.

132. Jews in the Westerbork camp in the Netherlands light Hanukkah candles inside a crowded barracks. This photograph, taken on 10 December 1944, came from the personal album of the camp commander Albert Konrad Gemmeker. According to one survivor, many of the young people shown here were sent to Auschwitz the day after the photograph was taken.

133. The main rail entrance of Auschwitz-Birkenau just after its liberation in January 1945, as seen from the rail spur (visible at left) inside the camp. Soup bowls and other personal effects of the prisoners can be seen strewn across the tracks.

134. This photograph comes from the 'Auschwitz Album', a book of photographs documenting the arrival, selection and processing of one or more transports of Jews from Subcarpathian Rus that came to Auschwitz-Birkenau in May 1944. The album includes 193 photographs. SS-Hauptscharführer Bernhardt Walter, head of the Auschwitz photographic laboratory and his assistant, SS-Unterscharführer Ernst Hofmann produced the album as a presentation volume for the camp commandant.

135. From the 'Auschwitz Album': Jewish women and children await selection on the ramp at Auschwitz-Birkenau in May 1944. Visible on the right is a prisoner in a striped uniform, part of the Sonderkommando assigned to unload people and possessions from the trains. A prisoner named Myszkowski who worked in the lab arranged the photographs in the album and wrote the captions.

136. Women and children from Subcarpathian Rus on the ramp at Auschwitz-Birkenau. Among those pictured are Irina Berkovits and her son Adalbert (age 5).

137. On the ramp at Auschwitz-Birkenau. Lili Jacob saw her Aunt Tauba on this picture (far left) with her four children. Lili, who was 18 years old when she arrived in the camp, was the only member of her family to survive Auschwitz. The woman in the centre with the two girls wearing rabbit-fur hats has been identified as either Bozsi Iskovics Engel from Beregszasz with her daughters Agota Engel and Judith Engel, or Breine Slomovics with her daughters.

138. These boys from Subcarpathian Rus, shown awaiting selection on the ramp at Auschwitz–Birkenau, were the brothers of Lili Jacob. After liberation, Lili (later Zelmanovic, now Meier), an Auschwitz survivor who appears in one of the photographs, found the album in an SS barrack where she was searching for some clothing.

139. Women and children who have been selected for death walk toward the gas chambers at Auschwitz–Birkenau, May 1944.

140. From the 'Auschwitz Album': Jewish women and children from Subcarpathian Rus walking toward the gas chambers in May 1944.

141. Richard Baer, Commandant of Auschwitz, in 1944. Baer presided over the camp during the final eight months of its existence. Under his command hundreds of thousands of Jews and thousands of Gypsies were murdered. After Auschwitz was evacuated in January 1945, Baer became commandant of Dora-Mittelbau. He evaded justice until 1960 when he was arrested in conjunction with the investigation for the Frankfurt Auschwitz Trial, he died of a heart attack in 1963, while in pre-trial detention.

142. SS officer Karl Hoecker lights a candle on a Christmas tree. This picture was included in an album of photographs of Auschwitz taken between May and December 1944, when Hoecker was adjutant to Commandant Baer. Hoecker joined the SS in 1933 and was assigned to the Neuengamme concentration camp in 1939. In 1943 he moved to Majdanek-Lublin where he served as adjutant during the peak period of mass murder there.

143. Karl Hoecker with his dog Favorit. Hoecker accompanied Richard Baer to his new post at Dora-Mittelbau. He managed to escape the camp before it was taken and joined a combat unit near Hamburg. Captured by British forces and held for eighteen months, he avoided identification and returned to his home town. At the Frankfurt Auschwitz Trial, he was charged and convicted of aiding and abetting mass murder and sentenced to seven years. Released on parole in 1970, Karl Hoecker died in 2000 at the age of 88.

144. SS officers and women auxiliaries (*Helferinnen*) in 1944 on a wooden bridge in Solahütte, the SS retreat centre outside of Auschwitz. Camp adjutant Karl Hoecker is pictured in the centre. The original caption, '*Regen aus heiteren Himmel*', literally means 'rain coming from a bright sky', but figuratively means that something unexpected has happened.

145. Members of the SS *Helferinnen* and SS officer Karl Hoecker turn over their bowls to show they have eaten all their blueberries. Although survivors often describe the camp as a site of total desolation, shunned even by birds, the Germans who worked at Auschwitz and lived in the model town created for them there enjoyed a comfortable life in a naturally lovely setting.

146. Survivors of the Hadamar Institute. These photographs were taken by an American military photographer in April 1945, soon after liberation of the site. The Hadamar Institute, near Wiesbaden in Hesse-Nassau, was one of six hospitals and sanitoria in Germany and Austria in which the so-called euthanasia programme was carried out. Code-named Facility E, Hadamar went into operation as a killing centre in January 1941. For the next eight months, busloads of patients arrived daily at the facility and a staff of approximately 100 did the work of receiving them, weighing and photographing them and getting them into the gas chamber located in the cellar of the Institute building.

147. In a later phase of operation, killings at Hadamar were done by lethal overdose of medication or starvation. In addition to the mentally and physically disabled who were Hadamar's chief victims, thousands of other people were murdered there. Among them were healthy Jewish *Mischling* children (children of mixed marriages), tubercular Eastern European forced labourers, German geriatric patients and disabled German soldiers. The Hadamar staff continued to kill 'patients' at the Institute until shortly before liberation by American troops in late March 1945.

148. Jewish youth liberated at Buchenwald lean out the windows of a train as it pulls away from the station. The train was en route to a home in France run by *Oeuvre de Secours aux Enfants*, a children's relief organisation in Geneva. This photograph, taken in June 1945, comes from the collection of Romek Wajsman (now Robert Waisman), one of approximately 1,000 Jewish child survivors found by American troops when they arrived at the Buchenwald concentration camp in April 1945. Born in Poland in 1930, Romek survived a ghetto, forced labour in a factory that made aircraft shells and digging anti-tank ditches before he ended up in Buchenwald. In 1948, with the help of the Canadian Jewish Congress, he and twenty other of the young Buchenwald survivors with him in France immigrated to Canada. Romek and his sister Lea were the only members of the family to survive the war.

149. Ruins of the Kovno ghetto, photographed in August 1944. German destruction of the Kovno ghetto began in July 1944, three weeks before the Soviets liberated the city. Aware that thousands of people had not appeared for the round-ups and likely remained hidden in bunkers, the SS ordered German troops to raze the ghetto area. They blew up every house, doused the ruins with gasoline and incinerated them. Thousands of people were burned to death or shot trying to flee. Only about 100 Jews survived the liquidation of Kovno.

150. In June 1945, German civilians from Burgsteinfurt watch a film in the local cinema about the atrocities of the Bergen-Belsen and Buchenwald concentration camps. Burgsteinfurt was known by some British soldiers as the 'village of hate' because of its silent but noticeable resentment of the Allied occupation. The military government began screening of a documentary on the concentration camps on May 29.

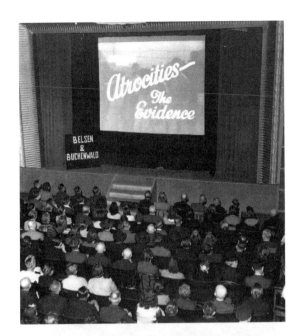

151. When few residents came to see the film, British military authorities ordered all 4,000 townspeople to attend showings. They were assembled and marched to the cinema. Here, German civilians from Burgsteinfurt exit the cinema after a screening. This photograph was taken on 30 May 1945.

152. Marion Kaufmann, later Cassirer (centre), a Jewish girl from Berlin, with the Gypsy family that hid her for a month in the Netherlands in late 1944, after the area had been liberated by the Canadians only to be reoccupied by the Germans. Marion had fled Germany with her mother in 1942. They were separated and Marion spent the war in a series of hiding places. She and her mother were reunited in 1945.

153. Jewish displaced women pose with Red Army officers in the Zittau camp for German POWs in July 1945. During the war Zittau was one of the sub-camps of the Gross-Rosen concentration camp system.

154. Ernst Mettbach testifies as a witness for defendant Wilhelm Beiglboeck at the 1946–1947 Doctors' Trial. Mettbach stated that he and thirty-nine other Gypsies volunteered for seawater experiments. The U.S. Military Government for Germany created the Military Tribunal I, which conducted the Medical Case Trial. Twenty-three SS physicians, scientists and officials were accused of committing 'murders, brutalities, cruelties, tortures, atrocities and other inhuman acts'. In August 1947, the Tribunal found fifteen of the defendants guilty. Seven of them were hanged in 1948.

155. Halina Mosinskis of Lithuania is presented with a certificate by Yad Vashem as one of the Righteous Among the Nations, in recognition of her 'compassion, courage and morality' because she risked her life to save the lives of Jews during the Holocaust. This photograph was taken in 1982. As of 2007, Yad Vashem had recognised close to 22,000 Gentile rescuers. The largest number – 6,004 – came from Poland; Halina Mosinskis was one of 693 Righteous from Lithuania.

Above: 156. Europe on the eve of the Second World War.

Left: 157. The division of Poland in 1939.

Opposite: 158. Major Concentration Camps, 'Euthanasia' Centres and Killing Centres.

Map by Michael J. Fisher, cartographer

Map by Michael J. Fisher, cartographer

6

Expansion and Systematization: Exporting War and Terror, 1940–1941

The previous chapter described the first year of the war as a period of Nazi experiments in conquest, persecution and mass killing. Just as Nazi revolution in 1933 had been followed by routinisation, the experimental phase in 1939 gave way to what might be labelled a time of expansion and systematisation. During 1940 and 1941 the size of Hitler's empire increased tremendously as German forces overwhelmed more and more of Europe. After Poland the Germans first turned their military attentions to the north and west, attacking Denmark, Norway, the Netherlands, Belgium, Luxembourg, France and Britain in the spring and summer of 1940. Able to conquer all but the British, they moved south and east – against Yugoslavia and Greece in spring 1941 and then in June 1941 against the Soviet Union.

Terror and suffering grew along with Hitler's empire as programmes of killing became both much larger and more efficient. By the end of 1941 German mobile killing units would have murdered close to a million Jews in Eastern Europe – men, women and children – many of them shot into mass graves. Preparation of killing centres to massacre even more stunning numbers of people would be under way. Millions of Soviet prisoners of war would be dead or dying in German captivity.

This chapter surveys the German campaigns of 1940 and 1941 that brought most of Europe under Nazi control. It explores the repercussions as Nazi Germans took their projects of supposed racial purification and territorial expansion ever farther from home.

War in the North and West

Within days of the German invasion of Poland on 1 September 1939, both Britain and France were officially at war with Germany. Bound by agreements to Poland, the British and French declared war on Germany on 3 September but initially remained fairly inactive. This early phase was known in Britain as the 'phoney war'. The French referred to it as a *drôle de guerre* – a 'funny war' – and the Germans spoke of a *Sitzkrieg*, an immobile 'war of sitting' in contrast to the rapid blitzkrieg – 'lightning war' – in Poland.

There were a few skirmishes on the border between France and Germany in 1939 but nothing otherwise on land. Siegfried Knappe, a young German artillery officer, describes in his memoir *Soldat* how he spent much of the autumn and winter of 1939–1940 in western Germany, mere miles from the border with Luxembourg. Days and then weeks passed as the Germans prepared for an attack from the French that never came. Rather than the dangers and strains of combat, Knappe and his men faced the challenge of readying their horses and themselves for action, tasks that left plenty of time to celebrate German victories in Poland by drinking beer and dancing with the locals. Knappe especially enjoyed an invitation to the Bismarck estate, where he and a group of fellow officers sipped cocktails and chatted with the vivacious, young granddaughter-in-law of Otto von Bismarck, the hero of German unification in 1871. From Knappe's vantage point, it must have been easy to view Hitler's early triumphs as confirmation of German superiority.

At sea there was more action as the Germans began their attack on Allied shipping. In return the British navy organised a convoy system and began breaking German codes. By mid-1940 this phase of the 'phoney war' in the west would come to an abrupt halt.

In the spring of 1940, after a winter spent consolidating their hold on Poland and continuing preparations for further offensives, the Germans moved north and west. Hitler and his generals knew that their plan to dominate Europe remained impossible unless they crushed and subordinated the European powers of France and Britain. That goal could only be achieved through war.

For Hitler war in the west was a prerequisite for grabbing land in the east. It had been part of the plan all along. The western conflict, however, did not take quite the form Hitler had foreseen. Already in 1938 Hitler believed Germany was ready for war against France and Britain. He had expected that war to precede hostilities with Poland. The German air force – the *Luftwaffe* – had been built up under Hermann Göring with an eye to campaigns in the west. It was in the west that Hitler anticipated the most difficult fighting for the Germans. After all, in Nazi eyes, Europeans to Germany's east were racial inferiors, surely easy opponents for members of a master race.

In keeping with Nazi racial theories, German warfare in the west would be less excessive than in the east. Nazi ideology regarded western and northern Europeans as 'racially valuable' people, suitable partners for German 'Aryans'. Still, Germans would do much stealing and plundering in these parts of Europe too. For leaders who believed that Germany had lost the previous war because of public discontent – the stab in the back from the home front – nothing was more important than placating the people back home. What easier way to do so than to let them enrich themselves at the expense of others?

In April 1940 German forces entered Denmark and that small nation surrendered without a struggle. The Germans moved on to Norway, where they had to fight their way in, but by June 1940 they had defeated the Norwegians too. The British and French tried to help Norway, but without adequate air support and thorough coordination their landings failed. The Norwegian government fled to London, where it established itself as a government-in-exile. Norwegian merchant ships also escaped to Britain, where they could be used in the war effort against Germany. A local fascist leader, Vidkun Quisling, took power – or more accurately, became the German puppet – at home. His name, 'Quisling', has become a synonym for 'cowardly collaborator'. The Norwegians would execute him as a traitor in 1945.

What did German military planners want with Denmark and Norway? A look at a map gives some explanation. The Germans needed to secure the supply route of Swedish iron ore for their war machine. They also sought to broaden their base for a sea war with Britain and eventually the United States. Scandinavia would provide naval bases from which to attack the British with submarines and access to routes around Britain.

In May 1940, just a month after the offensive against Denmark and Norway began, German forces invaded and conquered the neutral nations of the Netherlands, Belgium and Luxembourg. Here too victory was swift. In the Netherlands, German armoured forces penetrated the borders, while airborne units took strategic airfields and bridges. The Dutch soon surrendered. First, however, there were some significant developments. The queen and her government left Holland for Britain, where they too formed a government-in-exile on the side of the Allies. The Dutch were important to the French and British cause because they controlled a large colonial empire and a substantial merchant fleet, both of which would prove valuable in the war effort.

On 14 May the *Luftwaffe* bombed the Dutch city of Rotterdam in an attempt to terrorise the Dutch into surrender. The Germans clearly aimed at civilian targets to intimidate and demoralise their opponents. They destroyed the centre of the city and killed hundreds of civilians. At the time, the panicked British press reported the inflated figure of 30,000 Dutch casualties. For the Allies, the bombing of Rotterdam provided an early manifestation of German brutality and introduced a new kind of warfare: unlimited war from the air. Within a few years the Germans would reap what they had sown with the destruction from the air of their own cities.

One of the eyewitnesses to the German conquest of the Netherlands was Anne Frank, a young girl living in Amsterdam. She and her family of German Jews had left Frankfurt for Holland after Hitler came to power. As it turned out, they had not fled far enough. Unable to get out of Europe in 1940, their only option was to try to disappear within the city of Amsterdam. Anne's father began to use his contacts to prepare a hiding place for his family and some acquaintances. It was in their 'secret annex' between July 1942 and August 1944 that Anne would write a diary, now one of the most famous documents of the Holocaust. Betrayed by an anonymous tip-off to police, the Franks and the people in hiding with them were sent first to the Dutch transit camp of Westerbork and then on to Auschwitz. A group of them were later moved to the Bergen-Belsen concentration camp in Germany, where Anne died in March 1945. Of the eight residents of the hiding place, only Anne Frank's father, Otto, survived the war.

In May 1940 German troops entered France. They came through Belgium from two directions, the north and also the south. The French had concentrated their best forces in the north and were unprepared for a German attack through the Forest of Ardennes in southern Belgium. By 12 May, German soldiers were on French soil and by 20 May, they had broken through to the sea, to the coast of the English Channel. In effect the German attack cut the Anglo-French forces in two.

The Germans prepared to surround and annihilate the Allied forces converging on the French seaport of Dunkirk. Between the end of May and early June 1940, however, the Allies managed to evacuate some 338,000 of their own soldiers. Using merchant ships, motorboats, fishing boats, private yachts, destroyers and any other craft they could muster, the British rescued their men and more than 100,000 French people from the beaches of Dunkirk while under continued attack from the Germans. They had no choice but to leave most of their equipment behind.

German actions in the French campaign revealed the priorities of racial warfare. Some 100,000 men from French West

Africa served in the French military in 1939–1940. During May and June 1940, the Germans captured thousands of these soldiers, whom they separated from their white counterparts and targeted for special abuse. Sometimes on orders from their officers or on their own initiative, German soldiers shot them or blew them up with grenades. Supported by a massive propaganda campaign from Berlin, these slaughters of an estimated 3,000 black French soldiers within two months echoed German behaviour in Poland and anticipated the massacres of millions of Soviet POWs that began a year later.

By 14 June, German troops marched triumphantly into Paris. Hitler danced the jig that became famous from the newsreels when he visited Paris for the first time. Unlike the Dutch and Norwegian governments, the French government did not go into exile. Instead it remained and signed an armistice agreement on 22 June 1940. Under the terms of the armistice the Germans divided France into two parts: an occupied zone and an unoccupied zone known as Vichy France because its capital was located in the small, southern city of Vichy. Much of the French army entered prisoner of war camps, whereas the navy remained intact.

The head of the Vichy state was Marshal Henri Philippe Pétain (1856–1951), by 1940 an old man and a hero of the First World War. For at least part of the war Pétain's prime minister was Pierre Laval (1883–1945). Together those two names would become symbols of French collaboration with Nazi Germany. Some of the French, however, refused to accept defeat. Among those, General Charles de Gaulle (1890–1970) emerged as leader of the Free French forces and he too escaped to London. In the years before 1940, France had been a haven for refugees from all over Europe. Many communists and other supporters of the Spanish Republic had fled to France in 1939 when their side lost the civil war in Spain. Jews from other parts of Europe had taken refuge in France as their homelands fell prey to German aggression. Now all of these people came into the hands of the Germans and their new French partners.

Among the many foreigners residing in France in 1940 were a young boy named Saul Friedländer and his parents. Friedländer was born in Prague in 1932. He and his parents, middle-class, secular Jews, had left Czechoslovakia in 1938, even as German troops were moving in. France seemed a safe destination and it was hard enough to move that far, leaving behind property, career and relatives. It would prove difficult and for Friedländer's parents eventually impossible, to remain safe in a society where one was a stranger, without money, friends, or adequate language skills. For the Friedländers the collapse of France in 1940 was not primarily a national humiliation; it was a personal catastrophe that eventually put the parents in the clutches of the Nazis and left the son an orphan.

Britain was the only European power both to declare war on Germany in 1939 and to stand firm until 1945. Neither the Soviet Union nor the United States would enter the war against Germany until 1941. The British, however, were not entirely alone. The Dominions – Australia, New Zealand, Canada and, after considerable internal debate, South Africa – joined in declarations of war against Germany. The British-controlled government of India also did so, although without consulting the Indian political parties or, for that matter, the Indian public. For its part, the Irish Free State proclaimed its neutrality.

Support of the Allied cause by countries all over the world was significant, both to the outcome of the war and after the fact, to the national pride of citizens of the nations concerned. People in the Dominions would bear a substantial burden in the war and if the British Isles were to have fallen to the Germans, there would still have been the possibility of continuing the war effort. In fact, the British leadership planned to do so from Canada and moved large parts of Britain's gold reserves to Canada in case they would be needed to finance the war.

Within Europe Britain became the last refuge for many people fleeing Nazi Germany. The governments-in-exile – Polish, Norwegian, Dutch – were surrounded by communities of people forced to flee their homelands. Czech and French opponents of Germany also gathered in Britain, as did those Jews from the continent who could make it in. Among the people who had arrived before war began in 1939 were some 10,000 Jewish children from Germany, Austria, Czechoslovakia and Poland. A special programme organised by private citizens, known as the *Kindertransport*, brought them to Britain. Forced to leave their families behind on the continent, most of them never saw their parents again.

Two veterans of the *Kindertransport* were Ilona and Kurt Penner, children of a Polish Jewish father and a Hungarian Jewish mother. Born in Berlin in 1928, the twins were sent to England in March 1939, where they were placed separately. Their parents, owners of a dry goods store, managed to leave Germany in 1940, although they initially got only as far as France. Fortunately they were able to secure passage to the United States in 1941. Kurt joined them there that year; Ilona, two years later. Now, more than sixty years later, the children of the *Kindertransport* are adults, many of them grandparents. One girl who came to England from Vienna became known as an adult as Ruth Morley, an Academy Award–nominated costume designer who worked on such well-known American films as *Tootsie*, *The Miracle Worker* and *Taxi Driver*. Morley's daughter, a filmmaker named Melissa Hacker, included some of her mother's experiences in a documentary film titled *My Knees Were Jumping: Remembering the Kindertransports*.

By May 1940, with the fall of France, Hitler saw the British as Germany's main enemy in Europe. He proceeded with plans for an invasion, while Prime Minister Winston Churchill rallied the population against the Germans. One of Churchill's most famous speeches included the following challenge:

> The Battle of Britain is about to begin. Upon this battle depends the survival of Christian civilisation. ... If we fail then ... all we have known and cared for will sink into the abyss of a new Dark Age.

After the evacuation of Dunkirk, Churchill's rousing words helped strengthen and inspire British determination:

> Even though large tracts of Europe and many old and famous states have fallen or may fall into the grip of the Gestapo

and all the odious apparatus of Nazi rule, we shall not flag
or fail. We shall go on to the end. We shall fight in France,
we shall fight on the seas and oceans, we shall fight with
growing confidence and growing strength in the air, we shall
defend our island, whatever the cost may be. We shall fight
on the beaches, we shall fight on the landing grounds, we
shall fight in the fields and in the streets, we shall fight in the
hills; we shall never surrender; and even if, which I do not
for a moment believe, this island or a large part of it were
submerged and starving, then our Empire beyond the seas,
armed and guarded by the British Fleet, would carry on the
struggle, until, in God's good time, the new world, with all its
power and might, steps forth to the rescue and the liberation
of the old. (Sachse, 314–15)

The German plan for landings in Britain had the code name
Operation Sea-Lion. German planners were convinced that
successful crossing of the English Channel and establishment
of beachheads on the English coast depended on control of the
skies and Göring assured Hitler that the *Luftwaffe* could destroy
the Royal Air Force (RAF). In July 1940 the Luftwaffe began
massive attacks on British air and naval installations. Every day
for the next two months hundreds of planes fought in the skies
over Britain. The Germans, however, could not gain the mas-
tery they expected. On 15 September 1940, the RAF shot down
sixty aircraft and two days later, Hitler postponed the invasion
'until further notice'. He hoped among other things that invasion
and defeat of the Soviet Union – both of which were already
planned – would isolate and weaken Britain so that the Germans
could come back later for an easy victory. Those late-summer,
early-autumn months became known as the Battle of Britain.

Throughout 1941, the Germans bombed British cities, industrial centres and ports. Air raids became a nightly event, with
the inhabitants of London, Coventry, Plymouth and other cities
seeking safety in subways, cellars and homemade bomb shelters.
German bombing took a heavy toll on civilian lives and property,
but British morale remained firm. Meanwhile German air raids

spurred the Allies to develop radar technologies that would play a crucial role in winning the war in the air.

Events on the Periphery of German Warfare

Some European countries remained neutral throughout the Second World War, most notably Spain, Portugal, Switzerland, Sweden and Turkey. The neutrals would play different roles during the war. Some provided escape routes for victims of German persecution. For example, in October 1943 the small Jewish community of Denmark was smuggled out to safety in neutral Sweden. Others, such as Switzerland, turned many refugees away. Among those sent back at the border were the young Saul Friedländer's parents. In despair they ended up back in France and eventually they were sent to Auschwitz and killed there.

Some of the neutrals profited considerably from the war. Swiss banks grew rich on stolen gold sent there by German authorities and on deposits from European Jews desperate to protect some assets from the German predators. The Swedes delivered massive amounts of iron ore to Germany. Turkey offered refuge to some European Jews but charged special taxes intended to transfer wealth from the refugees to native Turks. After the war Turkey also provided an escape route to the Middle East for many Nazi criminals. Neutral or not, no nation in Europe would be untouched by the war.

In 1940 Germany entered into the Three-Power Pact with Italy and Japan. Later that arrangement would be consolidated into a formal military alliance, although coordination among the three powers was minimal. For the time being the three states committed themselves to aid one another against their enemies. Later in 1941, Hungary, Romania, Slovakia, Finland, Bulgaria and Croatia would join the pact. Why were these less powerful nations interested in allying themselves with Germany and Italy? A look at a map suggests an answer. All of these countries hoped to expand with German or Italian help at the expense of their neighbours. They operated on a common assumption:

'the enemies of my enemies are my friends'. By the end of the Second World War, that notion would prove disastrously false.

As evident in the division of Poland in September 1939, Germany was not the only belligerent power in Europe. Under the leadership of Josef Stalin, the Soviet Union had its own expansionist program, linked to the goal of crushing all threats to internal security. After seizing eastern Poland, Stalin turned his attention to the three tiny Baltic states, Estonia, Latvia and Lithuania. By October 1939 massive Soviet threats had compelled all three to accept Soviet military bases with tens of thousands of Red Army troops. In June 1940, as the victorious *Wehrmacht* marched into defeated Paris, Stalin grabbed the opportunity to transform those 'bases' into a full-scale invasion and occupation of the Baltic states.

Along with Red Army tanks came the Stalinist system of terror, presided over by the NKVD (People's Commissariat for Internal Affairs) and its political police, known after 1941 as the NKGB (People's Commissariat for State Security) or simply KGB. Soviet authorities organised a wave of purges and deportations of local nationalists of all ages. Hundreds of thousands of people simply vanished – into Soviet torture chambers, prisons and labour camps in Siberia. In Latvia alone, two per cent of the population 'disappeared' as NKVD operatives sought to destroy the possibility of any national resistance. For the next year, Soviet interrogators and guards and local collaborators followed Stalin's injunction to 'beat, beat and again beat'.

Likewise in June 1940, Stalin took advantage of the situation in Western Europe to seize northern Bukovina and the province of Bessarabia in northern Romania. There too NKVD rule and ruthless state terror followed, with the same deadly consequences as in the Baltic States.

By the time the Germans launched their own invasion of these regions in mid-1941, the people of the Baltic States and northern Romania had been brutalised by deprivation, abuse and violence. Small wonder that many of them in turn would seek revenge and scapegoats for their suffering by throwing their lot in with the Nazis. It can be tempting to set up competitions in evil between

Hitler and Stalin. Who was worse? Who caused more murder and misery? This brief survey of the events of 1940, however, is a reminder of an even more terrible reality; Nazism and Stalinism coexisted in time and place and for many Europeans the horrors of one vicious system served to increase the destructive force of the other.

Already in November 1939 the Soviets had invaded Finland, another neighbour to the west. The gigantic attack was intended to overwhelm the 3.5 million Finns in rapid blitzkrieg style. Instead the Finns mounted a resourceful, heroic resistance and held out until March 1940, when they were forced to sign a peace treaty and cede territories to the Soviet Union. In that conflict, known as the Winter War, Stalin again took advantage of British and French inability to aid the targets of his aggression and used the protective cover of German assaults elsewhere in Europe to pick up spoils of his own. At the same time, at least in the short run, Hitler and the Germans benefited from anything that further disrupted the stability of Europe and distracted attention from their own activities.

War had many repercussions inside Germany too. For one thing, German military successes brought floods of luxury goods into the hands of Germans back home. Men sent furs and jewels to their wives; German collectors, museums and galleries acquired costly art treasures; the finest wines, chocolate, cheeses, pâtés and other delicacies ended up on German tables. The wealthier the nation conquered, the richer the spoils of war.

In the words of the historian Robert Gellately, war also 'revolutionised the revolution' in Nazi Germany. War allowed German authorities to step up the pace of change at home and crack down hard on dissenters. For example, restrictions on public meetings and control over the press tightened considerably after 1939. Numbers of arrests continued to climb: for spreading so-called malicious rumours critical of the government or the Nazi Party, for violating state monopolies on information, for maintaining illegal organisations and for engaging in other activities considered subversive. The population of the ever-expanding network of concentration camps and their satellites grew accordingly.

War exported Nazi policies such as persecution of Jews and applied Nazi practices such as divide and conquer in new territories. Already between 1933 and 1939 Hitler's regime had built on the principle that nothing succeeds like success. In wartime that notion again proved extremely powerful. The pre-war triumphs of Hitler's rule – for example, the annexation of Austria and the seizure of the Sudetenland in 1938 – had helped to bring some reluctant Germans in line. Germany's spectacular military successes in 1939 and 1940 turned out to be even more effective. German patriots of all kinds, including many who consistently had voted against Hitler, rejoiced with him at the destruction of Poland and the victory over France. To German nationalists these successes seemed to vindicate old desires for revenge and to legitimate German aggression.

The family of Alfons Heck, an eager member of the Hitler Youth, illustrates this particular effect of Germany's war. Before 1939 Heck's father, a committed socialist and his grandmother, a devout Catholic, had both opposed Adolf Hitler. They also disapproved openly of Heck's enthusiastic involvement in the Hitler Youth. Nevertheless both were thrilled with the German conquest of France in 1940. Living as they did near the border with France they were particularly aware of Germany's long enmity with its neighbour to the west. By mid-May 1940, Heck's father and grandmother had stopped complaining about Hitler's government and joined Alfons as supporters of the German war effort.

War brutalised life in ways that did not alter the goals of the German leaders but did transform what it was possible for them to achieve. War provided a cover for mass murder; witness Hitler's false dating of his order to murder the handicapped to 1 September 1939 and his repeated claim that he had given his speech 'predicting' annihilation of the European Jews not in January 1939 but in September of that year. War also made possible the training of large numbers of experienced killers, beginning in Poland in 1939. War trapped the victims of Nazism inside Europe, making them ever more vulnerable. After September 1939 it became extremely difficult for Jews to

1. Nazi antisemitic propaganda borrowed images and accusations from Christian anti-Jewish traditions. This illustration comes from a 1938 German children's book. The text at the bottom reads, 'When you see a cross, think of the horrible murder of the Jews on Golgotha'.

„Wenn ihr ein Kreuz seht, dann denkt an den grauenhaften Mord
der Juden auf Golgatha…"

2. This poster promised that Der Stürmer would reveal the identity of the murderer in a case in the Saar-Palatinate, a region in western Germany. The words RITUAL MURDER in large letters and the Star of David made it clear that the answer given would be 'the Jew', represented here as a menace to the safety and purity of 'Aryan' womanhood.

3. A German race scientist, accompanied by a policeman, questions a Gypsy (Roma) woman. Pictured at the right is possibly Dr Robert Ritter, a child psychiatrist turned racial expert who directed the project to locate and classify the Romani population of Germany.

4. Cleaning up the broken glass in front of a Jewish-owned business on Berlin's Potsdamerstrasse the morning after the Kristallnacht pogrom of 9 November 1938 (the so-called Night of Broken Glass). At the suggestion of Propaganda Minister Joseph Goebbels, German Jews were forced to pay a huge sum for the damages.

5. A bright red 'enemy alien' identity card issued in September 1939 in British-controlled Cyprus to Kalman Haber, an Austrian Jewish refugee. The British classified Kalman as an enemy alien. He was imprisoned in 1941 then sent to a British refugee camp in Nyasaland (later Malawi).

6. One page of a German passport stamped with a red 'J' to indicate that the bearer was Jewish. In accordance with 1938 regulations, the passport also shows the middle name 'Israel', required for all German men defined as Jews. Jewish women and girls had to add 'Sara' to their names.

7. Inside pages of Kalman Haber's enemy alien registration identity card.

8. Drawing entitled 'Gurs II', by Gert H. Wollheim (1893–1974), a left-wing German Jewish artist and writer. When Hitler came to power in 1933, Wollheim fled to Paris. The Nazis' 1937 'Degenerate Art' exhibit included some of his works. Sent to Gurs internment camp in 1940, he escaped in 1943 and hid in the Pyrenees until the liberation of France. In 1949 he immigrated to the United States.

9. A chart of prisoner markings used in German concentration camps. The coloured triangles displayed horizontally designated the following categories of prisoners: political, professional criminals, emigrant/stateless, Jehovah's Witnesses, homosexuals, Germans deemed 'work shy', and non-German 'shirkers'. Listed vertically are additional markings to specify repeat offenders, members of punishment kommandos, and Jews. The remaining symbols, under the heading 'Special Indications', demonstrate marking patterns. The black triangle over a yellow triangle signified a 'Jew who has violated racial laws'; the combined red and yellow triangles with a bar above and dot below meant 'political, Jew, repeat offender, member of a punishment kommando'.

10. Nuns with patients in August 1940, at the Liebenau institution for mentally disabled people and others requiring long-term care. Like many hospitals and related institutions in Germany, Liebenau was run by the Catholic Church, and like a number of such institutions, Liebenau became a 'euthanasia' facility. The euphemistically labelled 'Euthanasia Programme', also known by the codename 'Operation T4', claimed at least 200,000 lives inside Germany.

11. Doctors and patients at the Liebenau 'euthanasia' facility stand outside a bus. Pictured in front at the left is a Catholic Sister.

Right: 12. Children in the Łódź ghetto waiting in line for the soup kitchen. Among those pictured are Aleksander Henryk Laks (b. Chaim Cale in 1928), standing below the central pane of the left window, and Sam Pakin (born Szlamek Pakin), to his left, holding two pails.

Above left: 13. A group of boys, one with a scooter, stand on a street corner in the Łódz´ ghetto, probably in 1940 or 1941. Established in 1940, the Łódz´ ghetto was second in size only to the ghetto in Warsaw. In September 1942, the Jewish children who remained alive in the Łódz´ ghetto (15,681 children) were murdered in the killing centre of Chelmno.

Above right: 14. A woman and two children, all of whom are wearing yellow stars, stand on a street corner of the Łódź ghetto. By the time of its liquidation in late-summer 1944, some 200,000 people had passed through the Łódź ghetto, the vast majority of them Jews.

15. Residents bring their goods to an open-air market in the Łódź ghetto. Conditions in the ghetto were terrible, and people used whatever methods they could to get food and other necessities: selling and trading remaining possessions, smuggling, performing, begging, stealing, and offering services of all kinds.

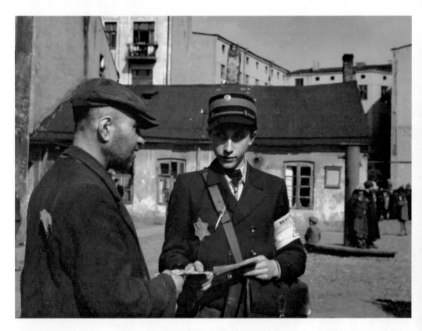

16. Izak Lefkowicz, a young ghetto postman, delivers mail or ration cards to a resident of the ghetto at Łódź. German authorities closely controlled mail into and out of the ghettos. Only postcards were allowed, with personal information only, written clearly and in German.

17. Ink drawing of a Łódź ghetto policeman by Kurant (?), dated 20 January 1941. Jewish men served as ghetto police. They worked for the Jewish Councils that implemented German orders inside the ghettos and tried, at the same time, to provide services to the ghetto population. Ghetto policeman had some privileges, but often the job also brought enmity from fellow residents.

18. A merchant at his stall at the outdoor market of the Łódź ghetto.

19. Jews board a passenger train during a transport action in the Łódź ghetto. The original caption reads, 'Judenaussiedlung (Resettlement of Jews), April 1942'. Photographs depicting the arrival and deportation of Jews into and out of the Łódź ghetto are often difficult to distinguish from one another. Here the date provides the additional evidence needed.

20. The front side of a special ration card issued to the Jewish Council of Rzeszów (Reichshof to the Germans) by the General Government of German-occupied Poland. The card is marked 'valid from 1 October 1941 to 30 April 1942'.

21. 'Vendor of Jewish Stars', drawing by Halina Olomucki. Born Halina Olszewski in 1919, Olomucki studied art in Poland until the outbreak of war. She was sent to Majdanek and in 1943 to Auschwitz. In both camps, she was assigned to paint slogans, signs and decorations. Prisoners asked her to draw their portraits, and she managed to hide over 200 of these drawings. Sent on a death march to Ravensbrück, Olomucki survived and settled after the war in Łódź´. In 1957 she moved to Paris and later to Israel.

22. View of the Gypsy camp in the Łódź ghetto. In November 1941, 5,007 Roma from around the former Austrian–Hungarian border were transported to Łódź and incarcerated in a designated part of the ghetto. They remained there until January 1942, when German authorities sent them to Chelmno and killed them in gas vans.

23. Street scene from the Lublin ghetto, June 1941, with Gypsy women in the foreground. In May 1940, approximately 2,800 Gypsies from Germany were sent to the Lublin district, designated by the Germans as a 'Jewish reserve'. The ghetto in Lublin remained more open than was the case in Warsaw or Łódź. In March 1942 the ghetto was closed and most of its inhabitants sent to the new killing centre at Belzec.

Hinter den Feindmächten:

der Jude

24. A German poster (from after 7 December 1941) with the slogan: 'Behind the enemy powers: the Jew'. Nazi propaganda insisted that the Allied war effort was only a cover for an international Jewish plot to destroy Germany. This accusation offered a way for killers to justify mass murder of Jews, as if the Holocaust were a defence of the German nation.

avvicinavano; bisognava, quasi, trattenere il respiro.

Sbucammo in una vasta prateria: bisognava allora fare il meno rumore possibile: eravamo vicino alla tanto desiderata frontiera.

Ah me ne dimenticavo! Prima di uscire dal bosco, ci fecero fermare per un quarto d'ora; intanto andavano ad esplorare i dintorni ed a tagliare la rete; poco dopo ci rimettemmo in marcia. Vedemmo dopo una garitta che era proprio davanti al buco della rete, fortunatamente la sentinella non c'era. Ad uno a uno, silenziosamente passammo attraverso il buco della rete. Che emozione! Finalmente eravamo in terra libera, in Svizzera. Se non piansero del nostro toppo mai i contrabbandieri ci dissero: "Andate in la"

25. Illustrated page of an Italian child's diary, written in a Swiss refugee camp in 1943–44. Born in 1934 in Milan, Bruna Cases (now D'Urbino) was raised in an assimilated Jewish family. In 1942, Cases fled bombardment with her mother and sister to Parma. The Germans entered Parma in September 1943; members of the family fled again, and a month later, Bruna, her mother and sisters crossed into Switzerland. There they were interned and eventually reunited with Bruna's father, Guido. After the war the family returned to Italy.

26. A special issue of Serbian stamps bearing antisemitic and anti-Masonic themes, dating from the German occupation. The series was issued for an exhibition on Jews and Free Masons in Belgrade in 1942.

27. German propaganda poster from 17 September 1941, issued by *Parole der Woche* (Word of the Week), a publicly displayed 'wall newspaper' from the Nazi Party propaganda office in Munich. The text reads as follows: '"Onward Christian Soldiers!" sang the hypocrites Roosevelt and Churchill, their eyes closed piously, as they met on the Atlantic. At the same time, they gave Stalin and his Bolshevik hordes new promises of help against Germany and the awakened Europe. This is how they look, the "Christian Soldiers": Their bestial deeds of murder in Lvov, Riga, Vilna and Dubno have filled the world with disgust and rage! But the German military, hard and without mercy, is destroying the Bolshevik enemy of the world. No hypocritical songs, no pharisaic false piety will help you now, Mr. Roosevelt and Mr. Churchill. At the end is Germany's Victory!'

28. Watercolour by Nellie Toll entitled 'Peasant Family Eating at a Table'. Nellie Landau Toll was born in 1933 in Lvov. After the German invasion in 1941, Nellie's father paid some Polish former tenants to hide his wife and daughter. Through a Christian friend, Nellie acquired a set of watercolours.

29. Watercolour by Nellie Toll entitled 'Teacher with Children Wearing Black Uniforms'. Most of Nellie's paintings depicted the opposite of what the little girl was experiencing: friendship, safety and the outdoors rather than isolation, terror and confinement.

30. Painting by Halina Olomucki, 'Le camp les litieres dans le bloc' (The camp of litters in the block). Olomucki, born Halina Olszewski, arrived at Auschwitz-Birkenau from Warsaw via Majdanek on 8 July 1943. She received prisoner number 48652.

Overleaf, left: 31. One page of an illustrated album produced by Gyorgy Beifeld, a Jew from Budapest who spent more than a year on the Soviet front. The top image depicts events of 28 August, when Beifeld was wounded. He survived the war and immigrated to Australia in 1949.

Overleaf, right: 32. Another page of Gyorgy Beifeld's illustrated album, showing scenes from the retreat of the Germans and their allies after the Battle of Stalingrad. In the drawing at the middle left, starving Hungarian soldiers use an axe to cut up a dead horse for meat. Implicit in Beifeld's images is a comparison to the retreat of Napoleon's 'Grand Army' from Russia.

"Megsebesülők és elkerülők
a veszélyes Kanyarból"... VIII. 28 án

Keep smiling!

Veszélyes Kanyar!

Paschli
943. II.

a szomy-i ut 1943. II.

33. View of the entrance to Auschwitz-Birkenau from inside the camp, photographed after May 1945. Auschwitz – often captured with this image of the tracks leading into the camp – has become a symbol of the Holocaust and, more broadly, of evil. It is a powerful image but cannot capture the Holocaust's enormity and complexity.

34. Untitled drawing of Birkenau by Franz Reisz, an Austrian Jewish artist born in 1909. In 1938, the year that Germany annexed Austria, Reisz fled to Paris. Arrested in 1941, he was sent to various internment camps and prisons. In June 1942, he was deported to Auschwitz, where he worked in the offices and produced drawings for his friends and, upon orders, for members of the SS. He survived a death march and ended the war at a hospital in France. The men's orchestra in Birkenau, depicted here, was in constant flux due to killing of the musicians.

35. Drawing by an unidentified artist of camp guards watching prisoners die in a gas chamber. In 1942, an SS man named Kurt Gerstein wrote an account of how he watched through a peephole at Belzec as about eight hundred Jews were murdered using diesel fumes. Once the gassing began, Gerstein reported, it took thirty-two minutes to kill the people in the chamber; he timed the procedure with his stopwatch.

36. Interior view of a gas chamber at Majdanek, showing a blue stain from Zyklon B. This photograph was taken after the Red Army liberated Majdanek in July 1944. Mass killings of Jews in Majdanek's gas chambers began in October 1942 and continued until November 1943. Majdanek was the first major concentration camp and killing centre to be liberated. Soviet authorities invited journalists to inspect the site and document its horrors.

37. German civilians conscripted by U.S. troops from the surrounding area dig mass graves for the dead found in Kaufering IV, a sub-camp of Dachau in Bavaria. This photograph was taken on 30 April 1945.

Opposite: 38. Former prisoners in the newly liberated Dachau concentration camp. Dachau, located just outside Munich, was the site of the first concentration camp opened by Hitler's government in 1933. At the time of liberation, death marches and transports from evacuated camps in the last months of the war meant that its population – dead and alive – included many Jews and non-Jews from every country of Europe (and some beyond).

39. Post-war view of the site of the Warsaw ghetto. During and after the Warsaw Ghetto Uprising in April 1943, the Germans killed most of the Jews remaining there and levelled much of the area the ghetto had occupied. Sixteen months later, in response to the Warsaw Insurrection of August 1944, German forces destroyed large parts of the rest of the city. Among the estimated 200,000 people killed were Jews hiding or passing as ethnic Poles on the 'Aryan' side of the city, many of whom had joined the revolt against the German occupation.

40. A view through the barbed wire fence of survivors in the newly liberated Buchenwald concentration camp. Buchenwald was opened in 1937, primarily for political prisoners. A year later, it became a major prison for German Jewish men, some 10,000 of whom were sent there following Kristallnacht. The Germans began to evacuate the main camp in the spring of 1945. On 11 April 1945, remaining prisoners seized control of the camp. The first American units arrived later that day.

41. An American soldier stands near a wagon piled high with corpses outside the crematorium in the newly liberated Buchenwald concentration camp. An estimated 250,000 prisoners passed through the Buchenwald camp network. Only 21,000 people were found alive there in April 1945.

42. An American soldier stands among the corpses of prisoners exhumed from a mass grave near Nammering, Bavaria, in May 1945. On 19 April 1945, a freight train with nearly 4,500 prisoners from Buchenwald pulled onto the railroad siding at Nammering. Destined for Dachau, the train was diverted because of bomb damage to the tracks. The commanding officer ordered the dead removed from the train and burned. Forced to carry some 800 bodies to a nearby ravine, another 524 prisoners were shot and interred. When U.S. troops discovered the site, SS men from a POW camp were forced to exhume the bodies. Inhabitants of Nammering were then ordered to walk through the gravesite before the dead were buried.

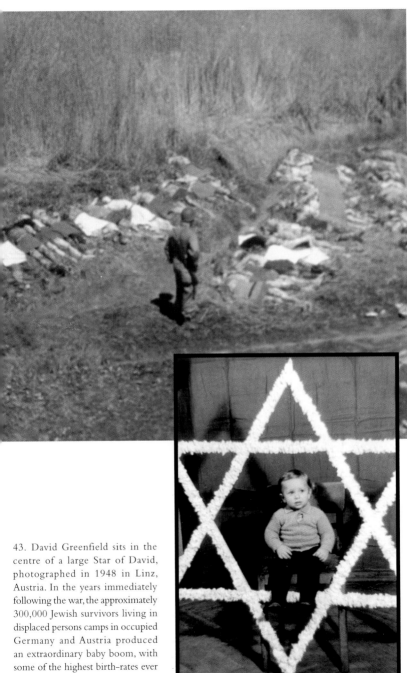

43. David Greenfield sits in the centre of a large Star of David, photographed in 1948 in Linz, Austria. In the years immediately following the war, the approximately 300,000 Jewish survivors living in displaced persons camps in occupied Germany and Austria produced an extraordinary baby boom, with some of the highest birth-rates ever recorded.

44. Survivors from Norway in the newly liberated Buchenwald concentration camp. There were Jewish and Gentile Norwegians in Buchenwald. A number of Norwegian university students were imprisoned in the main camp. Considered 'racially valuable' in the Nazi hierarchy, they were treated less harshly than many other inmates. According to some accounts, they even managed to refuse a labour assignment in a minefield.

45. A colour sketch entitled 'Aftermath', by Ernu Homanye-Grytze. No information is available on the artist except that he created this work in a concentration camp or displaced persons camp in 1945 or 1946 and probably came from Hungary.

46. View of the main camp at Auschwitz surrounded by a section of barbed wire fence, photographed after 1945.

No. 5 (16) פרײז 5 מארק

ייִדישע בילדער

JEWISH PICTURES

אומפּאַרטײיִשער אילוסטרירטער חודש זשורנאַל פֿאַר אַלע ייִדן

צווײטער יאָרגאַנג | „JIDISZE BILDER" | מינכן, מאי 1948

דער סימבאָל צייכנונג פֿון 3־טן קאָנגרעס פֿון דער שארית־הפּליטה:
אן אונטערגעהאקטער בוים מיט בליִענדע בלעטער אויפֿן פֿאַן פֿון דער קאָרעם פֿון דער ייִדישער מדינה.
אין דער ערשטער רײ: דאָס ערן פּרעזידיום פֿון קאָנגרעס, אין דער צווײטער רײ: די מיטגלידער פֿון אַפּטײרעמנדן 3־טן צ. ק. ק.

47. Cover page of the publication Jidisze Bilder (Jewish Pictures) with a photograph of participants at the Third Congress of the Shearit Ha-Pletah in May 1948 in Munich. Above the participants is a graphic of a branch growing from a chopped down tree. This image of destruction and new life became a symbol of the survivors, the She'erith Hapleitah – the saved remnant.

leave Europe. By 1941 it was practically impossible. The German police regulation of September 1941 that required all people defined as Jews to wear the identifying Star of David simply reinforced the obvious: Jews were now open targets.

War enabled Nazi propagandists to present attacks on innocent civilians of all ages as if they were defensive measures necessary to protect the German nation from its foes. For all these reasons, war was a necessary ingredient in what would develop into genocide – the deliberate effort at total annihilation of identifiable groups of people.

Assault on the Balkans and on the Soviet Union

In 1941, the Germans again turned east, first to the Balkans in south-eastern Europe. Mussolini's Italian forces had effectively failed in their campaign to conquer Greece in 1940 and were in urgent need of assistance. The German attack on the Balkans was also linked to preparation for an assault on the Soviet Union. Hitler and his generals considered it necessary to control the Balkan states in order to secure their south-eastern flank and safeguard access to Romanian oil. With Romania, Bulgaria and Hungary already bound to Germany through diplomatic arrangements, only Yugoslavia and Greece remained to be brought into the Nazi sphere.

On 6 April 1941 the *Luftwaffe* launched an air raid on Belgrade. German forces surrounded the Yugoslav army, which capitulated on 17 April. Italian, Hungarian and Bulgarian troops invaded Yugoslavia in aid of the Germans and the Yugoslavian king fled to Britain, where he too formed a government-in-exile.

Although the German offensive advanced rapidly, it faced tough resistance. Yugoslav partisans used the rugged terrain to their advantage and benefited from the effective, ruthless leadership of Tito (Josip Broz, 1892–1980). Aid from the British in the form of supplies and intelligence helped too.

In Yugoslavia the German forces stooped to new depths of organised brutality that may have surpassed even their behaviour in Poland. Here too they relied on familiar techniques of divide and conquer. Part of the country (Croatia, Bosnia and Herzegovina) became an independent Croatian state under Ante Pavelic (1889–1959) and his fascist *Ustasha* movement. The Germans used their ally Pavelic to carry out their will. At the same time they gave him and his henchmen license to do what they wanted against enemies of their own, which meant above all the Serbs. Meanwhile the Germans annexed some northern parts of Yugoslavia to the German Reich and set up a military government in Serbia. Everywhere, they encouraged thugs to attack Jews, Gypsies, communists, liberals and anti-German nationalists of any kind.

The Germans' brutal occupation policies ensured a steady flow of people into the partisan groups. In particular, the practice of reprisals roused hatred. For every one German whom Yugoslav partisans attacked or killed, German authorities ordered a certain number of Yugoslavs shot. Sometimes the ratio was fifty to one; sometimes it was one hundred or even two hundred to one. The victims seized included people of all ages, female as well as male. Germans used reprisals – often based only on fear or suspicion of partisan actions – as an excuse to massacre hundreds of thousands of Yugoslavs.

In Yugoslavia it was generally the regular German military, not some special SS units, who carried out mass shootings of civilians. Although soldiers were not forced to participate in these killings, there were always enough volunteers for such duties. Some of them even took photographs of their exploits to send home to their girlfriends and wives.

Often the Germans took their first victims from among the local Jewish and Gypsy populations, but they also took hostage and shot many Serbs. There were Croats, Bosnian Muslims and people with mixed backgrounds among those shot in reprisals too. Some of the most damning evidence of atrocities committed by the *Wehrmacht* – the regular German military – during the Second World War comes out of Yugoslavia.

Already in 1940, Hitler's Italian ally, Mussolini, had launched his own military campaign against Greece, but the Italian offensive bogged down until the spring of 1941, when the Germans took over. In April and May 1941 German forces overran Greece. Here too the Germans brutally assaulted civilians as well as the military. In so-called 'special actions', often in retaliation for resistance or partisan activity, they wiped out entire villages and towns. On orders from above, German soldiers tried to spare Greece's artistic treasures. Hitler had always been fascinated by Greek and Roman art. He held the notion that the best artistic achievements had been made by 'Aryans' who later migrated north and brought their superior creativity to Germany. According to Hitler, the Greeks of his own time were a lesser people unworthy of their country's glorious past. In Greece, as elsewhere, Hitler adjusted reality to fit his view of the world.

On 22 June 1941 German troops invaded the Soviet Union. The invasion was given the code name Operation Barbarossa. With this step Hitler's forces crossed the final line to what he called a 'war of annihilation'. War in the Soviet Union was extremely bloody. An estimated twenty-seven million Soviet citizens were killed, the majority of them civilians. Carnage on this scale was no mere replay of Napoleon's failed invasion of Russia 129 years earlier. The German assault on the Soviet Union was not a war of soldier against soldier or army against army. It was a war whose goal was total destruction of the Soviet Union, seizure of its land, colonisation, enslavement and murder of its people; in short, establishment of the Nazi new order in Europe.

By mid-1941 German forces were ready to wage a war of annihilation. Trained in conquest in Poland, proven capable of wholesale massacre of captured soldiers, flushed with successes in the west and brutalised by war on partisans and civilians in the Balkans, they were no longer likely to protest at atrocities as some had in 1939. From day one German operations in the Soviet Union would be characterised by a level of ruthlessness that has led the historian Omer Bartov to speak of the 'barbarisation of warfare'. Some people say that Germany would have won the war if Hitler had not made the mistake of attacking the Soviet Union. Given Hitler's worldview this claim makes little sense. For Hitler the whole point of the war was to conquer land and resources to support his purportedly superior 'Aryan race'. The *Lebensraum* – living space – he sought could only be found in the east. He was interested not in some limited European empire but in world domination. Hitler had always planned on war with the Soviet Union; it was only a question of when. Recently some writers have contended that Hitler's assault on the Soviet Union was purely defensive. According to them, Stalin was poised to attack Germany, so Hitler ordered a pre-emptive strike. This theory simply does not hold. Neither the German nor the Russian archival records support such a notion. Hitler made his intentions against the Soviet Union very clear, not only in *Mein Kampf* and in his second, untitled book, written in 1928 and never published, but in numerous conversations and speeches. Most significantly, German military planners had worked out the details of an offensive against the Soviet Union long before June 1941. Operation Barbarossa was no defensive reaction. Of course it is certainly possible that Stalin had his own violent plans for Eastern and Central Europe, but such schemes do not alter the fact of Hitler's aggression. Unfortunately there is no reason why two opponents cannot both be scoundrels.

What about the Hitler–Stalin non-aggression pact of 1939? Like all of Hitler's diplomatic agreements it was made to be broken. The deal had served Nazi goals well; it enabled rapid defeat of Poland in 1939, freed up German forces to concentrate in the west in 1940 and bought almost two years of time to prepare for war with the Soviet Union. It seems highly unlikely that Hitler or his generals even gave it a thought in June 1941.

The Soviet Union was a multinational empire that included many republics in addition to Russia. In fact some of the worst devastation of World War II occurred in Ukraine, Belorussia and the Baltic states of Latvia, Estonia and Lithuania. In June 1941, before the Germans reached Russia, they first entered territories that the Soviets had seized after the German attack on Poland in 1939. As a consequence, people in places such as Latvia and the eastern Polish city of Lvov – after the war part of western Ukraine and called L'viv – experienced two rounds of invasion in less than two years. In September 1939 Stalin's armies moved in; Hitler's troops arrived in 1941.

Some people in such areas had greeted the Soviets in 1939 as bearers of communism and protectors from Nazism. By 1941 almost all had become disillusioned. That year some people in Eastern Europe welcomed the German invasion, expecting Hitler's forces to crush communism and grant them independence. For example, many Ukrainian nationalists hoped the Nazis would let them set up their own state. They too would be disappointed. Very quickly most Eastern Europeans learned that they could expect only terror and destruction from a war fought not for them but on top of them.

One person who experienced Soviet takeover in the fall of 1939 and then the German invasion in 1941 was Nelly Toll. Born in 1935, Nelly was just a little girl in 1939. Her family was among the 110,000 Jews in Lvov, home to Poland's third-largest Jewish community, after Warsaw and Łódź. About one million Jews lived in the surrounding region, called eastern Galicia. Under Soviet rule more Jews streamed into the city to escape the Germans, but Soviet control brought its own hardships. Nelly Toll's father had to go into hiding to avoid being sent to a labour camp in Siberia. As the wealthy owner of a dry goods store he was considered an enemy of communism. Soviet officials seized much of the Tolls' property and took over their spacious apartment. Nelly remembers her family's relationship with the Russian officers as a mixture of fear, friendliness and contempt for people she and her relatives considered somewhat less civilised than themselves.

When the Germans came to Lvov in 1941 even some Jews there thought they might be an improvement over the Soviets. Nelly's grandfather, for example, at first regarded German takeover in 1941 as a good thing. In his view the Germans were more cultured and intelligent than the Russians. He was wrong. The Germans proved at least as barbaric.

In Lvov some of the local people saw arrival of the Germans as a chance to take revenge for all they had suffered under the Soviets. In particular Ukrainians in the region wanted to seize the chance to get back at the Russians as well as their Polish neighbours. Most of the Soviets had fled before the advancing Germans. So angry residents of Lvov attacked their Jewish neighbours as convenient scapegoats instead. They accused Jews of collaborating with the Soviets to oppress them. No doubt there had been Jews who supported the Soviet regime, but there had certainly also been Gentile Poles and Ukrainians who had done the same.

As usual German authorities encouraged ethnic strife and rewarded pogroms. They urged local Ukrainians to take out their grievances against the Polish majority, in particular against those elements the Germans targeted too: intellectuals, Catholic priests and other community leaders. They gave Gentile Poles and Ukrainians license to terrorise Jews and steal their possessions. In June 1941 Ukrainians in Lvov arrested some Jews on the charge that they had committed atrocities against Ukrainians during the Soviet occupation. Many of those Jews were executed in prisons and nearby forests. Others were taken to prison cells already stained with Jewish blood, forced to clean them and then shot. Pogroms raged in the city throughout July 1941 and thousands of Jews were killed. On one occasion little Nelly Toll watched from the balcony with her cousins as German soldiers beat an old Jewish man. A crowd gathered to laugh and applaud.

A local Jewish dignitary named Rabbi Levin appealed for help to Metropolitan Sheptitsky, the head of the local Ukrainian Catholic church. Sheptitsky called on Ukrainians to stop murdering Jews, but without effect. He then invited the rabbi to take refuge in his personal residence, but Rabbi Levin thought his place was with his people, so he left the metropolitan's residence to go home. He never made it. Instead rioters seized him and dragged him to prison, where he was murdered.

Nelly Toll was luckier than Rabbi Levin. She lived through 1941, although children threw stones at her in the street, her mother was beaten black and blue by a Ukrainian policeman and the family was forced into a ghetto. Eventually Nelly's mother sent her to hide with a Christian family. When that place proved too risky she returned to the ghetto to learn that her brother, aunt and little cousins had all been taken away by the Gestapo and put on a train. None of them returned.

In 1943, after more close calls and a failed attempt to escape to Hungary, Nelly and her mother went into hiding. They ended up with a Polish Catholic couple who sheltered them in exchange for money. The woman was kind and thoughtful but her husband was violent, paranoid and antisemitic, abusive to his wife yet over-attentive to Nelly's mother. It was a very difficult situation. Somehow both Nelly and her mother survived the war, but they never saw Nelly's father again. Nelly Toll emigrated to the United States in 1951, where she became an artist and a counsellor.

Crossing the Line to Annihilation

Hitler expected the campaign against the Soviet Union to be easy for the Germans. In this regard he and his military planners were caught in their own ethnic and racial stereotypes. They thought of Slavs as stupid and incompetent and believed that the communist Soviet Union was in the grip of Jews, whom they viewed as cowardly and perfidious. Such attitudes caused the German leaders to make some severe miscalculations.

The German invasion did not turn out as planned. The Soviets were better equipped than German planners had thought; the Germans themselves were over-extended and unprepared for winter. Contrary to what many German accounts claim, the winter of 1941 was neither unusually early nor extraordinarily harsh; it was more or less a typical Russian winter. Nor, as the historian Gerhard Weinberg has pointed out, did it snow only on the Germans; the Soviets faced the same winter conditions. Hitler and his generals, however, had anticipated quick victory, another 'lightning war' that of course they would win. They had not thought it necessary to prepare for winter.

From the beginning of war with the Soviet Union, the German leadership advocated unprecedented, ruthless measures. In instructions to the military and the SS, Hitler, Himmler and Heydrich made it clear that no mercy was to be shown

Germany's enemies, whether they were Jews, communists, or resistors. High-ranking officers passed the message down to their men. With the invasion of the Soviet Union the Nazi leadership would move to full implementation of their ideas of race and space on a massive scale. Their warfare reached new depths of brutality, especially against civilians but also against Soviet prisoners of war. Most noticeably they crossed the line from persecution and killing of Jews to a systematic attempt at total destruction.

Yet in many ways 1941 was not a radical break with earlier Nazi practices. All of the pieces were already in place. Hitler had spelled out the quest for *Lebensraum* in *Mein Kampf.* The Germans had begun to grab territory in Europe even before the war. They had assaulted civilians on a wide scale in Poland since 1939; they had used their enemies as slave labour, forcibly relocated enormous numbers of people and started to slaughter Jews, Gypsies and people deemed handicapped even before June 1941. In 1940 in France they had massacred black soldiers taken prisoner of war. All of these terrible developments culminated in the Soviet Union in 1941 and the years to follow.

Perhaps the most glaring sign of Germany's brutal style of warfare in 1941 was the use of special murder squads. German authorities dispatched mobile killing units to follow the regular military into Soviet territory. The main units, known as the *Einsatzgruppen* – 'special action groups' – included between 500 and 1,000 men each, many of them well educated, lawyers, theologians and other professionals. The *Einsatzgruppen* worked together with more numerous German units known as the Order Police. Both the *Einsatzgruppen* and the Order Police cooperated with the German military. The task of the mobile killing units was straightforward. They had explicit instructions from Heydrich to kill Jews, prominent communists and anyone suspected of sabotage or anti-German activity. Officially their goal was to combat Bolshevism and prevent guerrilla warfare. In fact, during the summer of 1941, they began to interpret their primary job as slaughter of all Jews, including women, children and old people. The *Einsatzgruppen* and Order Police also murdered

Gypsies and inmates of mental hospitals, although they seem to have been less systematic against those target populations.

Members of the mobile killing units tried to involve local people in their work. Many non-German auxiliaries – Ukrainians, Latvians, ethnic Germans from Eastern Europe, Belorussians and others – helped in their grisly task. Threats, bribes, massive amounts of alcohol and promises of privileges for recruits and their families all helped the Germans find willing henchmen. The *Einsatzgruppen* and Order Police attempted to stir up pogroms wherever they went. In some cases locals did take spontaneous action against Jews, but the mobile killing groups were less successful in this regard than they had hoped. Local individuals sometimes launched spontaneous attacks on Jews and took the initiative to steal their property, but generally the impetus and organisation for systematic killing came from the Germans.

Many of the actions of the mobile killing units more or less followed the same pattern. First they rounded up the Jews in a given area using various ruses to deceive them and relying on local collaborators for denunciations. The Germans ordered large pits dug in some convenient area – a local cemetery, nearby forest, or easily accessible field. Often they forced the prisoners themselves to dig what would be their own graves. At gunpoint they made the victims undress. Then they shot them by groups directly into the graves. In this manner the mobile killing units and their accomplices killed around a million people even before construction of killing centres for gassing had begun.

Of course, such mass killings in the open air could hardly be kept secret. Eyewitnesses of all kinds saw these shootings – German soldiers and workers, ethnic Germans who lived nearby, Russian, Polish, or Ukrainian families from the region and others. Some of those observers gave detailed, chilling accounts of what they saw. For example, a German builder named Hermann Graebe watched while mobile killing squads shot scores of people of all ages near Dubno in Ukraine. He was surprised to be allowed to stay, but he noticed three uniformed postal workers looking on as well. Elsewhere in Ukraine a fifteen-year-old Mennonite boy and his friends saw the slaughter of a group of Gypsies at a local cemetery.

Later someone came around the village to distribute clothes taken from the murdered people. According to the eyewitness's account, no one in that particular Mennonite (and ethnic German) community wanted anything to do with booty won in such a way.

Most of our information about the mass shootings comes from the perpetrators themselves or from onlookers. Few victims lived to tell about their experiences. One of the exceptions is a man named Zvi Michalowsky, whose account appears in a book by Yaffa Eliach called *Hasidic Tales of the Holocaust*. In 1941 on Rosh Hashanah, the Jewish New Year, Germans and their local helpers murdered the Jews in a Lithuanian town called Eisysky. Michalowsky, a teenaged boy at the time, was among those forced to strip and wait at the edge of a grave for a bullet. A split second before the Germans fired, Zvi threw himself back into the pit. Miraculously he avoided serious injury. For the rest of that day Zvi lay in the mass grave, feeling the bodies pile up on top of him. Only long after the shooting had stopped did he dare to climb out. He ran, naked and covered with blood, to the nearest house, but when he knocked, the terrified Polish Christians who lived there refused to let him in. Finally he approached an old woman. He told her he was Jesus Christ come down from the cross and she opened the door to him. Zvi Michalowsky went on to found a Jewish resistance group in the woods of Lithuania. He survived the war.

Probably the biggest slaughter carried out by the *Einsatzgruppen* and their helpers was the massacre at Babi Yar. In just two days in September 1941, German mobile killing units and local collaborators shot more than 30,000 Jews and an unknown number of other people at Babi Yar, a ravine on the outskirts of the Ukrainian city of Kiev. That act, just months after the invasion of the Soviet Union, destroyed the thriving Jewish community in Kiev and its surrounding area.

Germans continued to use Babi Yar as a killing field throughout the occupation of Ukraine. Some estimates of the total number of people killed there are as high as 100,000. The majority were Jews, although others targeted by the German occupiers were murdered at Babi Yar as well. That massacre has become emblematic of the vicious brutality of Nazi Germans in the Soviet Union generally and particularly in Ukraine. In Soviet times state authorities put up a monument to the victims of Babi Yar. The plaque dedicates the memorial to the more than 100,000 Soviet citizens killed there. Nowhere does it mention that most of those dead were murdered solely because they were Jews. Here the official act of remembering also became a way of forgetting.

The exact number of people killed by the mobile units cannot be known, although German records have allowed experts in the field to come to an estimate approaching 2 million total victims. Most were Jews – some 1.3 million – and there may have been as many as 250,000 Gypsies. The *Einsatzgruppen* and Order Police followed the regular military and in many cases even relied on them for provisions, security and intelligence. They could not have carried out such an enormous number of killings without the knowledge and cooperation of the *Wehrmacht*. How did the military respond?

At first it seems there might have been some misgivings. One incident illustrates the forms such doubts might have taken. In mid August 1941, German authorities in the Ukrainian town of Belaya Tserkov, more than two hundred miles east of Lvov, ordered local Jews to report for registration. Over the next few days, SS and German soldiers scoured the area for Jews, slaughtering hundreds of men and women. In the summer of 1941 some of the killers still seemed unclear as to whether their task included murder of Jewish women and children as well as men. Perhaps for this reason, the shooters at Belaya Tserkov did not initially kill all the children. Instead they dumped about ninety of them and a handful of women in a school.

German soldiers in a field hospital nearby heard babies crying in the night. Uncertain how to respond, they appealed to their military chaplains. The two German clergy, a Protestant pastor and a Catholic priest, went to see for themselves. They were appalled. It was hot, but the children were crammed into a small space without water, food, or adult care. Some of the mothers were locked in an adjoining room, from where they could see the misery of their children without being able to get to them.

The chaplains appealed to the local military commander, an elderly Austrian, to take pity on the children. Their effort failed, one of them later reported, because the man was a convinced antisemite. Together the chaplains persuaded another German officer to intervene. He got Army High Command to agree to postpone shooting of the children, but SS representatives and military officers on the spot prevailed, pointing to instructions from General Field Marshal Walter von Reichenau, commander of the German 6th Army, that they were to show no mercy. On 21 August 1941, the children were taken from the school and killed. It is unclear whether it was Germans or Ukrainian volunteers who did the job.

Killings of civilians did not end in the summer or autumn of 1941 but continued throughout the war. Presumably German soldiers and the military chaplains who ministered to them got used to the routine. The comfort of knowing they were backed by orders from above must have helped too. One of the most widely circulated of such orders came in October 1941 from German Field Marshal Walter von Reichenau. Reichenau admitted that there was 'uncertainty' among the German troops as to the current situation in the east. However, he told his men, given the nature of this war and the need to destroy what he called the 'Jewish-Bolshevist system' completely, it was necessary to break the conventional rules of war, to show no mercy to those defined as Germany's enemies, above all the people Reichenau labelled 'Jewish subhumans'.

It is certainly not common practice for military superiors to justify themselves and their decisions to their men. Reichenau, however, did just that. His order implies that there was some uneasiness in the ranks about military involvement in slaughter of civilians. We can assume that those reservations were overcome. After all, the killings continued with the necessary military support. Perhaps German soldiers accepted the official justifications offered to them, that such excesses were a necessary part of the German struggle against partisans, or later on, that they were some kind of revenge for Allied bombings of German cities.

Of course neither of those rationalisations actually makes sense. How could a baby be responsible for a partisan attack on

German rail lines? What could an old Jewish woman more than 1,000 miles away who spoke nothing but Yiddish possibly have to do with British planes dropping bombs on Hamburg or Cologne? Nevertheless these nonsensical explanations may have helped men live with themselves once they were already involved in killing. Many of their motivations for killing in the first place were undramatic. Their comrades were doing it and they did not want to stand out; they considered it part of their job; they had become used to it.

What we do know is that Germans were not forced to be killers. Those who refused to participate were given other assignments or transferred. To this day no one has ever found a single example of a German who was executed for refusing to take part in the killing of Jews or other civilians. Defence attorneys of Germans accused of war crimes during the Second World War have looked hard for such a case because it would support the claim that their clients were forced to kill. The Nazi system, however, did not work that way. There were enough willing perpetrators. For the most part coercive violence could be reserved for those deemed enemies.

Brutalisation, it seems, is contagious; violence tends to breed more of the same. This point is evident if we look briefly at Romania, one of Germany's Second World War allies, in 1941. The Romanian army took an active part in the German offensive against the southern Soviet Union. In the areas conquered, German and Romanian armies cooperated with the *Einsatzgruppen* in massacring Jews and Gypsies.

The case of the Jews in the Ukrainian city of Odessa provides an example. In the autumn of 1941, several days after German and Romanian forces occupied Odessa, an explosion rocked Romanian army headquarters there. In retaliation, Romanian leader Ion Antonescu ordered the execution of two hundred 'communists' for every Romanian officer killed and one hundred for each soldier. Most of the victims selected were Jews. *Einsatzgruppen* killers worked together with German and Romanian military, Ukrainian auxiliary police and recruits from the local ethnic German population to slaughter some 35,000 Jews. In February 1942, Odessa was proclaimed *Judenrein* – 'cleansed of Jews'.

Beginning in 1941, persecution of Jews also exploded within Romania. The Romanian government introduced laws restricting Jews in all kinds of ways and pogroms resulted in the death of well over 1,000 Romanian Jews. Antisemitism was not new to Romania, but the war and German leadership gave antisemites license to act on their hatreds in dramatic, large-scale ways.

In the autumn of 1941, Romanian authorities began moving Jews out of Romania and forcing them east across the Dniester River and then the Bug River into an area of intense *Einsatzgruppen* operations. First 50,000 and then another 120,000 Romanian Jews were driven into the hands of the Germans and their accomplices in Transnistria in the occupied Ukraine. Among those deported in this way was a young boy named Aharon Appelfeld. Separated from his father, he ended up in a makeshift Transnistrian camp. Somehow he escaped, dodged the killing fields of the *Einsatzgruppen* and evaded the reach of local collaborators. Just nine years old in 1941, he survived for four years working as a shepherd, hiding in the woods, stealing, begging and taking refuge with people who helped him. After the war Appelfeld moved to Israel. He is the author of many acclaimed works of fiction dealing with themes from the Holocaust.

Many Romanian Gypsies shared the fate of their Jewish compatriots. A woman named Drina Radu survived deportation to Transnistria as a girl of about ten. She remembers crossing the Dniester River into the part of Ukraine occupied by Romania. Everyone rushed to get on the first boatloads, she told the journalist Isabel Fonseca, not because they were eager to reach the other side but because, in her words, 'the boats were made of paper'. Hastily constructed from cheap, porous material, they became waterlogged and sank after three or four trips. That detail reveals the deadly cynicism of the Romanians in charge. Why go to any effort or expense to protect the lives of people they knew were slated for death anyway? Between 1941 and 1944, approximately 36,000 Roma were killed in Transnistria.

For the Romanian Jews and Gypsies murdered in the killing fields of Transnistria, there was nothing ambiguous about their government's plan for them. It was deadly, but there were ways in which the Romanian situation was complex too. For one thing, German authorities did not welcome Romanian initiatives, such as the expulsion of almost 200,000 Jews into territories the Germans held. The German masterminds of mass killing preferred to retain control themselves. Accordingly Antonescu was told to stop striking out on his own and to wait for Germans to take the lead.

Romanian Gentiles continued to have their own ideas about how to solve what they considered their 'Jewish problem'. The Romanian government set up an office to look after Jewish affairs. It tolerated the existence of Jewish mutual-aid activities and allowed them to try to help the Jewish expellees. Leaders of the Jewish community maintained relations with some heads of state and in some incidents even managed to mitigate anti-Jewish measures. There were prominent Romanians – including the queen – who approached the Germans on behalf of Romanian Jews. Those efforts were rejected.

In wartime Romania, traditional antisemitism and widespread persecution of Jews were the norm. Nevertheless the Romanian leadership, for all its viciousness, did not show the same single-minded and systematic dedication to eradication of the Jews that the Nazi Germans introduced in the countries they controlled. Traditional Jewish means of self-preservation – mutual aid, intercession with rulers, evasion and bribery – continued to have some effect in Romania. For all the horrors of 1941 and the years to follow, a higher percentage of Jews in Romania would survive the war than would be the case in Poland or the Netherlands.

Hitler's war of annihilation against the Soviet Union included killing of prisoners of war on a massive scale. Of the millions of non-Jews killed in German camps, by far the largest group of dead was Soviet POWs. Their brutal treatment violated every standard of warfare.

Statistics only begin to tell the story. Initial German successes in the summer and fall of 1941 brought an enormous number of POWs into German hands. In total, between 22 June 1941 and the end of the war, Germans took approximately 5.7 million Red Army soldiers prisoner. As of January 1945, about 930,000

Soviet POWs remained in *Wehrmacht* prison camps. About 1 million had been released as helpers of the German military and another estimated half million had escaped or been liberated by the Red Army. That still leaves 3.3 million – fifty-seven per cent – unaccounted for. They were dead. Such a staggering death rate was neither an accident nor an automatic result of war. It was deliberate policy. German treatment of Soviet POWs differed wildly from German handling of POWs from Britain and the United States. Of the 231,000 British and American prisoners held by the Germans, only about 8,300 – 3.6 per cent – died before the end of the war.

Death came in various ways to the more than three million Soviet POWs who died in German hands. In the early stages of the conflict the Germans shot many of the prisoners they took. They had made few provisions to accommodate their captives; they simply disposed of them. Eventually they erected some makeshift camps, but the lack of proper food, clothing and shelter took a terrible toll. By the end of 1941, epidemics – especially typhoid and dysentery – emerged as the big killers. In October 1941 alone, as many as 4,600 Soviet POWs died per day. Death rates fell off somewhat in 1942 as German authorities decided POWs could be a useful source of wartime labour. In 1943 and 1944, however, they soared again, due above all to hunger. Starvation of Soviet POWs was directly tied to the Nazi policy of making sure there was plenty of food for the German home front. No doubt Hitler and others remembered the food riots of the First World War, a war they believed Germany had lost because of its weak home front. This time they intended to keep food supplies – and morale – up, even if it meant starvation of what one bureaucrat called 'umpteen million people'.

German authorities viewed Soviet POWs as a particular threat, regarding them not only as Slavic subhumans but as part of the 'Bolshevik menace', linked in their minds to some imaginary Jewish conspiracy. They spared no violence against the Soviet prisoners. In the camp of Gross-Rosen, in Germany, the commandant had 65,000 Soviet inmates killed within six months by feeding them a soup made only of grass, water and salt. In

Flossenbürg, SS men burned Soviet POWs alive. In Majdanek, they shot them into trenches. In Mauthausen, in Austria, so many POWs were killed that people living near the camp complained about pollution of their water supply; for days the rivers and streams of the area ran red with blood.

The notorious German camps of Auschwitz, near Krakow and Majdanek, by Lublin, were originally built to shelter Soviet POWs and to exploit their labour for the industrial complexes Himmler planned there. In 1941 some 15,000 Soviet POWs were taken to those camps; by January 1942, only a few hundred remained alive. In early 1942, Himmler filled those sites with 150,000 German Jews and transformed the camps into killing centres. In this way camps constructed for Soviet POWs became part of the machinery for destruction of Jews.

It was when dealing with Soviet POWs at Auschwitz that camp commandant Rudolf Hoess and his assistants experimented with the means of killing that have become the symbol of Nazi genocide: Zyklon B. In early September 1941, 600 Soviet prisoners selected for execution by the SS arrived at Auschwitz. In order to avoid the cumbersome task of shooting so many people, Hoess and his men decided to gas them with the pesticide Zyklon B, also known as hydrogen cyanide. While they were at it they included another 250 inmates who had been designated unfit for work. The T-4 killers had already experimented with gassing as a way to murder people considered handicapped. Those lessons were subsequently applied first to Soviet POWs and then to Jews.

By the end of 1941, the German leadership concluded that mass shootings were not the most efficient way to carry out their so-called Final Solution. Their concerns were not about the victims but rather about the perpetrators, who found it physically and psychologically difficult to shoot people all day long at close range.

Led by Heydrich, top German officials met in early 1942 to coordinate and streamline their efforts to annihilate the Jews. This meeting was called the Wannsee Conference because it took place in a villa in Wannsee, a suburb of Berlin. At the conference were representatives from all of the offices and agencies in the

German government and Nazi Party who had a direct hand in
the killing process. High officials from the Foreign Office were
on hand as were representatives of the SS, *Einsatzgruppen*, Nazi
Party headquarters, Justice Ministry, Hans Frank of the General
Government in Poland and others. Heydrich himself chaired
the meeting. Eichmann, who would later be in charge of trans-
porting Jews to the killing centres, produced the official report.
Wannsee focused on Jews as the top priority of Nazi destruction. Eichmann's report makes it clear that all eleven million Jews
in Europe were targeted for murder in the current phase of a
plan for total annihilation. The list even included Jews in Sweden,
Ireland and England, places not in German hands in 1942. Also
specified were Jews in the 'European part' of Turkey, an indication
that Jews living outside Europe would be slated for destruction in
a subsequent phase of operations.

The Wannsee Conference marked another step in the killing
process. Mass murder was already underway when the conference met, but at Wannsee the SS asserted its leadership in the
annihilation of the Jews. Heydrich needed the cooperation of the
other agencies and offices represented, but he made it clear who
called the shots. Of course, by their very presence those other
bureaucrats, party functionaries and trained killers demonstrated
that they understood what was going on and endorsed it. The
line to genocide was not one Hitler would cross alone.

Participants at the Wannsee Conference also discussed methods
of killing and, according to post-war remarks by Eichmann, compared notes based on experiences in the field. Killing centres with
gas chambers emerged as a favoured means. Instead of bringing
the killers to their victims, it was deemed generally preferable to
transport the victims to their killers. Construction of new killing
centres, already begun, accelerated in the months that followed.
Meanwhile, existing camps such as Auschwitz were ordered
expanded and equipped with gassing facilities. At the same time,
the methods of killing already introduced continued, that is, gas
vans, shootings, starvation, death by lethal injection, overwork,
abuse and disease. It was remarkable how quickly things could
move forward once the line to annihilation had been crossed.

7

The Peak Years of Killing:
1942 and 1943

When it comes to human suffering, each year of a war tends to be worse than the year before. The passage of time adds further material deprivation, more wounded and more dead to the accumulated misery of the people involved.

This depressing observation certainly holds true for the Second World War. By the end of 1942 the Germans were heading into their fourth year of war. At least in the short term their victories insulated them from much of the bereavement and hardship that war brings. The same was not true for the people they conquered. The devastation of Poland – economically, politically, socially – became ever more terrible as the Poles endured year after year of occupation. The Nazi German hand may have been less heavy on Western Europe, but there too – in occupied Denmark, Norway, the Netherlands, Belgium, France and elsewhere – adversity and demoralisation continued to build. Meanwhile, in the Balkans and the Soviet territories overrun in 1941, German occupation practices produced an ever-escalating reign of terror.

It was not just the normal dynamic of war that served to multiply human suffering as the Second World War continued. The Nazi principles of spatial expansion and 'racial purification' meant that more and more killing was itself a direct goal of the German war effort. The more Hitler's empire extended its reach and consolidated its hold on subject lands and peoples, the more its forces sought to destroy those it deemed enemies – Jews above all, but also Slavs and others defined as unwanted inferiors. For this reason, 1942 and 1943 – the years when German power in Europe reached its height – were also the peak years of killing.

German Military Power at its Height

One point is so obvious it is often not stated: Hitler and the Nazis planned to win the war. War, Hitler believed, would not merely defeat the enemy militarily; it would create a 'new order'.

German planners developed in detail the implications of their notion of *Lebensraum* – living space – in an important memorandum called 'General Plan East'. Drafted in 1941, that document presented the Nazi vision for Eastern Europe. One of its primary authors was a young historian named Theodor Schieder. After the war Schieder pursued a successful academic career in West Germany. Only after his death, half a century after the war had ended, would his students and many people who admired his scholarship realise the use to which he had put his training and skills during the war.

General Plan East called for Germans and ethnic Germans to settle vast areas of Eastern Europe, where they would produce food and babies for the 'Aryan master race'. To make such settlements possible, the plan demanded expulsion of those currently living there. Those tens of millions of people, most of them Slavs, were to be forced into less desirable areas, allowed to die of starvation and disease, or turned into slaves for the German empire. According to General Plan East, Jews were to disappear altogether.

Like so much Nazi writing, General Plan East was full of euphemisms. Instead of spelling out the goal as to kill people or make sure they died of starvation, overwork, or disease, the document talked about 'reducing' or 'removing' certain populations.

Nevertheless its intentions were obvious. It also made clear that German policies toward different population groups were closely connected. Settlement of Germans and ethnic Germans in the east; expulsion, enslavement and decimation of Slavs; and murder of Jews were all parts of the same plan.

General Plan East envisioned 'Germanisation' of an enormous territory that stretched eastward from the old German Reich all the way to the Ural Mountains. Someday, according to the plan, 500 to 600 million people would live there: 'Aryan' Germans and their slaves. German population planners realised that even a massively increased birth rate could not produce enough children to achieve the rate of population growth they wanted. As a result, they proposed taking 'racially valuable' children away from supposedly inferior parents in order to 'Germanise' them, that is, to transform them into members of the 'Aryan race'. So-called racial experts estimated that about fifty per cent of Czech children were suitable for 'Germanisation'. They thought as many as seventy-five per cent of the children in some parts of western Belorussia might be acceptable, but under no conditions were Jewish children to be 'Germanised'.

Concrete steps were taken to increase numbers of Germans while weakening the peoples of the territories they occupied. Under a programme codenamed *Operation Heuaktion* (the 'hay action'), German agencies kidnapped thousands of children and adolescents from Eastern Europe and sent them to the Reich, in some cases to be raised by German families, in others to work in armaments factories or handicrafts. Meanwhile, German doctors, many of them working in concentration camps and using inmates as subjects, experimented with methods of mass sterilisation. At least those medical scientists working in Auschwitz knew full well that Jews would not be the people intended for mass sterilisation: the Jews were in the process of being annihilated. Sterilisation was to be the fate of the non-Jewish population of Eastern Europe.

Schemes of Germanisation remind us just how artificial Nazi notions of blood and race were. The case of two Polish women provides an illustration. Although the parents of Johanna and Danuta W. were 'pure Polish', the sisters both applied for

Germanisation. No doubt they hoped to get the benefits that being classified as German rather than Polish would bring. In 1944 SS racial authorities in one city approved Johanna's application and she became officially recognised as an ethnic German. A similar office elsewhere rejected Danuta. Meanwhile both women went to Germany to work as housemaids. Danuta became pregnant by an SS man. When her baby was born he received ethnic German status, but his mother was still classified as a Pole. The only reason German authorities gave for rejecting Danuta was that 'she did not look so good'. Danuta's status caused practical problems because the sisters lived together. Under the terms of Nazi racial law, ethnic Germans such as Johanna were to have no social contact with Poles like Danuta, nor was Danuta's own child permitted to interact with his mother. The post-war fates of Johanna, Danuta and her son are unknown.

During 1942 and 1943 Germans enslaved millions of people, women as well as men, from the Soviet Union and elsewhere in Eastern Europe. Some were forced to labour in the occupied areas; millions of others were sent to Germany to work in factories, on farms and in private homes. Hitler and other planners considered slave labour a way to keep the German home front happy. They did not want to introduce measures that might have been unpopular with many Germans; for example, recruiting large numbers of German women into factory work or curtailing supplies of food and consumer goods. After all, Hitler and others like him still believed that discontent at home had led to German defeat in the last war. So they brought in millions of people they considered disposable and used them to make waging a war of annihilation as comfortable as possible for the German people.

The German occupiers also seized agricultural produce in the areas they controlled, causing famine and starvation among the people left behind. They took over whatever industrial production had not been evacuated by the Soviet Army as it had fled in 1941. In the name of fighting partisans, German forces burned entire villages, often along with many of the people who lived in them. Public hangings, torture, rape and sexual slavery were all common occurrences in the occupied east.

Some German authorities worried that such brutality was counter-pro-ductive because it sparked opposition that could have been avoided. As one high-ranking German official observed, many of the Soviet people had suffered terribly under Stalin. It would not have taken much to persuade them that their lives under German rule would be better than they could expect with the return of communism. The extreme viciousness of German occupation, however, convinced the vast majority of Soviets that even Stalin was preferable to Hitler.

Hitler and propaganda minister Goebbels paid lip service to the need to soften up in order to prevent an explosion of opposition in the east, but German policies did not change. To the contrary, reprisals against guerrilla activity kept increasing in their ferocity. Meanwhile the Germans defined partisan activity, or 'banditry', as they preferred to call it, more and more broadly. SS leader Himmler summed up dominant German views in a speech to top SS men in October 1943:

> We must be honest, decent, loyal and comradely to members of our own blood and to nobody else. What happens to a Russian or to a Czech does not interest me in the slightest. What the nations can offer in the way of good blood of our type we will take, if necessary by kidnapping their children and raising them here with us. ... Whether 10,000 Russian females fall down from exhaustion while digging an anti-tank ditch interests me only insofar as the anti-tank ditch for Germany is finished. We shall never be rough and heartless when it is not necessary, that is clear. We Germans, who are the only people in the world who have a decent attitude towards animals, will also assume a decent attitude towards these human animals. But it is a crime against our own blood to worry about them and give them ideals, thus causing our sons and grandsons to have a more difficult time with them.
>
> [Noakes and Pridham 3:919–920]

In Himmler's mind Russians and Czechs merited nothing more than the self-interested care one would show a beast of burden.

Hitler and many top Nazis rejected Christianity. They considered it an offshoot of Judaism that encouraged weakness and humility instead of aggression. In wartime, however, they realised that it was counterproductive to deprive Germans of the comfort of traditional religion. Accordingly they allowed Christian military chaplains – Roman Catholic as well as Protestant – to minister to the men of the *Wehrmacht*. Accounts from these German clergy give another perspective on conditions in the east.

One Catholic chaplain buried 120 German soldiers in the first five months of 1942. In a report to superiors he admitted that the 'long duration of the war and the many dead have brought a certain indifference to death'. If the Germans had become numb toward their own casualties, how much less must they have cared about anyone else?

Christian clergy also heard confessions of terrible crimes. For example, a German Catholic priest stationed in Ukraine met a wounded soldier who confided to him about his past. The man had taken part in a mass shooting of Jews near Sevastopol in the Crimea. According to the priest, the soldier was ruined by his experience. He described the Jews, lined up, naked – women, children and men. Although he had manned one of the machine guns he insisted he had only shot in the air. What should he have done, he asked the priest? We do not know what the priest answered, but it seems evident that at least some Germans could not tolerate conditions in the east. Desertions and self-mutilations were not uncommon, although military authorities punished them severely, often with death. Nervous breakdowns generally led to transfers to less trying duties.

Not only military men but German civilians too were drawn into the war of annihilation. In Poland, for example, German employees of a bank found themselves assigned to guard the street between a Jewish ghetto and the train station as SS and Gestapo cleared out Jews and sent them on trains to be killed. Some people accepted such tasks, eager to win promotions or prove their hardness. Others sought transfers to places where it was easier to shut out the realities of the war, back home in Germany, perhaps, or in Western Europe.

When it came to his top military leaders, Hitler used bribery to make sure that their consciences did not protest too loudly. Every month, on orders from the *Führer*, German generals received special tax-free supplements of between 2,000 and 4,000 Reich Marks. They had their pick of the finest estates in Poland and elsewhere, stolen, of course, from the original owners. On special birthdays – when a general turned fifty, for example – he received a bonus of as much as 250,000 Reich Marks. Of course cooperation and good behaviour increased the amount. Such sums made the German generals fabulously wealthy. In contrast, German infantry who cleared mines during the war – an extremely dangerous job – received supplements to their regular incomes of only one mark per day.

Military Developments and Non-military Repercussions: Stalingrad, North Africa and Italy

Discussions of the Holocaust often pay little attention to the war itself, but without war and German victories there would have been no genocide of the European Jews. The vast majority of Jews murdered by Nazi Germans – about ninety-five per cent – came from outside Germany. Without military conquests the perpetrators would never have got those victims in their hands.

Yet even during the war itself many people on the Allied side did not see the links between the German war effort and mass murder. Soviet, British and American military planners tended to take a fairly narrow view of events. Their goal was to win the war, whatever that meant; their objectives were military ones. It is probably fair to say that they devoted little thought to what seemed bizarre, non-military 'sideshows' on the part of the Germans, such as attacks on handicapped people, Gypsies and Jews. Nevertheless military decisions and developments in 1942 and 1943 had repercussions far beyond the military sphere, as evident from Stalingrad, North Africa and Italy.

From 1941 to 1943 most of the combat in Europe occurred between German and Soviet forces on Germany's eastern front.

In 1941 the Red Army had checked the Germans and their Axis partners, but by mid-1942 the Germans took the offensive again. The new German offensive had two prongs. One entered the Caucasus region with an eye to the oil fields there. The other moved toward the city of Stalingrad – modern Volgograd – on the lower Volga River. What is now known as the Battle of Stalingrad began in the late summer and autumn of 1942 as the advancing Germans were blocked by the defending Red Army.

Hitler instructed the German 6th Army under General (later Field Marshal) Friedrich Paulus to take Stalingrad. In September the 6th Army and the 4th Panzer Army advanced into the out-skirts; by mid-November they had captured much of the city. Fighting was extraordinarily fierce. The Soviets, ordered by Stalin to defend the city with everything they had, contested every inch. Losses on both sides were staggering. Between 21 August and 16 October 1942, the German 6th Army alone suffered some 40,000 casualties. In late November, a Soviet offensive cut off the 6th Army, parts of another German army and two Romanian armies at Stalingrad and the Red Army surrounded them. German attempts to relieve their forces in December failed and the Soviets demanded capitulation.

Earlier, some of Hitler's generals had advised a withdrawal, but he and others were determined to hold on. The territory had been won at such a high cost and Stalingrad was an important hub of Soviet transport. Hitler did agree to retrenchment in the Caucasus, so it is not the case that he never authorised retreats. With Stalingrad, however, Hitler did not give in. On 31 January 1943, the German southern contingent under Paulus capitulated. A few days later the northern contingent followed. The Soviets took 90,000 German prisoners of war; there were hundreds of thousands dead on both sides.

Even after the Battle of Stalingrad, the outcome of the war was far from a foregone conclusion. Just a month later, in late February 1943, the Germans mounted a successful counter-offensive at the southern part of their eastern front. Still, at least in hindsight, Stalingrad appears to have been an important mili-tary and symbolic turning point.

Back home Goebbels' propaganda machine presented Stalingrad as a strategic retreat, but few were fooled. The Red Army victory at Stalingrad marked a visible departure from the way the war had gone so far for Germany, and at least some Germans were scared. SS reports indicate that the Nazi Party began to lose support. Many Germans had lost family members at Stalingrad; they wanted the war to end as soon as possible.

Discontent for the most part did not translate into open opposition to the regime. Instead the German public became more cynical and withdrawn. Distracted by increasing Allied air raids on their cities, Germans at home busied themselves with the practical matters of staying alive and keeping their families together. The regime did make some concessions to try to boost public spirits; it eased restrictions on the churches and slackened its campaign against cigarette smoking. Nazi reports indicate that many Germans knew quite a lot about the atrocities their country was committing in the east. In 1943, when mass graves of Polish officers shot by the Soviets were found at Katyn, there was little reaction within Germany. The Soviets would soon find plenty of mass graves of murdered Jews, some muttered, so it was better not to draw too much attention to similar crimes on the other side.

In the meantime, the German leadership cracked down tighter on its critics at home. Beginning in early 1943, offences such as 'defeatism' were often punished by death. For example, the sister of Erich Maria Remarque, author of the First World War classic *All Quiet on the Western Front*, was condemned to death for remarking that Hitler should resign. German authorities also introduced draconian measures against accused deserters and traitors in the military, at least 25,000 of whom they had shot over the course of the war, mostly in its later stages.

Still, being defined as 'Aryan' continued to offer considerable protection for Germans throughout the war. An important illustration involves a group of German Gentile women in Berlin who were married to German Jewish men. In early 1943, in preparation for Hitler's upcoming birthday, Goebbels planned to remove the last Jews from the city and send them east to be killed. Most of Germany's Jews had already been deported and killed, beginning in late 1941. Many of those who remained were married to non-Jews.

German officials had long been uncertain as to how to proceed against German Jews married to 'Aryans'. Participants at the Wannsee Conference in early 1942 had debated the issue without reaching a decision. On the one hand, Nazi principles of racial purity left no room for exceptions. According to that logic, any Jew left alive represented the possible pollution of generations of 'Aryan blood'.

On the other hand, however, practical considerations made it dangerous to strike against Jews married to 'Aryan' Germans or to attack the 'half-Jewish' offspring of such unions. Obviously any 'mixed' families had a 'pure Aryan' side, which meant plenty of relatives who would be antagonised by the deportation and murder of their husband, uncle, son-in-law, niece, granddaughter, or so forth. During wartime the Nazi regime was reluctant to risk stirring up discontent among its own public and its fighting men. Outside Germany of course the matter was easy. German officials hardly cared if they alienated Polish or Ukrainian Gentiles or mistakenly included some of them among the people they defined as Jews. Inside Germany the situation demanded much more delicacy.

By early 1943 Nazi planners decided the remaining Berlin Jews had to go. Police arrested most of the men at the factories where they worked and locked them in a building on the Rosenstrasse – German for 'Street of Roses'. From there they were to be deported and killed. In a spontaneous show of disobedience, the Gentile wives of those German Jewish men gathered in the Rosenstrasse to protest the arrest of their husbands and demand their release. Sympathisers joined them until there were several thousand people milling about. Hitler and Goebbels were furious, but they did not dare order police or military to open fire on a crowd of Germans. Instead they allowed the men to be released. Many of the internees of the Rosenstrasse survived the war. The historian Nathan Stoltzfus recounts these events in his book *Resistance of the Heart*.

Meanwhile the Nazi regime's air of invincibility was challenged from outside Germany too. In 1942, at German insistence,

Romanian and Hungarian troops had also been included in the advance on Stalingrad. Improperly armed and trained, those satellite forces were crushed in the Red Army offensives. Small wonder that by 1943 the leadership of those countries began looking for ways to get out of the war. Suddenly partnership with Germany seemed more a liability than an advantage.

After Stalingrad, Romanian and Hungarian leaders also became less willing to turn over the Jews among their populations to the Germans to be killed. It was not that those authorities suddenly became humanitarian. Rather they recognised that, should they need to negotiate with the Allies, Jews might be useful bargaining chips. Perhaps, they reasoned, they could barter Jewish lives for things they needed. Thus the German setback at Stalingrad might have had the unanticipated effect of prolonging and maybe even saving the lives of some Romanian and Hungarian Jews. On the whole, however, Stalingrad left the situation of Jews in Europe even more catastrophic than it had been before. The Battle of Stalingrad is often described as the beginning of the end for Nazi Germany, but it signalled no change in the assault on the Jews. To the contrary, Stalingrad occurred right in the peak of the killing process and genocide continued unabated.

Meanwhile, the guards, SS men and German bureaucrats who were attached to the programme for killing Jews found a new reason to step up their efforts. For them it was clearly preferable to be in the camps and offices overseeing mass murder of unarmed people than to face the Red Army on the eastern front. The chances of living through the war seemed quite good for Germans engaged in the slaughter of defenceless civilians. The odds were much lower for those assigned to fight armed opponents.

Even after Stalingrad the Germans had substantial military resources and a solid eastern front. Germany still held Poland and the killing centres built there – places such as Treblinka, Majdanek and Auschwitz. Forced to begin to pull back from the east, the Germans concentrated their forces and their destructive energies on the territories they still controlled. From that base of power the Nazi leadership would launch the effort in late 1943 to destroy the last remnants of the Jewish communities in Poland.

People often wonder why Nazi Germans wasted manpower and other resources slaughtering Jewish civilians when there was a war to be won. According to Nazi logic, however, murder of the Jews was just as much part of the war effort as were offensives against the Soviet Union. To the proponents of race and space, it was as urgent to use trains to transport Jews to killing centres as it was to move German troops from place to place. As Hitler had proclaimed in January 1939 and as Nazi propaganda insisted, Jews purportedly pulled the strings behind the allied war effort. Military setbacks in 1943 did not slow down the killing operations; if anything, they speeded them up.

In the autumn of 1943, the Germans launched a new offensive against the remaining Jews of Poland. Its code name was 'Harvest Festival'. Within just a few days in November 1943, Germans and their accomplices massacred 42,000 Jews in the Lublin area. The Harvest Festival relied heavily on mass shootings. In special 'Jew Hunts', the German Order Police and *Einsatzgruppen* worked with local collaborators to locate and kill as many Jews as they could. By the end of 1943, only a few thousand Jews remained alive in German-occupied Eastern Europe. Many of those were in hiding or fighting in partisan units. German officials kept some alive in the Łódź ghetto for economic reasons and a few survived in work camps. In the case of Stalingrad, a military setback for the Germans did not improve the immediate situation of European Jews or, for that matter, of other civilians under the German yoke. However, it may have helped to break down the myth of the invincible Germans and to encourage resistance.

The years 1942 and 1943 also brought German setbacks in North Africa. In this case too, military developments had enormous non-military results. Africa had been the focus of Fascist Italian ambitions ever since the 1920s when Mussolini's forces invaded Ethiopia. By 1940, the Italians requested German help against the British and their Allies in Africa. The following year saw formation of the German Afrika Korps under the popular General Erwin Rommel (1891–1944), the 'Desert Fox'.

In late October and early November 1942, the British 8th Army under Bernard L. Montgomery (1887–1976) defeated

Rommel's German–Italian forces at El Alamein. At the same time, the American and British 'Operation Torch' landed 106,000 Allied troops in Morocco and Algeria under the command of General Dwight D. Eisenhower. Soon Allied forces had pushed the Axis back into Tunisia and a small part of Libya.

The Germans managed to halt the initial Anglo–American advance and reinforce their position. By March 1943, however, Rommel was unable to supply his troops. He flew to Hitler's headquarters to request an evacuation, but Hitler refused. In May 1943 Tunis, the last Axis outpost in Africa, fell to the Allies, who took more than 230,000 soldiers prisoner. About half of them were German.

The reverberations of military action in North Africa were felt all over the world. Already in 1942 Hitler had blamed his Vichy French collaborators in North Africa for capitulating to the Allies and in November of that year, he ordered German occupation of Vichy France. From then on Germans would administer the territory directly, as they did the rest of France. There would be no more concessions to French independence.

Developments in North Africa also generated a chain reaction that affected the Soviet Union. Thanks to massive reinforcements in November 1942, the Germans held their bridgehead in Tunisia until May 1943. As a result, the Allies had to mount a campaign to crush those remaining Axis forces in North Africa. In turn it became impossible for the Allies to undertake the long-awaited invasion of north-western Europe in 1943.

Stalin nonetheless continued to call for the western Allies to invade north-western Europe as soon as possible. Since 1941 the Soviet Union had borne the brunt of German power and Stalin and the Red Army were desperate for relief. The western Allies could not liberate Tunisia and make the switch to operations in north-western Europe during the same year. Instead British and American planners decided on landings in Sicily, then on the Italian mainland for 1943 and postponed invasion of France until 1944. In the meantime, during 1943 and 1944, Germans in Soviet territories and other parts of Europe slaughtered millions of people: Red Army soldiers, Soviet civilians and Jews from all over Europe. Military developments in North Africa, worked out by both sides with little regard to the impact on Soviet civilians, Jews, or Italians, had enormous – and unforeseen – consequences for all those groups of people.

In 1942 and 1943, the territory that today is the state of Israel was still part of the British Mandate of Palestine. Arabs as well as some Jews lived in the area. During meetings with Arab leaders, most notably the Grand Mufti of Jerusalem, Hitler had promised that German forces would drive the British out of Palestine, occupy the territory and slaughter the Jews there. Thanks to Allied victories in North Africa, the Germans never occupied the British Mandate of Palestine, so the Jews there remained alive. Allied military planners probably gave no thought to the fate of the world's Jews as they made their moves in North Africa. Nevertheless their triumphs there in 1942 and 1943 made possible the eventual establishment of a Jewish state in Israel by saving the lives of those Jews already in the area.

Military developments in North Africa also affected Italy, Germany's longest-standing alliance partner. The loss of North Africa completed Italy's disillusionment with the Axis. German demands, German arrogance and German contempt for Italian officials and the Italian armed forces had also led to growing discontent.

In July 1943, Allied forces landed on Sicily. Soon they were advancing northward through the Italian peninsula. Committed Italian Fascists and their German backers retreated to the north of Naples, around the top of the ankle on the Italian boot. After more than twenty-one years, Benito Mussolini's regime collapsed. In July 1943 the Italian king assumed supreme command, dismissed Mussolini from office and had him arrested. A new Italian government under Marshal Badoglio dissolved the Fascist Party and surrendered to the Allies. Badoglio's government then fled to southern Italy and abandoned most of the country, as well as the Italian-occupied portions of France, Yugoslavia, Albania and Greece, to the Germans.

The Germans took severe countermeasures. German troops occupied Rome and disarmed Italian soldiers, discharged them from service, or placed them in POW camps. By December 1943, the Germans had interned 725,000 Italian soldiers and had sent 615,000 Italian men to Germany as forced labourers. Badoglio's government declared war on Germany. Meanwhile the Germans managed to free Mussolini by using a special para-troop unit and install him in a puppet state in northern Italy. Not until the end of April 1945 did the German forces in Italy capitu-late. That month Italian partisans shot Mussolini and his mistress as they tried to flee to Switzerland.

Events in Italy had devastating effects for civilians in Yugoslavia, Albania, Greece and France. In those countries the Germans had divided occupation duties with their Italian allies. The Italians tended to be less brutal than the Germans as occupi-ers, especially when it came to genocide of Jews. Neither the Italian military nor diplomatic officials would cooperate with the Germans in what they considered a barbaric procedure unwor-thy of any civilised society.

As a result, many Jews from German-occupied areas had fled into the Italian zones. When the Germans took over in 1943, those refuges disappeared. Already in the spring, Nazi Germans had begun to destroy the ancient Sephardic Jewish communi-ties in Greece and Yugoslavia, deporting their members to Auschwitz to be killed. Now, with the Italians out of the way, the job could be completed. They even sent boats to take the last old Jewish men from remote Greek islands.

In Italy itself, Jews had been fairly safe until 1943. In the late 1930s, under German pressure and for reasons of his own, Mussolini had introduced legislation limiting Jews' activities. In contrast to the leadership in Slovakia and Vichy France – partners who cooperated eagerly with German plans for the Jews – Italians had been reluctant to turn over their Jews for kill-ing. Beginning in 1943, Germans came in to Italy and took the Jews out themselves. Most of the Italian Jews murdered in the Holocaust died in 1944 or early 1945.

Primo Levi, an Italian survivor of the Holocaust, produced some of the most insightful reflections on that event ever written. Born in Turin in 1919, Levi was arrested with his Italian partisan group in December 1943. When his German captors discovered he was Jewish, they sent him to Auschwitz. Levi survived, but almost all of the inmates he knew in the camp did not. His closest friend in Auschwitz was another Italian named Alberto. Levi and Alberto shared what little food they received or 'organised' for themselves. They encouraged each other to muster the energy and will to try to stay alive, both physically and in some deeper, moral way that meant retaining an awareness of themselves as human beings.

Thanks to Levi's pre-war training as a chemist, he got a job in the camp that protected him from some of the harshest conditions there. Somehow he lived through the war. Alberto, however, did not. He too was a resourceful, intelligent young man full of the desire to survive. In early 1945, as the Red Army advanced from the east, the Germans evacuated the camp at Auschwitz. Guards marched Alberto, along with most other inmates, out of the camp to the west. Levi, sick in the infirmary at the time, was left behind with others too weak to walk. Who could have known that what seemed the chance for life – leaving the camp at last – would be Alberto's death, whereas Levi, abandoned by the guards as almost dead, would survive?

In his writings about the Holocaust, Levi described the camp as above all a place of dehumanisation. The English translation of Levi's memoir is called *Survival in Auschwitz,* but he originally titled the book *Se questo è un uomo* (If this is a man). For Levi, to be human meant more than merely to eat and breathe. It meant having an identity, relationships with others, ties to a past and a future and a sense of decency and dignity.

The camp took all that away. Physical abuses heaped on the prisoners – starvation, beatings, exposure – together with the many humiliations and indignities they suffered attacked their sense of humanity. In the camp, prisoners lost their names and became numbers. Emaciated, sick, shorn and forced to wear rags, they looked nothing like their former selves. Brutality and deprivation turned them against one another; pain and despair made them forget the values and ideals they had cherished. It was this destruction of people's humanity that Levi considered the most terrible crime of the

Holocaust. After the war Levi did everything he could to share his insights and to warn against dehumanisation and brutality in the post-war world. Already in Auschwitz he had nightmares that people 'outside' would not listen to his story. Toward the end of his life he expressed frustration that the world refused to learn from the past. Primo Levi died in 1987 when he fell down the stairs in his home. Many people believe he committed suicide.

The Holocaust at its Peak: The Killing Centres

By the time of the Wannsee Conference in January 1942, Nazi Germans and their helpers were already engaged in mass killing of Jews from all over Europe. Since late 1939 they had been starving Jews to death in the ghettos of Poland. Mobile murder squads followed the regular military into Soviet territory in June 1941 and began immediately to concentrate their slaughter on Jewish civilians. In September 1941 German police introduced a regulation forcing all Jews in Germany to wear an identifying Star of David. A month later they began deporting Jews from Germany and elsewhere in central and Western Europe to the east for killing. One killing centre, at Chelmno, near Łódź, started operations in December 1941.

Although it may have seemed impossible, for European Jews 1942 and 1943 went even beyond the horrors of the years before. At the beginning of 1942, even after three years of war, ghettoisation, torture and forced labour, seventy-five per cent of the Jews who would be murdered in the Holocaust were still alive. By the beginning of 1943, seventy-five per cent of the approximately six million who would be killed were already dead.

In December 1941 the SS opened its first killing centre at Chelmno, called Kulmhof by the Germans. Located just forty miles from Łódź, the Chelmno facility used specially equipped gas vans to kill Jews and also Gypsies. Guards loaded their victims into the cargo compartment and sealed the doors. As the van drove, pipes brought the diesel exhaust directly into the back so that the people there were asphyxiated. T-4 killers had developed this technique, which they used first against people deemed handicapped. Within months of the Wannsee Conference of January 1942, five more killing centres were in operation, all of them, like Chelmno, in territories that had once been part of Poland. Contrary to popular notions, German mass killing of Jews was not some perfectly coordinated, 'clean' enterprise. Like the entire Nazi regime it was characterised by confusion and rivalry, which only served to exacerbate the horror.

The killing centre at Chelmno was located in the incorporated territory, that is, the part of Poland annexed to the Reich and earmarked for Germanisation. Chelmno was a small village on a railway branch line. An unoccupied castle proved useful as headquarters for the killing process. Trains brought Jews, mostly from the surrounding area, to Chelmno and then trucks drove them to the courtyard of the castle. There an SS man addressed them. They were to be sent to Germany, he told them, but first they had to take a shower. Ordered to strip, they were handed towels and soap and pushed through a corridor labelled 'washroom' into the vans. About ninety people were forced into a van at once.

The vans drove slowly for a few miles into the forest. There personnel opened the doors and dumped the bodies. Guards shot anyone who was still alive. The Germans kept a few Jews around to unload the corpses and bury the bodies. Known as the *Sonderkommando* – 'special unit' – this small group of men handled twelve to thirteen vans – about 1,000 bodies – each day. Jews were also assigned to sort the clothing left behind and clean out the vans. The more lucrative task of extracting any gold teeth went to the Nazis' Ukrainian helpers.

Most members of the Jewish *Sonderkommando* did not hold that position for long. As additional shipments of Jews arrived the German guards selected new workers and killed the old ones. Some of the Jewish workers tried to escape and a few succeeded. The Germans responded to those attempts by chaining the legs of *Sonderkommando* members. By the spring and summer of 1942, the area around Chelmno was filled with the stench of rotting bodies. German officials ordered ovens brought in so that the mass graves could be opened and the bodies exhumed and burned. Of course they delegated this gruesome job to members of the Jewish *Sonderkommando*. Mordechai Podchlebnik, a Jewish man assigned to the task found the bodies of his wife and two children in a mass grave. He begged the SS guards to shoot him. When they refused, he tried to commit suicide. This time his comrades stopped him. Eventually he escaped. One of very few survivors of the killing centre at Chelmno, Podchlebnik later served as a central witness at the post-war Chelmno trial.

Rumours about the killing centre at Chelmno soon spread. Jews in the region struggled to know how to react, but their options were extremely limited. In December 1941, German authorities demanded that Rumkowski, head of the Jewish Council at Łódź, hand over 20,000 members of his community for 'special treatment'. Aware that selection most likely meant death, Rumkowski and his committee tried to fill their list with outsiders and people considered asocial. Among those early victims were the remainder of some 5,000 Gypsies who had been sent to Łódź from the Reich. Located in a separate part of the ghetto, many had already died from hunger and disease. Now those left would be murdered in Chelmno.

By mid-1942, the German district commander reported to Himmler that in the next two to three months, the 'special treatment' of some 100,000 Jews from the area would be complete. Given the 'success' of the project, he suggested a similar programme for Poles with tuberculosis.

From December 1941 to the end of 1942, Germans and their henchmen killed about 145,000 people, most of them Jews, in Chelmno. About 5,000 Gypsies from the ghetto in Łódź were murdered in the gas vans at Chelmno as well. In late 1942 the SS closed the killing centre until 1944, when it was reactivated briefly. Its job in the area had been completed.

Only one inmate of the killing centre at Belzec survived the war. Located near the Polish city of Lublin, Belzec began operations in March 1942. German governor Hans Frank of the General Government in Poland had boasted that Jews in his territory would be the first victims of the so-called Final Solution.

To that end, after the Wannsee Conference, the labour camp at Belzec was outfitted as a killing centre.

Belzec had a fixed installation for gassing that used diesel fumes. On 1 April 1942, the first night of the Jewish holiday of Passover, the SS brought more than 15,000 Jews from the city of Lvov to Belzec to be killed. By the time the camp was dismantled in the spring of 1943, some 600,000 Jews had been murdered there, along with perhaps several thousand Gypsies.

We have an early account of a gassing at Belzec from an unusual source: an SS man named Kurt Gerstein. Gerstein was a Nazi Party member and devout Protestant. He had served a brief term in a concentration camp himself for criticising the anti-Christian attitudes of the SS. Nevertheless, thanks to family connections, he was able to have his name cleared and join the SS. Gerstein was an engineer with some training in sanitation and medical matters. Accordingly he received a post as SS chief disinfection officer. Early in 1942, a deputy of Eichmann's assigned Gerstein to transport Zyklon B to a secret place. The destination was Belzec.

At Belzec the commandant, Dr Christian Wirth, an old T-4 expert invited Gerstein to witness the killing of Jews using diesel fumes. That day the diesel motor broke down. About eight hundred Jews were forced to wait naked for nearly three hours until the gassing began. The killing itself took thirty-two minutes; Gerstein timed it with his stopwatch. Horrified by what he had seen, Gerstein decided to try to use his position to stop the killings. He destroyed some of the Zyklon B he was supposed to deliver to Auschwitz and he tried to get the word out about German mass murder of Jews in Poland. When he met a Swedish diplomat on a train, Gerstein blurted out the whole story. He went to the papal nuncio – the Vatican's representative – in Berlin to pass the news to the pope. Gerstein's efforts met with little response.

At the end of the war, Gerstein was captured by the French. Arrested and charged with war crimes, he died in prison, either by his own hand or as a victim of foul play. Only half a century later, due to efforts by his family, did he gain a reputation as a hero. Gerstein's story is instructive. A lone individual who tried to sabotage a murderous process from within, he ended up caught in the system himself and destroyed. Gerstein did not have the public backing within Germany that allowed someone like Bishop von Galen to protest the killing of the handicapped with some effect. Nor would or could the foreigners he told about what he knew grasp what must have seemed to them the ravings of a madman.

The camp at Sobibor was constructed solely for the purpose of killing. Its first commandant was an Austrian named Franz Stangl, a policeman trained in the T-4 program. Sobibor was one of the Operation Reinhard camps, named after Reinhard Heydrich, Himmler's deputy and the driving force at the Wannsee Conference. Mass slaughter of Jews began there in April 1942. Sobibor functioned as a killing centre until October 1943.

At Sobibor, Germans and their accomplices murdered 250,000 Jews from eastern Poland, the occupied Soviet Union and other European countries. Many Dutch Jews, for example, were killed in Sobibor. Trains brought the victims right into the camp. Guards selected some Jews as workers in the killing process and the rest they gassed immediately.

In October 1943 Sobibor was the site of an uprising by its Jewish workers, who staged a mass escape. Most were killed or recaptured, but some survived the war. The Germans closed the camp shortly after the revolt. It is not clear whether the revolt hastened the camp's closure, but by the time Sobibor stopped operations, most of the Jews in the territories from which it had drawn its victims were already dead.

Another Operation Reinhard camp built solely as a killing centre, Treblinka began operations in July 1942. Just eighty miles from Warsaw, it became the grave of a staggering number of Polish Jews. Its first victims were some 300,000 Jews from Warsaw, but Gypsies from the Warsaw ghetto and Jews from all over central Poland, Germany, Austria, Czechoslovakia and Greece were killed there. In all close to a million Jews were murdered at Treblinka.

Treblinka too had its *Sonderkommando*, more than eight hundred Jews who worked in the camp. They included craftspeople employed by the SS as well as men assigned to work in the gas chambers, cutting hair and burying and burning bodies. In August 1943 Jewish workers at Treblinka revolted, after which German authorities gradually shut the camp down.

A number of high-ranking Nazi officials visited Treblinka. Eichmann, for example, paid a call. He described the fake railway station that greeted arrivals to Treblinka as looking 'just like Germany'. Camp organisers intended the facade to create a semblance of normalcy so that people would not suspect they were about to be killed. Eichmann also saw guards chase Jews into the gas chambers through a path between barbed wire fences that the Germans in charge of the camp called the 'hose', the 'funnel', or the 'way to heaven'.

Treblinka was far from perfectly organised. Often corpses littered the train tracks both inside and outside the compound. Eventually the commandant of Sobibor, Franz Stangl, was transferred to Treblinka to clean the place up. Even Stangl's 'improvements' – increased efficiency and a beautification scheme that included planting flower beds – could not conceal the unbearable smell that surrounded the place. Fields came right up to the security fence, so that Polish farmers who lived nearby could see much of what happened inside. No one in the area could be unaware of the massive killing operations at Treblinka.

Majdanek combined a labour camp with a killing centre. Just a mile from the city of Lublin, the camp, modelled after Dachau in Germany, was built in the winter of 1940–1941 for prisoners of war. In fact, the Jewish POWs from the Polish army who were its first inmates did much of the construction. In July 1941 the Germans brought Soviet POWs to Majdanek. Over time they added many Polish Gentiles, especially political prisoners. They built gas chambers in 1942, but death vans and shooting were also widely used at Majdanek. All of Majdanek's inmates were subjected to terrible abuses and many were worked to death. Most of the Soviet POWs died from torture and starvation. The SS guards were known as sadists who enjoyed killing children in front of their mothers and forcing the prisoners to engage in deadly 'sports'.

At Majdanek, gassing, for the most part, was reserved for Jews. Guards brought most transports of Jews straight to the gas chambers. Those kept alive to work had a precarious existence. In late 1942 Eichmann visited Majdanek. Guards forced the inmates to spend the entire day on parade. Eichmann looked at them and said, 'Get rid of the whole lot'. In Nazi eyes, the lives of the inmates at Majdanek were worth less than nothing. In just one day, 3 November 1943, guards mowed down some 17,000 prisoners with machine gun fire and forced the few left alive to conceal the evidence. In all, 200,000 people were killed in the camp. About 75,000 were Gentiles; the other 125,000 were Jews.

Auschwitz-Birkenau was the last camp established as a killing centre, but it functioned the longest in that capacity. Like Belzec and Majdanek, Auschwitz started as a labour camp. Many of the early inmates were political prisoners from Poland. Facilities for mass killing were added later as were a number of factories using slave labour drawn from the camp; the chemical company IG Farben had a plant at Auschwitz III (Buna-Monowitz) to produce artificial rubber.

In the summer of 1941 – before the Wannsee Conference – Himmler decided to transform the camp at Auschwitz into a killing centre. He assigned a man named Rudolf Hoess, trained at Dachau, to the task. Auschwitz seemed an ideal location to Himmler. It was near the small Polish town of Oswiecim and convenient to rail lines yet securely distant from the front. The prisoners already on hand provided a ready source of manpower.

Germans conducted some early trial gassings at Auschwitz. In September 1941 they killed nine hundred Soviet POWs using Zyklon B. By March 1942 Jews were being sent there from the surrounding area to be gassed. The killing centre was known as Auschwitz II or Birkenau. Eventually Birkenau would be the destination of Jews rounded up for killing from Slovakia, France and then all over Europe. An estimated 6,400 Gypsies would be gassed at Birkenau too. The killing procedure at Auschwitz-Birkenau was similar to that elsewhere. Often German officials met the transports of Jews right at the ramp as they came off the trains. There they made their 'selections' – the decision as to who would go immediately to the gas and who would be kept alive in the camp for a time as labourers.

Many survivors remember selections conducted by Dr Josef Mengele. Mengele was a scientist and SS doctor who had his own special projects that involved experiments with dwarfs, twins and others. Mengele's abusive experiments killed the vast majority of his subjects. With a wave of the hand, Mengele and his counterparts sorted those deemed useful for work from those considered fit only for killing. Children, women with children, pregnant women, the elderly, the sick and the weak were sent to one side and then on to the gas. Others were admitted into the camp.

The officials who presided over the killing process developed a series of tricks and deceits to keep their victims calm. Often SS men addressed those selected for gassing in polite, helpful tones as they entered the gas chambers. 'You have been on a journey and you are dirty', the SS informed their victims. 'You will take a shower'. Sometimes they even handed out soap and towels before cramming the people in the 'Shower Room'. Hoess was proud of arrangements at his camp; he had a sense that he had perfected procedures.

Auschwitz represented other refinements to the Nazi system of killing. From early in the process German officials had worried about conflicts between German economic interests and the goal of annihilating Jews. In Auschwitz, those two aims were combined. The SS found they could make money by essentially renting out slave labourers to manufacturers and industrialists. Employers need not worry about keeping their workers alive; there were always more where they came from.

In addition to the concentration camp and the killing centre known as Birkenau, the Auschwitz system included a massive industrial complex and labour camp called Monowitz. There was also a model town where thousands of employees and their families, Germans and ethnic Germans, enjoyed the fruits of state-of-the-art urban planning.

Bizarre as it may seem, some Germans made a rather pleasant life for themselves at the killing centres. Ambitious Nazi doctors had an endless supply of disposable human subjects on whom to conduct experiments. Commandants and other high-ranking administrators often brought their wives and children to be near them. They had access to every luxury and of course to free labour. Hoess's wife supposedly said about Auschwitz, 'Here I want to live until the end of my days'. Himmler authorised fish farms, gardens, brothels and even zoos on the sites for the employees' enjoyment. As for the guards, assignment to a killing centre was certainly preferable to being sent to the front.

The killing centres marked the culmination of the killing process. They were not separate from the Nazi German war for race and space but were an integral part of it. In all, an estimated three million Jews were murdered in the six killing centres outlined here. The number of Gypsies killed with them is even harder to pin down, but it was certainly in the tens of thousands. Approximately 20,000 Roma died in Auschwitz-Birkenau alone – two thirds of them from starvation, disease, experimentation, beatings and shootings; the rest in the gas chambers.

Women's and men's experiences in the Holocaust converged and diverged in significant ways, summed up in the scholar Myrna Goldenberg's phrase 'different horrors, same hell'. Jewish men were more likely to be killed in labour camps in Poland in 1939 and 1940, but more women were among the groups 'selected' from the ghettos in 1941 and 1942 for transport to killing centres. In places like Auschwitz, men had a better chance of being chosen for work; SS authorities regularly consigned women, particularly if pregnant or with small children, directly to the gas chambers.

Accounts by Jewish women in Auschwitz and other Nazi camps often emphasise the physical transformation that their bodies underwent. Isabella Leitner, a survivor from Hungary, described her feelings in Auschwitz in May 1944:

> Our heads are shaved. We look like neither boys nor girls. We haven't menstruated for a long time. We have diarrhea. No, not diarrhea – typhus. Summer and winter we have but one type of clothing. Its name is 'rag'. Not an inch of it without a hole. Our shoulders are exposed. The rain is pouring on our skeletal bodies. The lice are having an orgy in our armpits,

their favourite spots. Their bloodsucking, the irritation, their
busy scurrying give the illusion of warmth. We're hot at least
under our armpits, while our bodies are shivering.

(Rittner and Roth, 67)

German authorities tried to keep the operation of the killing
centres secret, just as they had attempted to conceal the murder
of people deemed handicapped and the mass shootings of Jews
and others in 1941, but in no case was secrecy really possible.
The killing operations were simply too big and involved far too
many people to keep them quiet.

Local populations watched full trains pull in and saw them
depart empty. The air for miles around was thick with the ashes
of burning bodies and heavy with the stench of death. Civilians
of all kinds came from Germany and elsewhere for jobs in the
camps. There were guards, of course, but also architects and engi-
neers, suppliers, telephone operators and secretaries. What did the
German and Polish women think whose job it was to type up lists
of the dead and prepare statistics of the numbers of people killed?

Presumably perpetrators, bystanders and onlookers found ways
to live with their knowledge of the killing centres. One individual's account illustrates some of the forms denial and rationalisation
could take. Teresa Stangl was married to Franz Stangl, commandant first of Sobibor and then of Treblinka. A devout Catholic, she
had initially opposed her husband's involvement with the Nazi
Party. According to Mrs. Stangl, she had never really understood
his position in the T-4 programme; she claimed she did not know
the nature of the programmes he administered.

Later Teresa Stangl moved to Sobibor to be near her husband.
From their house near the camp she could not see the activities
inside. One day a drunken co-worker of her husband's called on
her. He told her the details of Franz's job. Horrified Mrs. Stangl
confronted her husband. He denied any direct connection with
killing and assured his wife that he was just responsible for routine administration. Nevertheless she found herself unable to have
sexual relations with him for some time. Eventually she moved
away and they continued their marriage from a distance.

Despite her misgivings Mrs. Stangl stood by her husband. He loved her and would have done anything for her, she said. Once, she admitted in an interview that he would have chosen her over his work if she had given him an ultimatum, but later she insisted that she could have done nothing.

What of the Jews? What could Jews in Europe know in 1942 and 1943 of the killing centres? The answer is complicated by geography. Clearly Jews farther away – in Greece, for example – might have access to very little reliable information, but even Polish Jews, at least in the early stages of the killing centres' operation, could have problems grasping the reality of genocide. The word 'genocide' did not even exist until after the Second World War. Perhaps one account can illustrate. Piotrków Trybunalski, in the incorporated territories, was home to about 11,400 Jews, some twenty-two per cent of the overall population. Since October 1939 the Jews of Piotrków had been confined to a ghetto. In the spring of 1942, two young Jewish men escaped from Chelmno. They arrived in Piotrków and revealed the truth about German gassings of Jews. Most people refused to believe their ears. Why, during wartime, when it was well known that Germany had a serious shortage of labour, would the Germans try to slaughter every Polish Jew?

The leaders of the community met. Desperate to reassure themselves, they decided that the excesses the two young men had witnessed must be regional aberrations. Everyone knew that the SS commander Odilo Globocnik in Lublin was exceptionally vicious. Surely nothing so terrible could happen in their district. Were the Jewish leaders of Piotrków naive? Maybe, but perhaps that innocence is to their credit. Who could imagine mass gassings as part of systematic annihilation of Jews? Such a thing had never happened. Nazi planners in turn manipulated and exploited that inability to believe the worst.

Hope, even false hope, had some advantages over despair. One of the chroniclers of the Warsaw ghetto wrote, 'It is good that we console ourselves, for even if these are false hopes, they keep us from collapsing'. For the most part those Jews who grasped German intentions toward them could do nothing anyway. In the summer of 1942, Adam Czerniaków was head of the Jewish Council in Warsaw. When the Germans ordered him to hand over the children of the ghetto, he knew that they would be killed. Powerless to stop the slaughter, Czerniaków took the only way out still left to him: he committed suicide.

Not all of the Jews targeted in the Holocaust ended up in killing centres. Many Jews fled, taking refuge where they could. Others hid and still others 'passed' as Gentiles. An estimated 80,000 to 120,000 Jews were hidden in Poland; maybe half of those survived the war. Many of the Jews in hiding were children. It was easier to persuade non- Jews to have pity on children than on adults, who took up more space, ate more and were harder to explain. It tended to be more difficult to find hiding places for Jewish boys than for girls. In Europe very few Christian parents had their sons circumcised. So Jewish boys had their religion marked on their bodies in a visible way. It was not uncommon for police or local collaborators hunting for Jews to demand that men or boys pull down their pants so that they could see if they had been circumcised.

The decision to put a child into hiding was agonising for parents. Whom could one trust? When was hiding the best option? Was it not better to stay together no matter what? How could one leave a child one might never see again? Only as adults have many of the people hidden as Jewish children during the war recounted their experiences publicly. Here are two of their stories.

Henny. Henny was the daughter of Lithuanian Jews from Kovno. When she was just a year and a half old she and her parents were forced to move into the ghetto. For more than two years Henny's parents hid her in a small room that had been a walk-in pantry, but when she developed whooping cough it became too risky to keep her there. So they arranged for a Lithuanian Christian family outside the ghetto to take her in.

Henny's mother also arranged a hiding place for her two-year-old niece, Shoshana, after Germans shot the little girl's father. She made contact with a Lithuanian priest who got false papers for Shoshana and placed her in a convent. Later the nuns passed her on to a family of pig farmers. Miraculously, Shoshana,

Henny's parents and Henny (Henia Wisgardisky Lewin) all survived the war.

Rudy. Rudy was a little boy in the Netherlands. He survived the war in about twenty different hiding places, most of them in rural Holland. He remembers spending three days with a Jewish family in the woods while Germans searched the area. He heard German vehicles and dogs at night, but he stayed hidden under branches and leaves and they did not find him. Later two young women hid him with a group of ten other children. Several times a local Dutch policeman warned them of an impending raid. Once, they stayed in a cave for two days until it was safe to return. Eventually the group had to be split up. Only after the war, as adults, did some of them, including Rudy, now known as Yehudi Lindeman, find one another again.

Concentration Camps: Microcosms of the Third Reich

Killing centres were just one part of the vast network of German camps that had been expanding since 1933. Those who passed through the killing centres were overwhelmingly Jewish, although Gypsies were murdered there as well. Other kinds of camps included a much wider range of inmates. The years 1942 and 1943 were also a time when the Germans incarcerated huge numbers of people from all over Europe. A closer look at the concentration camps belongs in this discussion of the peak years of killing.

The total number of Nazi German camps of various kinds is not known, but it must be in the thousands. An estimated 18 million people passed through the camps; some 11 million died there. Many of those who survived bore deep scars, physical and psychological. In crucial ways Nazi concentration camps were microcosms of the Third Reich. The camps reflected the nature of Nazism and the Nazi system would have been impossible without the camps. German practices inside the camps echoed methods used elsewhere. The principle of divide and conquer was evident, for example, as was promotion of rivalry among German authorities with the end result of increasing brutality toward the victims.

Political prisoners, such as communists, Jehovah's Witnesses, homosexual men, common criminals, so-called asocials and critics of the regime, all served terms that in some cases proved fatal. Representatives of all those groups were still found in large numbers in the German camps during the war.

German conquests brought influxes of new kinds of prisoners too. German police arrested Polish and French communists and socialists as well as members of resistance groups from all over Europe. These inmates were not gassed, but they were beaten, starved, used for experiments and forced to do backbreaking labour. Some of them survived only a few weeks. Others lived for months and a few made it longer, often because they managed to wrangle some kind of privileged position in the camp.

Camps often used for political prisoners included Gross-Rosen, Stutthof, Bergen-Belsen, Flossenbürg and Ravensbrück for women, but there were many others. Even these names often encompassed a vast network of satellite facilities; Buchenwald, for example, included some 134 satellite camps. Another type of mass-detention facilities was the labour camps. Most of their inmates were non-Jewish women and men from conquered nations. German authorities used them for work connected to military requirements, in factories, mines, quarries and production of armaments. One example was Dora-Mittelbau, a camp in north-central Germany not far from the city of Göttingen. In its extensive underground facility slave labourers built V-2 rockets.

The German state viewed slave workers as a renewable resource; their lives had no value. Death tolls in such camps were astronomical. Toward the end of the war, as more Jews were kept alive for labour, they died in even greater numbers than the rest of the prisoners. Camp organisers quartered the Jews separately, gave them less food and treated them even more harshly than they did the Gentile inmates.

Like the killing centres, concentration camps specialized in brutality, with an eye to comfort and ease for the staff. Buchenwald had a zoo; many had gardens and, beginning in

1943, brothels staffed by sex slaves from the occupied territories. Sometimes camp authorities also assigned German 'asocial' women – lesbians, communists and criminals – to brothels. Clients included staff and especially privileged male prisoners.

All of the big camps, even places such as Dora-Mittelbau, had orchestras. Often they included Gypsies, popular as musicians in Europe, or trained classical musicians. There was no shortage of candidates; Europe in the 1940s was a very musical place. Orchestras performed to entertain the guards, to send the prisoners off to work and sometimes during executions in the camps. They played well-known marches, arias, folk songs and even Christmas carols. The cynicism of those behind the camp system is evident in other ways too. A sign over the gate of Auschwitz read *Arbeit macht frei* – 'work liberates'. Buchenwald, built in 1937, had its own slogan: *Jedem das Seine* – 'to each his own'.

German authorities recruited for high-ranking positions at the camps from within the German police. They hired unskilled or semiskilled workers to be guards at the lower levels. At Ravensbrück, for example, women guards were recruited through ads that promised job security, a responsible position and wages higher than many unskilled positions. Successful candidates underwent only a very short training course.

Outside of Germany, SS men took the top positions in the camps. Often they had been trained at German camps such as Dachau. Lowlier guards commonly came from subject populations; for example, ethnic Germans from Eastern Europe, Ukrainians, Latvians or Croatians. Jobs in the camps gave individuals a chance to enrich themselves at the expense of the inmates. They also provided an opportunity to lord it over one's local enemies. For example, the Germans hired Croatians to guard Serbs, Yugoslavian Gypsies and Jews; they often used Ukrainians against Poles. Working conditions that tolerated and even encouraged drunkenness, rape and brutality appealed especially to sadists and thugs.

Women occupied almost all of the same positions that men did, at least at the lower levels. Generally women prisoners had women guards. There were also female SS auxiliary units, usually assigned to communication duties and housekeeping for SS men at the front. It was no secret that these women, chosen on the basis of their supposedly valuable 'blood', were expected to help German SS men resist the temptation of sexual liaisons with 'non-Aryans' by making themselves available.

About 2,000 female guards assisted the SS at the Ravensbrück camp for women. Some women, like some men, were notorious for cruelty. Most infamous were Irma Grese, a guard at Auschwitz and the 'Bitch of Buchenwald', Ilse Koch, wife of Commandant Karl Koch. Frau Koch, though not herself a guard, was active and visible in the camp. After the war, wild rumours circulated about her sexual deviancy and fondness for lampshades and other household decorations made of tattooed human flesh. Some of the most horrific stories about Ilse Koch were never proven, but what seems clear is that to prisoners and outside observers alike, the involvement of women in Nazi brutality seemed even more shocking than the behaviour of men.

German authorities in the camps also appointed some prisoners to supervise and control other inmates. Such prisoner functionaries became known as kapos. Often the leaders of labour gangs, kapos had access to some power and privilege. At the same time they remained answerable to camp authorities. The use of kapos encouraged development of elaborate hierarchies of power within the camps. Such divisions, of course, benefited the Nazis, who needed to invest less time and energy to control prisoners who were at odds with one another. By rewarding kapos for brutality against fellow prisoners, German officials continued to undermine solidarity. Every kapo realised that he or she could be replaced at a moment's notice. There were plenty of prisoners eager to increase their chances to survive by accepting positions of privilege within the camp.

To reinforce divisions among prisoners, camp officials introduced a system of coloured badges to identify the various groups. Criminals wore a green triangle; communists received red. Gypsies and 'asocials' were marked with a black badge and Jehovah's Witnesses with purple. A pink triangle designated homosexual men. A yellow triangle – or more often two triangles together to form a six-pointed star – identified Jews.

Camp authorities recruited most kapos from the green and red triangles, the two groups at the top of the hierarchy. Kapos from the other groups were not unknown, but it was hard for people to assert authority over those considered above them. Jews, marked as they were for death, invariably occupied the bottom of the hierarchy. Often the other prisoners ostracised and tormented homosexual men in particularly vicious ways. Nevertheless, in a few cases Jews and homosexuals too served as kapos or in similar positions.

The perpetrators devised special humiliations for members of each of their victim groups and even the same treatment was experienced in different ways by people whose own values and taboos set them apart from one another. German aggressors often launched attacks on Jews on the Jewish holidays. Camp officials frequently put tough, homophobic kapos in charge of gay prisoners. Nakedness of adults in front of their own children was particularly taboo among Sinti and Roma, so orders to strip carried extra humiliation for members of those groups.

Many accounts from the camps stress the importance of support from other prisoners. German officials tried to divide and conquer their prey. They set people against one another by forcing competition for absurdly small prizes – an extra crust of bread, a button, a piece of string. Some of the most powerful stories of the camps explain how inmates countered such efforts to isolate them. Primo Levi, an Italian Jew, tells how he reminded himself and a co-worker of their humanity by reciting lines from Dante's *Divine Comedy*: 'Think of your breed; for brutish ignorance / Your mettle was not made; you were made men, / To follow after knowledge and excellence'. Sara Nomberg-Przytyk, a Jewish communist woman from Poland, attributes her survival to an anonymous woman in the next train car who sacrificed her own blanket so that Sara would not freeze to death.

Almost every memoir of the concentration camps mentions Gypsies. For Gypsies, like Jews, 1942 and 1943 were the peak years of killing. As German forces consolidated their hold on subject territories, they located more and more groups of Roma. In all, German perpetrators and their accomplices killed an estimated one-quarter to half a million Roma, including many children. Thousands of others were sterilised.

Nazi ideology considered Gypsies impure and unworthy to live. One of the absurdities of the situation was that according to Nazi terminology, Gypsies were in fact more 'Aryan' than the Nordic Germans. Gypsies originated in India, home of the original Aryan tribe, whose name was appropriated by European racists for their own purposes. The Romani language even bears some similarity to Indian languages.

SS leader Himmler was fascinated by Gypsies. He set up an office within the German Ministry of Health called the Racial Hygiene and Population Research Centre. Its main task was to study the approximately 30,000 German Gypsies, draw up gene-alogies of them and identify those considered 'pure'. Information it gathered made it possible to locate Gypsies and kill them.

Initially Himmler wanted to preserve some 'pure Gypsies' in a kind of reservation or zoo, where they could be examined by future German scientists. 'Experts' estimated that between three and four per cent of the Gypsies would fall into that category. Later Himmler abandoned that idea. The German government provided generous funding for research on the Roma and many scientists got involved in the project, especially social scientists such as anthropologists.

Gypsies shared many of the experiences of Jews in the Holocaust. Classified, dispossessed, deported, forced into ghettos, shot into mass graves and gassed, they too were marked for anni-hilation, but Nazi authorities never devoted the same fanatical energy to killing Gypsies as they did to eradication of Jews. They seemed to regard Gypsies as a nuisance rather than part of some diabolical, international conspiracy. Either way, however, Sinti and Roma were targeted for murder.

The experience of Nazi persecution highlighted just how iso-lated Gypsies were within Europe. Church leaders in Germany protested the killing of people deemed handicapped in 1941. In the 1943 Rosenstrasse protest, the Gentile wives of German Jewish men forced cancellation of plans to deport their husbands to the east to be killed. In Poland, the Netherlands, Ukraine,

Yugoslavia and elsewhere, non-Jews risked their lives to hide Jewish children and adults, sometimes for years. Who protested on behalf of the Roma? Who beyond their own circles sheltered Gypsy children from death? There may have been some people who did so, but their stories are not well known.

Hitler's regime had harassed and persecuted homosexuals since its early years in power. Between 1933 and 1945 German courts convicted 50,000 men on charges related to homosexuality. The year 1942 brought a record number of arrests, mostly of Germans. Nazi ideology regarded homosexuals, particularly men, as a threat to 'Aryan racial health' because they refused to take part in producing children for the fatherland. In wartime, especially in 1942 and 1943, as German casualties began to climb, the German leadership took that offence very seriously. German police arrested thousands of men accused of homosexual activity. Between 5,000 and 7,000 of these men perished in the Second World War, perhaps half of them in concentration camps.

Like every group targeted by Nazi Germany, homosexuals had experiences unique to them. For one thing, Nazi theorists and practitioners were confused as to whether homosexuality was biological or acquired. So German officials vacillated between treating gay men as if they were racial enemies or handling them as candidates for re-education. In 1933 Himmler had estimated there were between one and four million homosexually inclined men in Germany, but even the homophobic Himmler never mounted a systematic effort to wipe out homosexuality as such. Instead police made arrests on the basis of denunciations and raids.

By 1942 many concentration camps had homosexual inmates. Sachsenhausen and Buchenwald housed the largest numbers, at times in separate 'queer blocks'. Gay men, like Jews and Gypsies, fell near the bottom of the camp hierarchy. Viewed even by many fellow prisoners as the scum of humanity, they suffered severely from torture, beating and medical experimentation. Perhaps their isolation from other prisoners explains the extremely high death rate among gay inmates in Nazi camps; it was about sixty per cent as compared to forty-one per cent for political prisoners and thirty-five per cent for Jehovah's Witnesses.

As the war went on and German demands for labour increased, officials allowed some of the homosexuals in Sachsenhausen to be released as civilian labourers, but there were strings attached. In order to be pronounced 'cured', a candidate for rehabilitation had to perform 'properly' with a prostitute from the camp brothel. If he failed but agreed to castration, he might still be released for heavy labour. Some gay men also won release by volunteering for special penal units sent to the very worst areas of the front. Few of those individuals survived.

Harry Pauli, an actor from Berlin, was one of the rare exceptions. Sentenced on grounds of homosexual activity to twenty months' imprisonment, he served eight months before being drafted into the *Wehrmacht*. Ridiculed and abused by the other men, he tried to desert but was caught. His punishment was a year with the penal battalion *Dirlewanger*. Thanks to a non-fatal wound, he witnessed the end of the war from a military hospital in Prague.

In significant ways persecution of homosexual men in Nazi camps continued what went on outside. After liberation of the camps in 1945, occupation authorities arrested again some gay men, reconvicted them and sent them back to prison. Homosexual activity remained a criminal act in West Germany until the 1960s. Illegality and social stigma account for the silence that shrouded the treatment of gay men in Nazi Germany until the 1970s and 1980s.

Resistance

All over Europe people resisted Nazism in many ways. There were individual acts of defiance and heroism; there was sabotage and rescue of people targeted for killing. The Communist Party organised resistance groups, often with backing from the Soviet Union. The British Special Operations Executive supported nationalist guerrilla movements from France to Yugoslavia and Greece.

Any discussion of resistance has to define the term. Does opposition have to be effective to count as resistance? Does it need to be organised? Armed? Unmixed with collaboration or opportunism? I define 'resistance' as any actions taken with the intent of thwarting Nazi German goals in the war, actions that carried with them risk of punishment. Under this definition, resistance could be individual or group, armed or unarmed. Whether we talk about intelligence as resistance, Jewish resistance, or resistance within Germany, all discussion of resistance serves to counter some popular misconceptions about the Second World War.

Resistance can take many forms. Many anti-Nazi organisations took enormous risks to collect and transmit information that would undermine the German war effort. One of the most remarkable examples of intelligence as resistance involved a member of the Polish underground named Jan Karski. Born in 1914 Karski made a career before the war in the Polish Foreign Service. He joined the Polish Army in 1939 and was taken prisoner by the Soviets. Karski escaped and became part of the Polish underground. In the fall of 1942, Karski was charged with a mission to London. He was to carry a report to the Polish government-in-exile that described the situation in German-occupied Poland.

Leaders of two Jewish organisations learned of Karski's impending trip to London and asked if he would also carry a report for them. Karski agreed. The Jews of Poland were being exterminated, the Jewish leaders told Karski. Eventually Hitler would lose the war, they said, but he would win his war against Polish Jewry. The Jewish leaders asked Karski to tell the highest circles of the Allied governments that Hitler planned to kill every Jew regardless of the outcome of the war. Polish Jews and even Polish Gentiles were helpless to stop the destruction. Only the Allied governments could save the Jews.

Before they sent him off with their message, the Jewish leaders wanted Karski to see for himself what they meant. They smuggled him into the Jewish ghetto in Warsaw and then into the killing centre at Belzec. Karski was devastated by what he saw. After an hour in Belzec disguised as a guard he broke down and had to be taken out, vomiting blood. Karski became one of the first eyewitnesses to present to the West the whole truth about the fate of the Jews in occupied Poland.

Karski delivered his reports as promised. He met with British, American and Polish representatives; he spoke directly with

Prime Minister Churchill in Britain and President Roosevelt in the United States and sought out journalists and other opinion leaders. All of Karski's perseverance and heroism did not get the results he so desperately wanted. People simply did not comprehend. After U.S. Supreme Court Justice Felix Frankfurter listened to Karski's report, he responded that he could not believe it. Frankfurter did not mean he thought Karski was lying; he simply could not grasp the enormity of what he had heard. Karski found no effective help for the Jews of Poland from any nation, government, or church. Only a few courageous individuals like him were willing to act. Karski survived the war and moved to Washington, D.C., where he taught political science for many years. He died in 2000.

Jan Karski's experience highlights the issue of Allied knowledge of Nazi crimes. What did the British or the Americans know and when? By late 1942, when Karski prepared his report, at least some people within the Allied leadership had access to a great deal of information about German atrocities. Already in 1941 British code breakers were reading German dispatches, including those from the Soviet Union describing the Order Police's murders of Jews and other civilians. Reports from eyewitnesses and individuals who had managed to escape from Nazi prisons and camps reached world leaders through all kinds of channels and every government had its own sources of intelligence. The press offered considerable detail for the reading public – in the United States, Canada, Switzerland and elsewhere – so that it is not possible to speak of mass murder as if it were a Nazi secret.

Nevertheless a number of factors prevented the Allies from broadcasting their knowledge of slaughter of European Jews and other people. Most important there was a war to be won, a war whose outcome was by no means clear in 1942 or even 1943. In particular military leaders in the United States and Britain emphasised the need to stay focused and avoid being distracted by 'sideshows'. No doubt some individuals were indifferent to the fate of Europe's Jews or even had antisemitic notions of their own. Nevertheless it is probably fair to assume that many people simply could not grasp the unprecedented nature of this war of annihilation and even those who could tended to be preoccupied with their own issues and struggles.

Jewish resistance of various kinds was much more widespread than many people used to assume. All across German-occupied Europe, Jews and other opponents of Nazism took to the woods, often forming partisan units to combat the Germans. The existence of Jewish partisans was precarious at best. They lived from hand to mouth, stealing when necessary, arranging secretly for deliveries of food and spending hours and even days in holes in the ground when danger threatened. Afraid that the presence of Jews nearby would jeopardise their own security, Gentiles often denounced or killed their Jewish counterparts. Nevertheless, as German police records for 1943 indicate, Jews in the woods of Eastern Europe managed to acquire explosives and weapons and to perform acts of sabotage against the Nazi system. In some cases, young Jewish men and women even married in the woods and gave birth to children there.

In Lithuania in early 1942, about 10,000 Jewish men and women were fighting as partisans. At least thirty different Jewish partisan groups existed in the General Government alone. Jews also revolted in such major ghettos as Warsaw and Bialystok. In general, the groups that banded together were desperate, pitifully small and barely armed. Their chances of success were minimal, but still they defied Nazi power.

Even in the camps, under the most adverse conditions, resistance in many forms occurred. Numerous survivors' memoirs tell the story of the beautiful dancer in Auschwitz who seized a gun from an SS man and shot him. Both Sobibor and Treblinka had revolts in 1943. In October 1944, Jewish prisoners at Auschwitz-Birkenau blew up the camp's fourth crematorium. Starved, abandoned by the world and robbed of their property, the Jews were in a weak position to offer resistance to the Germans. Nevertheless, like others they did resist – violently, passively, spiritually, physically and emotionally – throughout the entire process of the 'Final Solution'.

The Jewish ghetto in Warsaw must have been one of the last places the Germans expected an uprising in the spring of 1943.

By then eighty per cent of the population of the Warsaw ghetto was already gone, most of them murdered at Treblinka in the summer of 1942. Initially the Warsaw Jewish rebels had little support even within their own community. The Jewish fighting organisation had fewer than five hundred fighters. Armed only with gasoline bombs, hand grenades, pistols, one or two submachine guns and about ten rifles, they must have seemed unlikely to accomplish anything other than rapid mass suicide. Yet this ragtag band managed to mount the largest armed resistance organised by any targets of Nazi mass murder during the Second World War. What happened?

In January 1943 German SS planned to liquidate what was left of the Warsaw ghetto. To their surprise they met with organised resistance from ghetto Jews. Unwilling to risk casualties they gave up the attempt a few days later. Four months later, on 19 April 1943, the Germans returned much better prepared. More than 2,000 men came with armoured vehicles, artillery, flame throwers, heavy-calibre machine guns and even aircraft. For their part Warsaw Jews had prepared an elaborate system of bunkers and underground passages. Determined to make a stand they held off the Germans for four weeks.

The SS burned down buildings, dynamited and smoked out the Jews' bunkers until they won the upper hand. The Jewish fighters' tenacity was astounding, especially because the ghetto was sealed off and it was almost impossible to get weapons or supplies in. The Germans crushed the uprising at a huge cost in human lives, almost all of them Jewish. The SS commander reported sixteen German dead; the actual number may have been slightly higher. Small pockets of Jewish resistance continued for weeks, but in the end, more than 56,000 Jews surrendered. The Germans shot many on the spot and transported the others to killing centres and labour camps. Thousands of Jewish dead remained buried in the rubble.

The Warsaw ghetto uprising marked the first large-scale urban revolt against German occupation in Europe. It did not save Jewish lives. To the contrary, it may have led the Germans to use more force more quickly in the future when they set out to liquidate ghettos. Given their intention to kill the Jews anyway, however, it could hardly have worsened the Jews' situation. Certainly its moral and symbolic importance as an assertion of life cannot be underestimated.

Examples of resistance within Germany are few although so-called Aryan Germans were certainly in the strongest position to oppose the Nazi regime. The early years of Hitler's rule had paralysed organisations that might have been the focal point for resistance activities. Members of the Communist Party, for example, had been dispersed, although they managed to retain some links to one another and preserve some pockets of resistance. The time to oppose Nazism had been in the first phases of its rule in Germany. By 1942 and 1943 the stakes were much higher. Only in 1944, once Germany was clearly losing the war, would more opponents of the regime be emboldened to acts of resistance. Still there were some important incidents earlier on.

In the winter of 1942 a professor and a handful of students at the University of Munich formed an organisation they called the 'White Rose'. The key figures were Kurt Huber, a professor of philosophy; Willi Graf, a devout Catholic; Alexander Schmorell, son of a Russian woman; Christoph Probst and Hans Leipelt, both of whom had Jewish family members; and a brother and sister, Hans and Sophie Scholl. Both Scholls had been enthusiastic Nazis as children, but as students they broke from those ideas. Hans's tour of duty as a medical orderly on the eastern front gave him first-hand exposure to the horrors of Nazi German warfare.

Under the name 'the White Rose', the group printed a series of leaflets decrying the crimes of Nazism. The last issue, in February 1943, was called 'The Spirit Lives!' In it the students protested the moral destruction of German youth. Nazism, they wrote, had turned German young people into godless, shameless, unscrupulous murderers.

Police caught Hans and Sophie Scholl along with three of their friends, including Professor Huber. They were interrogated and tried for spreading malicious and defeatist rumours against the state. Sophie, a twenty-two-year-old philosophy student at the time, addressed the court as guards led her away: 'What we have written is in all your minds, but you lack the courage to say it aloud'. Hans and Sophie Scholl and Christoph Probst were executed in February 1943. Schmorell, Huber, Graf and Leipelt were tried and executed later. The university remained silent; there was neither protest nor any show of solidarity from administrators, faculty or students on behalf of the members of their community. After the war the University of Munich named its main quadrangle after the Scholl siblings.

There were enormous barriers to resistance, especially for members of groups targeted for persecution and death, in German-controlled Europe. One of the most significant was the Nazi policy of exacting reprisals. The Germans made entire communities suffer for acts of resistance on a scale massively out of proportion to the supposed offence.

In June 1942 members of the Czech underground, with support from the British Special Operations Executive, assassinated Reinhard Heydrich. The Germans responded with total destruction of the town of Lidice, near Prague. They murdered all 199 men there as well as many of the women and children. Those remaining were removed for Germanisation.

In 1943 a group of Jewish fighters from Vilna escaped from the ghetto to join partisans in the forest. Somehow they got their hands on a few weapons and attacked some Germans outside the city. In retaliation, the Gestapo seized the entire family of each Jewish fugitive or everyone who lived with him or her. They also arrested the leaders of all of the Jewish work parties in the vicinity, together with their families. All of those people were shot.

The policy of reprisals was a major deterrent. It probably explains why revolts in the Jewish ghettos often occurred only after the rebels were certain that death was planned for them and those close to them anyway. Divisions within communities could present another obstacle to resistance. What would be the prospects? What were the best tactics? Were some would-be heroes risking increased horror for other people? After years of war and occupation few people had the prerequisites for resistance. Overwhelmed by events, isolated, exhausted and hungry, they could not hope for much success when it came to stopping Nazi Germany. Given those conditions we should perhaps be surprised at how much rather than how little resistance there was in German-occupied Europe.

The topic of resistance easily lends itself to manipulation and stereotypes. For decades the insistence of the post-war French governments that they were the heirs of the heroic French resistance made it impossible to face the realities of French collaboration. The fact that Jews were enormously over-represented among French resisters was rarely acknowledged. Old stereotypes of Jewish passivity in turn blinded many scholars and other observers to the abundant evidence of specific Jewish resistance. It is tempting to offer resistance as a sort of antidote to the depressing subject of the Second World War and the Holocaust, but some caution is in order. For one thing, a focus on heroism – those 'lights in the darkness' who dared to defy the Nazi juggernaut – can serve both to encourage us with the possibilities for resistance and to remind us of just how many people participated in the crimes of the Third Reich or stood by silently.

It is also important to keep in mind that resistance arguably did not change the course of the war. It was military might that defeated Nazi Germany; with very few exceptions it was the Red Army and the western Allies that liberated occupied territories from German control. Nevertheless resistance had a crucial impact. To other conquered peoples it sent a message that they were not alone and that the Germans were not invincible. Resistance also left a positive legacy for a post-war world in which so many people had been compromised by collaboration and opportunism or paralysed by death and misery.

Thaddeus Stabholz experienced many of the events that have been addressed in this chapter. 'Teddy' Stabholz grew up in a middle class, assimilated Jewish family in Poland. He was a young medical student in Warsaw when the Second World War began. Months after the Germans defeated Poland, they forced Teddy, his father, his grandmother and the rest of his relatives to move into the Warsaw ghetto. Teddy's mother had died in 1938 of cancer; in 1941 his father was killed by the Germans.

Teddy was left alone 'like a homeless dog', he wrote later. With his fiancée, Fredzia, he survived as best he could on the food they could scrounge. Teddy cared for his grandmother too, until January 1943, when Germans beat her to death in the street. By that time, many of the Jews – especially the old, very young and sick – had already been taken out of the ghetto and sent to the gas chambers at the killing centre of Treblinka.

In early 1943 some of the young Jews left in the Warsaw ghetto organised an uprising against the Germans. Teddy and Fredzia were among them. They fought desperately with whatever weapons they had, but they were no match for the SS firepower. The Germans burned the ghetto, killed most of the people in it and sent the remaining few to Treblinka. There Fredzia was murdered, but Teddy, for some reason, was sent on to Majdanek, a labour camp as well as a killing centre. He remained a prisoner of the Germans in various camps for two more years.

Through extraordinary luck – if one can speak of good fortune in the context of genocide – Teddy Stabholz survived. Guards selected him to be killed at Majdanek but at the last minute pulled him out of the group and made him a medic. At Auschwitz-Birkenau he was starved, beaten and forced to carry enormous loads of water and cement for miles. He almost died of pneumonia. For a time he even had a 'job' delousing the body hair of fellow prisoners with Zyklon B, the same insecticide used in the gas chambers. Stabholz managed to win the favour of some senior prisoners and guards by 'operating' on the corns and calluses on their feet. In the summer of 1944, he witnessed the murder of all of the Gypsies in Auschwitz.

Stabholz endured excruciating work, plagues of typhus and lice and transfers to camps farther from the front lines. At one point he resigned himself to death, but a vision of his father and mother encouraged him and revived his will to live. In April 1945 American troops fighting their way through southern Germany found Stabholz and some fellow prisoners who had escaped from the SS and hidden in the woods. After spending time in a displaced persons camp in Germany, Teddy emigrated to the United States. He graduated from medical school and opened a practice in Ohio. Dr Stabholz's memoir of the Holocaust is called *Seven Hells*.

8

Death Throes and Killing Frenzies, 1944–1945

If the Germans were to lose the war, Hitler once said, they would bring down with them 'a world in flames'. Hitler kept that promise. The last stage of the war in Europe, from 1944 until May 1945, brought German retreat, defeat and collapse, but the Nazi Empire remained bloody and destructive until its very end.

At the beginning of 1944, many Germans still expected to win the war. By the end of the year, few persisted in that hope. Germany was under assault – from the air, from the Red Army in the east and after D-Day in June, from the Allies in the west. Even internally there were some signs of weakening, but it still took until May 1945 for total collapse.

The death throes of the Third Reich were deadly themselves – far less for the privileged elite of the regime than for its victims. Even as defeat became ever more certain, killing went on in many settings. The Allies, both eastern and western, had to fight hard and suffer many casualties to advance. When a plot to assassinate Hitler and stage a coup failed in July 1944, the Nazi regime responded with a vicious crackdown on its own population.

Well into 1945, Nazi programmes of mass murder continued in the ever-shrinking territories that Germany controlled. Most of the Gypsies in Auschwitz were gassed in 1944. The murder of almost 400,000 Hungarian Jews took place that summer too. Throughout the last year of the war, the Germans kept opening new labour camps. As they abandoned killing centres and camps in areas lost to Allied advances, guards sent the inmates still left alive on murderous treks known as death marches. None of that killing halted the disintegration of German power, but it ensured that the defeat of Nazism was accompanied by the maximum amount of carnage.

Allied Advances and Conditions in Germany

From late 1943, the Soviets remained on the offensive against Germany. The Red Army made rapid advances in 1944 and on the third anniversary of Operation Barbarossa – in June 1944 – the Soviets launched a massive offensive against the German Army Group Centre.

By the end of 1944, odds on Germany's eastern front were heavily in favour of the Soviets. Against the total German strength of between 2 and 3.5 million men loomed 6 million Red Army soldiers. A German disadvantage of one German to every five Soviets was common; in some places the odds were closer to one to thirty or forty. Still the Soviets fought at a tremendous cost. Even at the end of 1944, the Germans were still killing or wounding four Soviets for every casualty of their own. The huge Soviet advantage in replacements – and the need to send in wave after wave of those troops – itself implied the staggering death toll that the fighting took on the Red Army. It is estimated that the battle for Berlin alone cost half a million people their lives or their health. Small wonder that as soon as it could, the Soviet leadership would demand massive territorial gains and enormous reparations from the Germans.

Air raids on Germany by the Royal Air Force and the U.S. air force peaked between January 1944 and January 1945. In the words of U.S. President Franklin Roosevelt, 'Fortress Europe' had no roof. American planes alone made some 755,000 sorties that year and dropped 1.4 million tons of bombs on Germany and German-controlled territories. Much of that aerial bombing was inaccurate, so that planes often dropped their loads indiscriminately in and around major German cities. Allied bombing may have killed as many as 500,000 German civilians.

Attacks from the air hit the petroleum and chemical industries hard. By September the Germans could supply only ten per cent of their needs in aviation fuel. By early 1945, the flow of fuel and ammunition to the German fronts had almost stopped. Nevertheless the German war machine demonstrated remarkable resilience to the assault from the air. Electric power stations continued to function and German war production persisted during the last stage of the war. Of course a regime obsessed with public opinion ensured that these achievements were accompanied by massive 'armaments propaganda'. Did manufacturing of fighter planes peak in late 1944? Was total German military output in 1944 really more than five times the country's 1939 level? Eager to depict Germany as invincible in the face of economically superior enemies, Goebbels and his minions exaggerated and celebrated the triumphs of mass production and trumpeted the imminent appearance of new miracle weapons.

Such claims were encouraged and supported by Albert Speer (1905–1981), Hitler's minister of armaments and war production from 1942. A trained architect and a friend and confidante of Hitler, Speer also indulged the *Führer*'s passion for designing giant buildings for the Nazi world of the future. The Allies captured Speer at the end of the war and brought him to trial for his role in German crimes against foreign labour. He served twenty years in prison and published memoirs and a diary. Unlike almost all of his Nazi counterparts, it appears that by the end of his life Speer was repentant toward victims of the Third Reich and regretted his role in German crimes.

The real key to German wartime production was the massive use of slave labour. In 1939 there were about 300,000 forced labourers in Germany. By 1944 that number had skyrocketed to 7.5 million. It was above all these non-Germans – from Russia, Ukraine, Belorussia, Poland, France, the Netherlands, Italy,

Hungary and elsewhere – who bore the tremendously high human cost involved in outfitting the German war machine.

The impact of the attack from the air on the morale of German civilians is hard to gauge. Certainly air raids alone did not destroy German support of Hitler's regime, although it is possible that the destruction of German cities made it easier for Germans to recognise defeat and surrender at the end of the war. Much easier to measure was the physical impact of the bombing. Allied raids destroyed between 4.5 and 5 million habitations, so that Germans experienced an incredible shortage of housing in the last stages of the war. Production of consumer goods fell dramatically at the same time.

By 1944 the German economy was in serious trouble. Hitler's insistence on protecting the home front from the costs of war meant deficit financing on a huge scale. The idea, of course, was that the vanquished would pay for the war. As long as the Germans were victorious they supported themselves through theft and plunder. Once the tide of the war turned, however, they were left with the hollowness of their own economy. Printing large amounts of money sparked inflation. Rapidly rising prices, in conjunction with stringent wage and price controls, led – as that particular combination always does – to the emergence of an active black market. In the German case, even before the war was over cigarettes began to overtake the official currency as the preferred medium of exchange.

On 6 June 1944, in a massive action with the code name Operation Overlord, the western Allies landed in Normandy in north-western France. D-Day, as it became known, was the greatest amphibious assault ever. The numbers alone are staggering. More than 4,000 Allied ships landed 176,000 troops after 10,000 aircraft dropped 10,000 tons of explosives on the German defenders of the French coast.

By the end of July, after hard fighting and heavy casualties, Allied forces broke out of the beachheads and began to drive the Germans eastward. In August 1944 the Allies liberated Paris. The next month the western Allies under General Dwight Eisenhower crossed the German border. Germany's new 'wonder weapons' –

the V-1 and V-2 rockets – were deadly enough for those targeted, but they were no match for the onslaught of Soviet, British and American artillery and tanks during 1944.

In the wake of D-Day and the Soviet offensive of June 1944, Hitler named Goebbels the Reich plenipotentiary for total war. Together the *Führer* and his loyal associate painted a gruesome picture for the Germans of what lay in store if they were defeated. Germans could expect only the harshest of treatment from the vengeful Allies, they warned. Their scare tactics assumed widespread knowledge of the atrocities that Germans had committed throughout the preceding years, especially in the east. It was as if Hitler and Goebbels were taunting the German public with its complicity – we Germans are all in this together, they insisted, and all of us will have to pay the price if we surrender.

Meanwhile Hitler and Goebbels instructed the German press to keep blaming the Jews for the war. U.S. President Roosevelt held out to Europeans the promise of the four freedoms: freedom of speech, freedom of worship, freedom from want and freedom from fear. Hitler, for his part, threatened the German public with his own version of what Allied victory would mean: 'Jewish poison, Bolshevik slaughter, capitalist exploitation and Anglo-American Imperialism'.

It was not love for his people that motivated Hitler's raving but an obsessive fixation on his own goals of race and space. 'I will shed no tears for the German people', he had once said in contemplating what defeat would mean. According to Hitler's logic, any people that allowed itself to be conquered proved its own unworthiness to wear the mantle of the master race.

Not internal dissension but military defeat eventually brought down the Nazi regime. Nevertheless there was one important attack from within Germany during the last year of the war: the plot of 20 July 1944. The plot was the work of a fairly disparate network of opponents of Hitler's regime. The conspirators included high-ranking military men who resented the way Hitler was conducting the war effort. Some of them hoped to overthrow his government and then join up with the western Allies against the communist Soviet Union. Others more loosely involved in the plan had moral and humanitarian motivations. Appalled by German crimes against civilians in the east, such people saw no option but overthrow of the dictator if Germany's soul were to be saved.

Typical of the humanistic side of the opposition to Hitler was Count Helmuth James von Moltke (1907–1945), a lawyer and devoted Christian who, from 1939 to 1944, was a war administration counsellor in the international law section of the German Armed Forces Supreme Command. Moltke organised a group of anti-Nazi friends and likeminded individuals who met during the war to make plans for a new, democratic Germany. Moltke, who struggled with issues of violence, did not support assassination, but he did urge military leaders to overthrow Hitler. Arrested already in January 1944, Moltke was hanged in Berlin-Plötzensee a year later.

Anti-communists, conservatives, liberals, monarchists and dedicated Christians all numbered among those who hoped to see Hitler assassinated or at least removed in July 1944. Although their visions for a reorganised Germany differed, they all saw the need to replace Hitler's rule with a government that would seek peace with the Allies and introduce reforms at home.

The plan for 20 July 1944 itself was straightforward. A high-ranking General Staff officer named Colonel Claus Schenck von Stauffenberg (1907–1944) would plant a bomb at a meeting in the 'Wolf's Lair', Hitler's East Prussian headquarters. The death of Hitler would then give the signal for a coup d'état in Berlin.

The plan failed. Stauffenberg set the bomb in his briefcase, placed it under the table around which the meeting was taking place and then left the building. As he drove toward Berlin he heard the explosion and assumed Hitler had been killed. In fact only part of the explosives went off and Hitler was barely injured. Instead of a successful coup the conspirators experienced the *Führer's* terrible revenge.

Stauffenberg was captured and shot by firing squad on the evening of 20 July 1944. He went to his death shouting, 'Long live Germany!' Others accused of participation in the plot were hauled before the so-called People's Court, publicly humiliated

and sent to prison. Hitler had many of them killed, some immediately, others only after some months. The assassination attempt
provided an excuse for a general crackdown within Germany on
anyone suspected of opposition.

In September 1944, Hitler ordered full deployment of
Germany's resources against the enemy through creation of a
Volkssturm – a 'people's storm'. The *Volkssturm* was to mobilise
all men between the ages of fifteen and sixty, adding a total of
1.5 million men under arms. Not just intended for local defence,
Volkssturm units were to close gaps in the regular *Wehrmacht* and
engage the enemy in combat.

Some of the *Volkssturm* boys and men fought valiantly and
desperately against the Red Army and the western Allies. Some
Volkssturm units were well organised and fairly well equipped.
Others were thrown together; thirteen-year-old boys stood on
bridges expecting to take on men in tanks and men in their sixties
took up arms to try to hold their villages. Some units took appall-
ing losses of life; others collapsed in the face of the Allied advance.

By early 1945 even Nazi true believers had to see that the war
was lost. The German army was falling apart. Increasing numbers of men deserted, although military authorities continued
to shoot those they caught and in many cases to arrest members of their families. Special courts-martial were set up with the
intent of frightening the German troops into reckless resistance.
Propaganda announced the existence of the Werewolf organisation to continue Nazi efforts behind enemy lines. Roving SS
units sought out and punished German civilians who expressed
defeatism, advised surrender or made contact with the enemy.
None of these measures slowed the Allied advance, but they did
reveal for anyone who had not yet noticed the heartless ruthlessness of National Socialism.

On 19 March 1945, Hitler gave what became known as the
Nero Order. He instructed Germans fleeing before the advancing Allies to destroy everything they left behind and leave nothing
for the enemy. The 'Nero Order' called for the destruction of all
installations serving military purposes, transportation, communication, industry and supply. At the same time Hitler ordered

the defence of German cities under threat of the death penalty for anyone disobeying his orders. When Speer suggested that the Germans too would starve if such measures were implemented, Hitler showed no concern.

A World in Flames

The unravelling of German power emboldened the regime's opponents in occupied Europe. Once again, as in 1943, the city of Warsaw was the site of a major revolt. By August 1944 the Red Army was approaching Warsaw from the east. Leaders of the Polish Home Army decided to try to liberate the city from the Germans themselves. The Home Army was the non-communist wing of the Polish resistance linked to traditional Polish nationalists and the Polish government-in-exile. Drawing on an armed force of about 25,000 people, Home Army leaders launched a large-scale uprising.

Instead of continuing their advance into Warsaw, Red Army units stopped on the east bank of the Vistula River and waited. Perhaps they did not want to risk confrontation with the Germans massing on Warsaw, or perhaps Stalin preferred to let German forces wipe out the anti-communist elements inside the city to clear the way for his own takeover. Whatever the reason, the Soviets abandoned the Polish insurgents.

German forces outnumbered and vastly outgunned the struggling Poles. Throwing everything they had into the effort, the Germans crushed the revolt by 2 October 1944. In the process they killed some 170,000 people in Warsaw. By the fall of 1944 the Germans' overall position was weak. Nevertheless they still had the might to wreak terrible destruction, especially on civilians. Soon after the Warsaw Uprising began, Hitler ordered the city levelled. German forces carried out the command. Unlike Moscow and Leningrad, which the Germans never conquered, or Paris, which they spared, Warsaw was flattened. It was an act of revenge unique even in the gory history of the Second World War, but typical of the killing frenzies of the last stage of Hitler's war.

The year 1944 also brought dramatic changes within those countries that had been partners in the German war effort. In September Finland signed an armistice with the Soviet Union and withdrew from the war. Finnish authorities had never handed over the small community of Jews in their country to the Germans to be killed. There had even been a few Finnish Jewish soldiers fighting alongside the *Wehrmacht* against the Soviet Union. The history of the Second World War and the Holocaust is full of such strange twists.

For some time already the authoritarian regimes in Romania and Hungary had been eager to get out of the war. By mid-1944 the Germans had to abandon hope of getting their hands on Romanian oil. By the autumn of 1944 the Soviets occupied Romania and Bulgaria and were moving toward Hungary and Yugoslavia. Both Romania and Bulgaria signed armistices with the Soviet Union and declared war on Germany.

In March 1944 the Germans had taken steps to prevent Hungary from capitulating. That month German forces occupied Hungary, their ally, to keep control of the territory and safeguard access to its resources. In October 1944, when the Hungarian leader Admiral Miklos Horthy was caught trying to cut a deal with the Soviets, Hitler had him overthrown. The Germans installed a Hungarian Fascist regime dependent on their support.

Until the spring of 1944 the Jews of Hungary had managed to stay out of German hands. In March 1944, however, when German forces moved into Hungary, they brought with them experts led by Adolf Eichmann who were intent on making sure that Hungarian Jews, too, would be annihilated. In the summer of 1944, Germans and Hungarian collaborators worked together to deport a large proportion of Hungary's Jewish population to Auschwitz-Birkenau. In hindsight it is clear that the war was lost for the Germans. Nevertheless, they continued to pursue their goal of racial purification in those areas still in their control. Between 15 May and 9 July 1944, German and Hungarian police crammed some 437,000 Hungarian Jews into 147 transports and sent them north to Auschwitz. As usual, Roma from Hungary shared that fate.

One of those Gypsies was fifteen-year-old Karoly Lendvai, who came from a town near Budapest. Rounded up by Hungarian police, he and his family walked forty miles to an internment camp, where they stayed for two weeks. Decades later Lendvai remembers his hunger and the pits overflowing with corpses as typhus raged among the prisoners. Among his most vivid memories is the double-barrelled curse a Hungarian guard shouted at him: 'Rot, you Jew-Gypsy!'

Because of Germany's acute shortage of labour, German officials decided to postpone the killing of some of the Hungarian Jews until they had been exploited as slave workers. In 1944 Hitler allowed Himmler and Speer to bring some Jews into Germany to add to the labour force needed for military production. Under those terms, about 100,000 Hungarian Jews slated for killing were brought to German labour camps. There these men and women were used to excavate underground bunkers and make armaments. Conditions were terrible, but they had at least a chance to live, something denied to their more than 300,000 relatives and friends sent directly to the gas at Auschwitz.

Why did the Germans persist in the slaughter of the Hungarian Jews? Some scholars have suggested that such determination even in the face of impending defeat showed just how deeply committed many Germans were to the project of annihilating the Jews. Many German functionaries, however, showed similar dedication in the last stages of the war in their efforts against other victim groups, for example, Polish Gentiles, Slavic slave labourers, Soviet POWs and homosexual men.

At least some of these last-minute brutalities were motivated by the common drive of self-preservation. By 1944 and 1945 the prospect of the front looked worse all the time. Many German guards, police and officials of various kinds who were involved in attacks on civilians worked feverishly to prove how crucial their jobs were – jobs they could do in relative safety. Even in Nazi Germany, cowards were probably more common than fanatics.

Some Hungarian Jews survived within Hungary, thanks to rescue efforts on the part of many people, including foreign diplomats and international Jewish groups. The most famous rescuer in Hungary was Raoul Wallenberg. Wallenberg was a Swedish businessman and diplomat who rescued as many as 100,000 Hungarian Jews from deportation. Using money raised largely from the Jewish community in the United States, Wallenberg set up safe houses under the jurisdiction of the Swedish embassy, issued Swedish passports, bribed German and Hungarian officials and even rescued some Jews from transports slated for Auschwitz. At the end of the war Wallenberg wound up in Soviet hands. His fate is unknown, but it seems likely that he was sent to Siberia as a suspected spy and perished there.

Elie Wiesel is no doubt the best-known Jewish survivor from Hungary. His book *Night* is probably the single most widely read personal account of the Holocaust. It recounts the experiences of Wiesel, at the time an adolescent boy, in the hell of Auschwitz in the deadly last months of the war.

Another Hungarian survivor is Judith Magyar Isaacson, who recorded her experiences in *Seed of Sarah*. Like Wiesel just a teenager in 1944, Judith Magyar landed in Auschwitz with her mother and a young aunt. Somehow the three women managed to stay together. Once, Judith faced down an SS man who tried to send her to one side of a selection, her mother to another. He let her go with her mother. Camp functionaries offered Judith a position as a kapo, but she refused.

Judith, her mother and her aunt were among the Hungarian Jews taken out of Auschwitz and sent as slave labourers to Germany. Beaten, half-starved and terrified of rape, Judith lived through the final stages of the war. Later she married an American soldier and moved to Maine, where she taught mathematics and served as dean of students at Bates College until she retired.

The Hungarians suspended transports of Jews to Auschwitz in July 1944, and it was only in November that the new Arrow Cross government installed by the German coup ordered the Jews remaining in Budapest into a closed ghetto. The Arrow Cross was brutal: over the next two months its men shot 20,000 Jews and dumped their bodies into the Danube River. But it could not approach the efficiency of Auschwitz. When the Red

Army liberated Budapest in February 1945, there were 100,000 Jews still alive in the city.

The killing centre of Auschwitz reached new records of destruction in the final phase of the war. In the summer of 1944, as the transports from Hungary poured in, camp functionaries murdered as many as 12,000 Jews per day.

There was one large operation against Gypsies that summer too, in which the entire Gypsy 'family camp' was wiped out in one night. Of the 23,000 Gypsies sent to Auschwitz, almost 20,000 died there. By 2 August 1944 more than 13,000 were already dead. That night on orders from Berlin, the remaining 6,000 Sinti and Roma in the camp were gassed. Camp leaders had time now that they had suspended killing of Hungarian Jews. German military setbacks, however severe, did not save the lives of those thousands of Gypsies any more than they spared the Jews of Hungary.

The last year of the war also saw several important incidents of armed resistance within German camps and killing centres. In mid-May 1944, when SS and camp workers first tried to liquidate the Gypsy camp at Auschwitz-Birkenau, they encountered violent resistance. Roma inside the camp improvised weapons as best they could or fought with their bare hands. That defiance may have helped postpone killing of all the Gypsies in Auschwitz until early August 1944.

The most dramatic example of resistance within Auschwitz came in October 1944. Jewish *Sonderkommando* prisoners blew up and destroyed Crematorium IV. Some of the necessary explosives were provided by a young Polish Jewish woman named Roza Robota. Assigned to work in an ammunition factory, Robota, along with some other women, began to smuggle small amounts of explosives to the *Sonderkommando*. The SS arrested and tortured her, but she refused to divulge any information. Robota was hanged in January 1945, shortly before the arrival of the Red Army.

Beginning in the autumn of 1944, as the Germans lost control of much of the territory they had occupied, they began to evacuate many of the camps and killing centres. At the same time, they opened new labour camps in areas still safe from Allied advance. On orders from Himmler, camp officials began to empty the camps of prisoners. They sent the inmates, under guard, marching in columns toward places farther from the ever-advancing front. Throughout late 1944 and early 1945, these trails of half-dead prisoners made their way through the Polish, German and Czech countryside. Because of the awful numbers killed and dying along the way, these treks have come to be known as death marches.

A few examples give some idea of this new form of torture and killing. In the late autumn of 1944, Germans sent about 1,000 Jewish women, many of them Hungarian, from Auschwitz to Gross-Rosen. There the women were forced to dig antitank ditches, in the snow, with little or nothing to eat and often without shoes. In early January 1945, as the front advanced, that camp too was evacuated. Guards forced the remaining 970 women to begin a new march. In eight or nine days they had covered only about sixty miles. One hundred and fifty of the women died along the way. Perhaps twenty succumbed to starvation; guards shot another 130.

The remaining 800 women were soon evacuated again from their next destination, with about 1,000 additional prisoners. The group was divided into two, with half of the women being marched toward Helmbrechts in Bavaria, a satellite camp of Flossenbürg. In the middle of winter the women walked about three hundred miles. After five weeks, 621 of them arrived at the camp. A few had escaped and around 230 had remained at various camps along the way. Between 150 and 250 of the prisoners did not survive that march. Many were shot by guards. The camp at Helmbrechts was quite new. Established in the summer of 1944, it housed women prisoners set to work for an armaments firm. As always, they suffered brutal beatings and deadly privation.

In April 1945 Helmbrechts too was emptied. German guards forced some eleven hundred women on yet another death march to nowhere. The group was about half Jewish and half Gentile. Guards refused food and water and forbade inhabitants of the surrounding area to help the prisoners. By many accounts Jewish women received even worse treatment than the others.

Another 175–275 of the Jewish women died during this stage of
the march, just weeks before the war ended. Every one of them
would have died had they not been rescued by American forces.

On 15 April 1945, the same day that British troops reached
the concentration camp of Bergen-Belsen, SS and camp guards
forced 17,000 women and 40,000 men to march westward from
the concentration camps of Ravensbrück and Sachsenhausen into
territories still in German hands. Hundreds of women died of
exhaustion on the march from Ravensbrück. Retreating guards
and SS men shot hundreds of others. Some were killed by Allied
bombs. Having made it so far, thousands died by the roadside
just days from the end of the war. Death marches continued right
up until German surrender on 8 May 1945. In all, an estimated
250,000 to 375,000 people died in such forced marches.

Final Collapse

On the military front too, Hitler's Germans exacted a high
price from their enemies. At the end of December, Hungary
finally completed the reversal of its allegiances. Declaration of
war on Germany was followed a month later by an armistice
with Moscow.

The Germans came back with a final onslaught in the west.
The Ardennes Offensive, called the Battle of the Bulge by the
Allies, began in December 1944. That grandiose effort failed, but
only after it had cost many lives on both sides. By early March
1945 the German front in the west had collapsed. U.S. and
British forces were advancing in the north, centre and south.
German authorities responded by lowering the age for the draft
to include boys born in 1929.

In the last months things unravelled quickly. March brought
a partisan offensive by Tito's forces against German troops in
Yugoslavia. By April the Red Army was in Vienna and German
forces in Italy capitulated at the end of that month. In early May,
Czechs revolted against German occupation in Prague. In this
climate, even the death of U.S. President Roosevelt on 12 April

1945 did not weaken the Allies' demand for Germany's uncondicional surrender.

Finally, in the last stage of the war, many Germans came to feel something of the reality of the conflict their leadership had inflicted on Europe. More Germans died in bombings, expulsions and the collapse of the military fronts in the last six months of war than in the previous four years together. Approximately 160,000 German soldiers died in 1940–1941. In 1944 that number increased almost fourfold to some 600,000. The all-or-nothing mentality of Hitler's Social Darwinism made all lives cheap, including those of the German people. Many books on Nazi Germany label the last days of the Third Reich the *Götterdämmerung*, or 'twilight of the gods'. The reference is to the end of the *Ring Cycle*, a group of operas by Richard Wagner. Hitler loved those operas and the massive, tragic cataclysm at the end fit his own obsession with heroic death. That morbid fascination came to the fore in the last months of Hitler's regime.

In his poem 'The Wasteland' (1922), T. S. Eliot wrote the following lines: 'This is the way the world ends, not with a bang but a whimper'. Eliot's description could be applied to the Third Reich, which ended with both an explosion of death and destruction and a whimper of cowardice and defeat. In a small way, Hitler reaped what he had sown with the principle of divide and conquer when it came to the behaviour of his inner circle in the last days. Whimpering treachery turned out to be more characteristic of Hitler's henchmen than that iron loyalty they had loved to espouse.

Everyone, it turns out, seemed to have a plan as to how to salvage the Reich – and of course, save his own neck. In February 1945, Goebbels suggested that Hitler should remain head of state but appoint a new chancellor and foreign minister. Goebbels's preferred candidate for the job: himself, obviously. In deference to Himmler's control of the SS Empire, Goebbels proposed Himmler for minister of war. Himmler himself had toyed for a long time already with the idea of a separate peace with Britain. He used his contacts to test the waters, but they were icy cold. Efforts on the part of *Luftwaffe* commander Göring and German foreign minister Ribbentrop to negotiate a separate peace with the western powers also failed.

Hitler was determined to continue the fight, but on 22 April 1945, two days after his birthday, he fell into depression. Hitler realised that the war was lost and knew he could not negotiate a peace himself. Göring, he decided, was the man for the job. When Göring heard about Hitler's remarks he decided it meant he was to take over. Outraged by that presumption, Hitler denounced Göring as a traitor, dismissed him from his many posts and had him arrested by the SS. Göring would eventually be captured and brought to trial at Nuremberg, where he committed suicide before his scheduled execution.

Just days after he dismissed Göring, Hitler got word of Himmler's treachery. Furious, he ordered the arrest of the SS leader as well, but Himmler slipped through his hands. Himmler too would manage to kill himself before the Allies could exact justice. In the last days of April, Hitler swung briefly from depression into a kind of manic activity. He ordered a massive counterattack to drive the Soviets back from Berlin. He announced that the western Allies would soon be at war with the Soviet Union and that Germany would be saved. Nothing came of any of these notions.

On 29 April 1945, holed up in his bunker in Berlin, Hitler dictated one final document: his last will and political testament. In it he admonished Germans 'punctiliously to observe the racial laws' and to fight on against 'the poisoner of all the nations of the world, international Jewry'. True to form he blamed the entire course of the lost war on 'international Jewry and its helpers'. Consistent to the end, Hitler implied that annihilation of the Jews of Europe was his greatest achievement.

That same day Hitler married Eva Braun. On 30 April the 'first soldier of the German Reich' deserted by committing suicide in his bunker. Dead beside him by their own hands were his new wife, the loyal Goebbels and Goebbels's wife and six children. Hitler's war would end as it had started – with a lie. His chosen successor, Admiral Karl Dönitz, reported by radio to the nation that its *Führer* had sustained 'heroic death in battle'.

Two days later, the city of Berlin surrendered to the Soviets, and Hitler's successors signed documents of unconditional surrender on 8 May 1945.

The reality of how Nazi rule ended sweeps away the myth of order that has grown up around Hitler's regime. There was neither order nor glory to his demise. No heroic struggle marked his death, only cowardice, the ruin of his own people and lies. The Nazi revolution had promised a new awakening. Instead it brought destruction and death far beyond the borders of Germany. An estimated 55 million people died world-wide in the Second World War. Among them were over 5 million German soldiers. At least 27 million Soviet citizens were dead, as well as millions of Poles, over a million Yugoslavs and scores of other people from all over Europe. Close to 6 million Jews had been murdered and Jewish civilisation was almost eradicated from Europe. The list could go on and on and the world continues to feel the effects of hatreds sown for the Nazi goals of racial purification and territorial expansion.

Epilogue:
The Legacies of Atrocity

This book ends in May 1945, but the legacies of Nazism, the Second World War and the Holocaust extend much further. Perhaps one account can begin to illustrate some of the personal and political repercussions of the history described in the previous chapters. Like many stories that end in death, the details can only be pieced together in a fragmentary way, but they are nonetheless significant.

This account begins in the mid-1930s in the Soviet Union. Frightened by manifestations of antisemitism under Stalin, a young Russian Jew whom we will call N decided to leave his home and move west. He settled in France, where he built a life for himself until the Germans invaded in 1940 and his existence again became precarious.

For a while N succeeded in evading the Nazi dragnet, but sometime in 1942 or 1943 German or French police rounded him up, along with many other foreign Jews living in France and sent him east to a Nazi camp. Against terrible odds, N survived more than a year as a prisoner and slave of Nazi Germany. In mid-April 1945, when British troops arrived at the concentration camp Bergen-Belsen, N was one of the inmates liberated.

Under the terms of an Allied agreement, N, a citizen of the Soviet Union, was turned over to Soviet authorities. Instead of relief from years of torment at Nazi German hands, he soon found himself again on a deportation transport, this time to Siberia. Suspicious of the loyalty of Soviet citizens who had spent years outside the country, Stalin had tens of thousands of people like N – Jews, POWs, forced labourers – sent directly from their 'liberation' to labour camps and prisons in remote regions, where they toiled in massive industrialisation projects.

N did not survive this second round of abuse. N's son, who lived through the war in France and later moved to New York, spent years trying to trace his father through the Red Cross and other international organisations. Decades after the war ended, he received the news he had long feared: his father had died in Siberia.

The fate of N highlights several facts about the end of the Holocaust and the Second World War. The arrival of Allied forces and the collapse of Nazi Germany were not miracles that could undo or even stop the spirals of violence and misery unleashed by years of brutality. Although in hindsight it is easy to speak of liberation, for many individuals and groups of people, the end of the war meant continued and even new forms of misery. The defeat and demise of Hitler's Germany unleashed a massive movement of people within Europe, some of it voluntary, much of it coerced. Wartime atrocities created urgent demands for justice, even as the enormity of the crimes committed and the overwhelming death and destruction made any kind of restitution painfully inadequate and often impossible. Whether they had been victims, perpetrators, or bystanders in Nazi barbarity – and many Europeans had reason to count themselves in more than one of those categories – people faced the challenge of building lives for themselves and what was left of their families and communities with scarce resources and restricted freedom and in a climate of distrust and grief.

As Allied troops moved into German-held territory in the last stages of the war, they encountered shocking scenes. The Soviets were the first to reach the major killing centres. Even they, many of whom had experienced and witnessed Nazi German brutality firsthand, were stunned by the horror of places like Auschwitz-Birkenau. Soldiers from the United States and Britain who fought their way into Germany from the west were even less prepared for what they found: mass graves, abandoned camps, cattle trucks full of corpses and emaciated, dying prisoners.

On 15 April 1945, the first British tanks entered the concentration camp of Bergen-Belsen. Terrorised and enfeebled, inmates of the camp could not believe they were free. And in fact, freedom did not come easily. After initial contact, the British tanks moved on. For the next forty-eight hours, the camp was only nominally under British control. Hungarian soldiers whom the Germans had stationed there as guards remained in command. In two days they shot more than eighty Jews and non-Jews for such offences as taking potato peels from the kitchen. Even after British troops entered Belsen in force, for more than two weeks three hundred inmates continued to die daily of typhus and starvation. Horror on the scale of the Holocaust did not simply disappear with the arrival of the Allied liberators.

The images captured on film by photographers and journalists who accompanied and followed Allied forces horrified people back home, just as the sights themselves stunned and sickened the soldiers who saw them first hand. Decades later those images continue to haunt us and to shape the way we perceive and present atrocities in our own time. The questions they raise remain pressing even though they have almost become clichés: How could human beings do such things to other people? How can we go on living in a world where crimes and suffering of such magnitude are possible?

For those who survived, the end of the Second World War brought the realisation of all that had been destroyed. Alone, without family or friends, often far from what had been their homes, many survivors, particularly Jews, had nowhere to go. Separated from their parents for years, some Jewish children no longer knew their birth names or even that they came from Jewish families. Many Jews had seen their Gentile neighbours turn against them, denouncing them to Nazi officials and stealing their possessions.

Could they now simply go back as if nothing had happened? In Poland, Ukraine, Hungary and elsewhere, Jewish survivors who returned home to search for family members or reclaim their property were often met with violent hostility from the new 'owners'. Some Jews were attacked and beaten; some were killed.

Non-Jewish victims of Nazism faced their own problems as they discovered that true liberation was impossible in hostile surroundings. Gypsies who had managed to live through the Nazi assault were no more welcome in many places after May 1945 than they had been before or during the war. Few non-Gypsies realised or cared that Nazi Germany had singled out the Roma for particular abuse. Only decades after the war would Gypsies gradually begin to be acknowledged legally and unofficially as victims of Nazism. In some places – for example, in the western zones of occupied Germany – homosexual men were released from Nazi prisons and concentration camps only to be arrested again and incarcerated under old or new laws that criminalised homosexuality. Jehovah's Witnesses, thousands of whom endured imprisonment in Hitler's Germany, faced renewed persecution, especially under communism in East Germany. Looking back at Nazism and the Holocaust, we often vow 'never again', but for the Jews hounded out of Polish cities and towns by pogroms in 1945 and 1946, the Jehovah's Witnesses sitting in communist jails in the 1950s and the Gypsies crippled and left homeless by arson attacks in Romania in the 1990s, a more apt slogan might have been 'Still?'

The Second World War sparked the movement of the largest number of people in the shortest period of time that the world had ever known. Refugees, fugitives, displaced persons, deportees and expellees jammed the roadways and waterways of Europe and spilled over into Central Asia and the Americas. Hundreds of thousands of people, like the Russian Jew N, were transported eastward, against their will, as prisoners and labourers of the Soviet Union. More of the wave of motion, however, was westward. An estimated ten million refugees poured into the western zones of occupied Germany alone, those parts controlled by the United States, Britain and France.

The motivations of those fleeing west varied. Some had experienced communism in Stalin's Soviet Union and would risk anything to avoid a return to that misery. Some were ethnic Germans whose families had lived in Eastern Europe for generations. Nazi authorities had begun evacuating them already before the war ended, aware that they would be targets for revenge. Many ethnic Germans had eagerly served the cause of race and space and benefited from the deprivation and expropriation of their neighbours. In some cases, Soviet and local authorities expelled ethnic Germans, both to remove potential troublemakers and to free up space for resettlement programmes of their own. Ethnic Germans were forced out of western Poland, for example, at least partly because the Soviets needed homes for Poles they had pushed out of the eastern parts of the country, territories annexed to the Soviet Union after 1945. Other East Europeans, who like many ethnic Germans had collaborated with Nazism, also had reasons to flee west, now that their German protectors had retreated. Fearing the wrath of their neighbours, they sought security or at least anonymity. The Red Army's horrific record of rape and plunder as its troops penetrated deeper into central Europe added another urgent reason for many people to try to escape westward.

Throughout 1945 masses of weary travellers crisscrossed Europe – Hungarian Jews trying to go home; ethnic Germans from the Sudetenland making their way north and west; demobilised soldiers, prisoners of war, former slave labourers from Ukraine and Poland. Amid the chaos it is no surprise that war criminals and other fugitives often found it easy to blend in and evade detection. Under such conditions, whose documentation was in order anyway? Who would know if a former SS man or high-ranking Nazi Party boss, or even Heinrich Himmler himself, had simply buried or burned his papers, put on old clothing and assumed a new identity? Paradoxically, the Nazis, with their obsession with race, blood and homeland, had created a situation where all of those identities were in flux.

Building on the creation of the U.N. Relief and Rehabilitation Administration during the war, the United Nations tried to address some of the most pressing humanitarian concerns stemming from the refugee crisis. U.S. occupation authorities set up camps for displaced persons (DPs) in their zone, which became the first destination of many Jewish survivors. Initially DPs were organised by country of origin, so that Jews, ethnic Germans and non-German collaborators might find themselves grouped together as Ukrainians, Poles, or Yugoslavians. Subsequently the Americans set up separate facilities for Jews, who had different needs and options from most Gentiles.

By late 1946 more than 150,000 Jews lived in DP camps in the U.S. zone, bringing a Jewish presence to parts of Germany that previously had been home to relatively few Jews. Jewish DP camps were sites of Zionist activity, as survivors, especially young people, were urged to leave Europe for Palestine and, after 1948, Israel. Many Jews preferred to wait for visas to the United States, Canada, or Australia and some accepted options that were often quicker, such as relocation to South Africa, South America, or the Caribbean. An estimated 20,000 Jews remained in Germany even after the last Jewish DP camp finally closed in 1957. Some of them were too old or sick to travel or be granted visas; some had ties to Germany.

Jewish DP camps were more than just holding places for people waiting to exit. They developed an internal leadership and communal spirit, with cultural and religious activities, educational opportunities and social and family life. The immediate post-war years saw a baby boom as the birth rate among Jewish DPs rose to remarkable heights, especially in contrast to the unusually low rates for other people in Germany. Those Jewish children must have represented faith in new beginnings and hope for life after so much death.

Despite the urgent demands of daily existence, many people in post-war Europe concerned themselves with questions of justice. Perpetrators and organisers of Nazi crimes went to immense lengths to avoid being brought to account for their deeds. They set up self-help networks and used connections in Turkey, the Middle East, South America, Canada and the Vatican to get themselves to safety. For example, Franz Stangl, former T-4 operative and subsequently commandant of Sobibor and Treblinka, fled via Turkey and the Middle East to Argentina, where Hitler's expert on Jews, transportation and deportation, Adolf Eichmann, also found refuge. Josef Mengele, the doctor and medical scholar whose vicious experiments at Auschwitz killed thousands of people, made his way to Brazil, where he died in the 1980s.

Of course those victimised by Nazism had very different interests in justice. No acts of revenge or restitution could make up for the deaths of millions, the annihilation of Jewish life in much of Europe, the destruction of property and the shattering of trust and coexistence. Nevertheless survivors had to begin new lives and for that they required at least minimal material resources, some acknowledgement of their suffering and a measure of confidence in the world around them. Seeing some key criminals brought to justice could begin to address those needs as well as combat the sense of meaninglessness that must have threatened to overwhelm many survivors.

Already during the war Allied leaders had agreed that the defeated Germany must be denazified and top perpetrators brought to justice. Doing so was necessary for post-war stability, at least some of them believed, because it would make it possible to effect some kind of separation between 'Nazis', who needed to be punished and 'Germans', who could and should be integrated into a peaceable world. The International Military Tribunal with the Nuremberg Trials of 1945–1946, a joint effort of all the Allies, served this purpose.

Contrary to what detractors claimed, the trial of twenty-one major war criminals and a handful of central Nazi German organisations at Nuremberg was not sham 'victors' justice' or a reflection of some Allied notion of German 'collective guilt'. Although the trials were not perfect and Allied cooperation was severely strained at times, they were real legal proceedings, with witnesses, massive amounts of documentation and counsels for the defence – and without torture. Some individuals and organisations were acquitted and those convicted received varying sentences, including death sentences in about half of the cases. The most famous defendant, Hitler's favourite, Hermann

Göring, committed suicide in his cell before the order for his execution could be carried out.

The Nuremberg Trials were just one step. The occupying powers and subsequently local authorities, including Germans and foreign governments – like Israel with the Eichmann trial in 1961 – conducted their own hearings, trials and deportation proceedings of camp guards, doctors, bureaucrats, members of the *Einsatzgruppen* and former SS men accused of lying on their immigration applications to the United States, Canada and elsewhere. Property of all kinds – art, gold, land, buildings, factories – has been grounds for other kinds of legal cases, commissions and settlements. These processes are all important, although they can never bring closure to a past that remains an open wound despite remarkable – perhaps unprecedented – efforts by Germans to come to grips with their nation's cruel past.

This history has no happy ending, no uplifting message of redemption. It leaves us only with human beings, with their startling capacities for good and evil and with an awareness of the complex ties that connect the fates of people and nations all over the world. One final account may best express these points. This time the story begins in the Netherlands with the birth of a baby girl in 1943. When she was two weeks old, her Jewish parents and older brother were rounded up by German and Dutch police, sent to the transit camp of Westerbork and from there to Sobibor, where they were murdered.

Somehow the baby escaped that fate. Perhaps her parents hid her or a sympathetic policeman took pity on her. Either way, she ended up in a beauty parlour run by two young women with connections to the Dutch underground. They helped find hiding places for Jewish children, on the understanding that potential rescuers would return the children to their families after the war.

Details are no longer clear, but it seems the women found a family to take the baby, but the arrangement fell through, perhaps because the couple would not agree to surrender the girl when the war was over or perhaps because the two young women could not bear to give up the beautiful baby girl. So one of the beauticians took the child herself and cared for her until 1947, when an uncle from New York managed to locate his niece. True to her promise, the Dutch woman gave the girl up. She never saw her again. Growing up in the United States, the girl remembered little from her early years, and her uncle and his wife discouraged all contact with her Dutch foster mother. Meanwhile the Dutch woman suffered severe emotional problems and died quite young. Only decades later would the orphaned girl, now a mother and grandmother herself, find a way to restore contact with members of her Dutch 'family'. In the process she met people who had known her parents and brother, saw photographs of them and even received a few of their belongings.

One could present this account as an inspirational example of heroism and miraculous luck and those are indeed important messages to take away from a study of the Holocaust. At least as significant, however, are the crushing themes of loss and violence and the unavoidable, heartbreaking decisions that no one should have to make, decisions the scholar Lawrence Langer has dubbed 'choiceless choices'. These are the realities of the Holocaust and its bitter legacy, a history specific and unique but at the same time firmly embedded in the all-too-familiar global experiences of war and genocide.

Sources and Suggestions
for Further Reading

Note: Books are listed in the first chapter to which they directly relate. Many of the titles given in one place are relevant elsewhere too. To the extent possible, I have limited this list to materials available in English.

1. Preconditions: Antisemitism, Racism and Common Prejudices In Early-Twentieth Century Europe

Bartlett, Roger and Karen Schönwälder, eds. *The German Lands and Eastern Europe: Essays on the History of Their Social, Cultural and Political Relations.* New York: St. Martin's, 1999.

Bartov, Omer. *Mirrors of Destruction: War, Genocide and Modern Identity.* New York: Oxford University Press, 2000.

Berenbaum, Michael. *A Mosaic of Victims.* New York: New York University Press, 1990.

Berenbaum, Michael and Abraham J. Peck, eds. *The Holocaust and History: The Known, the Unknown, the Disputed and the Reexamined.* Bloomington: Indiana University Press, 1998.

Breitman, Richard. *The Architect of Genocide: Himmler and the Final Solution.* New York: Knopf, 1991.

Burleigh, Michael. *Death and Deliverance: 'Euthanasia' in Germany c. 1900–1945*. New York: Cambridge University Press, 1997.

The Third Reich: A New History. New York: Hill and Wang, 2000.

Burleigh, Michael and Wolfgang Wippermann. *The Racial State: Germany 1933–1945*.

New York: Cambridge University Press, 1991.

Crowe, David and John Kolsti, eds. *The Gypsies of Eastern Europe*. Armonk, N.Y.: Sharpe, 1991.

Evans, Richard J. *Rituals of Retribution: Capital Punishment in Germany 1600–1987*. Oxford: Oxford University Press, 1996.

Fout, John C. *Forbidden History: The State, Society and the Regulation of Sexuality in Modern Europe*. Chicago: University of Chicago Press, 1992.

Friedlander, Henry. *The Origins of Nazi Genocide: From Euthanasia to the Final Solution*. Chapel Hill: University of North Carolina Press, 1995.

Gay, Peter. *My German Question: Growing Up in Nazi Berlin*. New Haven, Conn.: Yale University Press, 1998.

Gellately, Robert and Nathan Stoltzfus, eds. *Social Outsiders in Nazi Germany*. Princeton, N.J.: Princeton University Press, 2001.

Gutman, Israel. *Encyclopedia of the Holocaust*. 3 vols. New York: Macmillan, 1990.

Hancock, Ian. 'The Roots of Antigypsyism: To the Holocaust and After'. In *Confronting the Holocaust: A Mandate for the 21st Century*, edited by C. Jan Colijn and Marcia Sachs Littell, 19–49. Studies in the Shoah 19. Lanham, Md.: University Press of America, 1997.

Hilberg, Raul. *The Destruction of the European Jews*. Rev. ed. 3 vols. New Haven. Conn.: Yale University Press, 2003.

Hull, Isabel. *Absolute Destruction: Military Culture and the Practices of War in Imperial Germany*. Ithaca and London: Cornell University Press, 2005.

Kenrick, Donald and Grattan Puxon. *Gypsies under the Swastika*. Hatfield: University of Hertfordshire Press, 1995.

King, Christine Elizabeth. *The Nazi State and the New Religions: Five Cases in Non-Conformity*. New York: Edwin Mellen, 1982.

Langmuir, Gavin I. *History, Religion and Antisemitism*. Berkeley: University of California Press, 1990.

Levy, Richard S., ed. *Antisemitism in the Modern World: An Anthology of Texts*. Lexington, Mass.: Heath, 1991.

Marks, Sally. 'Black Watch on the Rhine: A Study in Propaganda, Prejudice and Prurience'. *European Studies Review* 13, no. 3 (1983): 297–334.

The Illusion of Peace. New York: St. Martin's, 1976.

Milton, Sybil. 'The Context of the Holocaust'. *German Studies Review* 13, no. 2 (1990): 269–83.

Mosse, George. *Fallen Soldiers: Reshaping the Memory of the World Wars*. New York: Oxford University Press, 1990.

The Nationalisation of the Masses. New York: Howard Fertig, 1975.

Müller-Hill, Benno. *Murderous Science: Elimination by Scientific Selection of Jews, Gypsies and Others in Germany, 1933–1945*. Translated by George R. Fraser. Plainview, N.Y.: Cold Spring Harbor Laboratory Press, 1998.

Naimark, Norman. *Fires of Hatred: Ethnic Cleansing in Twentieth-Century Europe*. Cambridge, Mass.: Harvard University Press, 2001.

Poliakov, Léon. *Harvest of Hate: The Nazi Programme for the Destruction of the Jews of Europe*. New York: Holocaust Library, 1979.

Pomerantz, Jack and Lyric Wallwork Winik. *Run East: Flight from the Holocaust*. Urbana: University of Illinois Press, 1997.

Siegal, Aranka. *Upon the Head of the Goat: A Childhood in Hungary, 1939–1944*. New York: Puffin, 1981.

Stern, Fritz. *The Politics of Cultural Despair*. Berkeley: University of California Press, 1961.

Stopes, Marie Carmichael and Ruth E. Hall, eds. *Dear Dr Stopes: Sex in the 1920s*. London: Deutsch, 1978.

Weinberg, Gerhard L. *Germany, Hitler and World War II: Essays in Modern German and World History*. New York: Cambridge University Press, 1995.

Weiss, John. *Ideology of Death: Why the Holocaust Happened in Germany*. Chicago: Ivan R. Dee, 1996.

2. Leadership and Will: Adolf Hitler, the NSDAP and Nazi Ideology

Allen, William Sheridan. *The Nazi Seizure of Power*. Rev. ed. New York: Watts, 1984.

Bessel, Richard. *Germany after the First World War*. Oxford: Clarendon, 1993.

Bukey, Evan Burr. *Hitler's Hometown*. Bloomington: Indiana University Press, 1986.

Bullock, Alan. Hitler: *A Study in Tyranny*. Rev. ed. New York: Bantam, 1962.

Burrin, Philippe. *Hitler and the Jews: The Genesis of the Holocaust*. Translated by Patsy Southgate. London: Arnold; New York: Routledge, Chapman and Hall, 1994.

Childers, Thomas. *The Nazi Voter: The Social Foundations of Fascism in Germany, 1919–1933*. Chapel Hill: University of North Carolina Press, 1983.

Eubank, Keith, ed. *World War II: Roots and Causes*. 2nd ed. Lexington, Mass.: Heath, 1992.

Fischer, Conan. *Stormtroopers: A Social, Economic and Ideological Analysis 1925–35*. London: Allen and Unwin, 1983.

Fischer, Klaus P. *Nazi Germany: A New History*. London: Continuum, 1995.

Friedländer, Saul. *Nazi Germany and the Jews*. Vol. 1, *The Years of Persecution*. New York: HarperCollins, 1997.

Haffner, Sebastian. *The Meaning of Hitler*. Translated by Ewald Osers. Cambridge: Harvard University Press, 1983.

Hamann, Brigitte. *Hitler's Vienna*. Translated by Thomas Thornton. New York: Oxford University Press, 1999.

Hamilton, Richard F. *Who Voted for Hitler?* Princeton, N.J.: Princeton University Press, 1982.

Hitler's Table Talk, 1941–1944: Secret Conversations. 1953. Updated ed. edited by Hugh Trevor-Roper. Introduction by Gerhard L. Weinberg. New York: Enigma, 2008.

Jäckel, Eberhard. *Hitler's World View: A Blueprint for Power*. Cambridge: Harvard University Press, 1981.

Kater, Michael. *The Nazi Party: A Social Profile of Members and Leaders, 1919–1945*. Cambridge: Harvard University Press, 1983.

Kershaw, Ian. *Hitler*. Vol. 1, *1889–1936: Hubris*. New York: Norton, 1998.

Vol. 2, *1936–1945: Nemesis*. New York: Norton, 2000.

Lochner, Louis P., ed. *The Goebbels Diaries 1942–43*. Garden City, N.Y.: Doubleday, 1948.

(More complete editions of the diaries are available in German. See, for example, *Die Tagebücher von Joseph Goebbels. Sämtliche Fragmente*, Vol. 1, *Aufzeichnungen 1924–1941*, edited by Elke Fröhlich. 4 vols. Munich, 1987.)

Marks, Sally. 'The Myths of Reparations'. *Central European History* 11, no. 3 (1978): 231–35.

Marrus, Michael. *The Holocaust in History*. New York: Meridian, 1989.

Orlow, Dietrich. *The Nazi Party 1919–1945: A Complete History*. 2 vols. New York: Enigma, 1969–73.

Patch, William L., Jr. *Heinrich Brüning and the Dissolution of the Weimar Republic*. Cambridge: Cambridge University Press, 1998.

Pauley, Bruce F. *Hitler and the Forgotten Nazis: A History of Austrian National Socialism*. Chapel Hill: University of North Carolina Press, 1981.

Reck-Malleczewen, Fritz Percy. *Diary of a Man in Despair*. Translated by Paul Ruebens. New York: Macmillan, 1971.

Sax, Benjamin and Dieter Kuntz. *Inside Hitler's Germany*. Lexington, Mass.: Heath, 1992.

Turner, Henry Ashby, Jr. *Hitler's Thirty Days to Power: January 1933*. Reading, Mass.: Addison Wesley, 1996.

Wistrich, Robert S. *Hitler and the Holocaust*. New York: Modern Library, 2001.

3. From Revolution to Routine: Nazi Germany, 1933–1938

Abel, Theodore. *Why Hitler Came into Power.* 1938 Reprint, Cambridge, Mass.: Harvard University Press, 1986.

Abrams, Alan. *Mischlinge: Special Treatment, the Untold Story of Hitler's Third Race.* Secaucus, N.J.: Lyle-Stuart, 1985.

Bankier, David. *The Germans and the Final Solution: Public Opinion under Nazism.* Cambridge, Mass.: Basil Blackwell, 1992.

Bergen, Doris L. *Twisted Cross: The German Christian Movement in the Third Reich.* Chapel Hill: University of North Carolina Press, 1996.

Engelmann, Bernd. *Inside Hitler's Germany.* Translated by Krishna Wilson. New York: Pantheon, 1985.

Friedländer, Saul. *Pius XII and the Third Reich: A Documentation.* New York: Knopf, 1960.

Fromm, Bella. *Blood and Banquets: A Social Diary.* New York: Harper and Brothers, 1942.

Giles, Geoffrey. 'The Most Unkindest Cut of All: Castration, Homosexuality and Nazi Justice'. *Journal of Contemporary History* 27, no. 1 (1992): 41–61.

Grossmann, Atina. *Reforming Sex: The German Movement for Birth Control and Abortion Reform 1920–1950.* New York: Oxford University Press, 1995.

Heck, Alfons. *A Child of Hitler.* Frederick, Colo.: Renaissance House, 1985.

Jaskot, Paul. *The Architecture of Oppression.* London: Routledge, 2000.

Johnson, Eric A. *Nazi Terror: The Gestapo, Jews and Ordinary Germans.* New York: Basic, 2000.

Kaplan, Marion. *Between Dignity and Despair: Jewish Life in Nazi Germany.* New York: Oxford University Press, 1998.

Kershaw, Ian. *The 'Hitler Myth': Image and Reality in the Third Reich.* Oxford: Clarendon, 1987.

   The Nazi Dictatorship: Problems and Perspectives of Interpretation. London: Arnold, 1993.

Klemperer, Victor. *I Will Bear Witness: A Diary of the Nazi Years, 1933–1941.* Vol. 1. Translated by Martin Chalmers. New York: Random House, 1998.

Koehn, Ilse. *Mischling, Second Degree: My Childhood in Nazi Germany.* New York: Bantam, 1977.

Koonz, Claudia. *Mothers in the Fatherland: Women, the Family and Nazi Politics.* New York: St. Martin's, 1987.

   The Nazi Conscience. Cambridge, Mass.: Harvard University Press, 2003.

Koshar, Rudy. *Social Life, Local Politics and Nazism: Marburg, 1880–1935.* Chapel Hill: University of North Carolina Press, 1986.

Lewy, Guenter. *The Nazi Persecution of the Gypsies.* New York: Oxford University Press, 2000.

Maschmann, Melitta. *Account Rendered*. Translated by Geoffrey Strachan. London: Abelard-Schuman, 1964.

Merkl, Peter. *Political Violence under the Swastika*. Princeton, N.J.: Princeton University Press, 1975.

Mommsen, Hans. *From Weimar to Auschwitz: Essays in German History*. Translated by Philip O'Connor. Cambridge, Mass.: Polity Press; Oxford: Basil Blackwell, 1991.

Opitz, May, Katharina Oguntoye and Dagmar Schultz, eds. *Showing Our Colors: Afro-German Women Speak Out*. Translated by Anne V. Adams. Amherst: University of Massachusetts Press, 1992.

Owings, Alison. *Frauen: German Women Recall the Third Reich*. New Brunswick, N.J.: Rutgers University Press, 1993.

Petropoulos, Jonathan. *Art as Politics in the Third Reich*. Chapel Hill: University of North Carolina Press, 1996.

Peukert, Detlev. *Inside Nazi Germany: Conformity, Opposition and Racism in Everyday Life*. New Haven, Conn.: Yale University Press, 1987.

Plant, Richard. *The Pink Triangle*. New York: Henry Holt, 1986.

Rosenberg, Otto, as told to Ulrich Enzenberger, trans. Helmut Bögler. *A Gypsy in Auschwitz*. London: London House, 1999.

Steinweis, Alane. *Studying the Jew: Scholarly Antisemitism in Nazi Germany*. Cambridge, Mass.: Harvard University Press, 2006.

Thimme, Annelise. 'Geprägt von der Geschichte. Eine Aussenseiterin'. In *Erinnerungsstücke: Wege in die Vergangenheit*. Edited by Hartmut Lehmann and Gerhard Oexle, 153–223. Vienna: Boehlau, 1997.

Welch, David A. *The Third Reich: Politics and Propaganda*. London: Routledge, 1993.

4. Open Aggression: In Search of War, 1938–1939

Bridenthal, Renate, Atina Grossmann and Marion Kaplan, eds. *When Biology Became Destiny: Women in Weimar and Nazi Germany*. New York: Monthly Review Press, 1984.

Bukey, Evan Burr. *Hitler's Austria*. Chapel Hill: University of North Carolina Press, 2000.

Conway, John S. *The Nazi Persecution of the Churches 1933–45*. London: Westfield and Nicolson, 1968.

Ericksen, Robert P. and Susannah Heschel, eds. *Betrayal: The German Churches and the Holocaust*. Minneapolis, Minn.: Fortress, 1999.

Friedländer, Saul. *When Memory Comes*. New York: Farrar, Straus and Giroux, 1979.

Gellately, Robert. *The Gestapo and German Society: Enforcing Racial Policy, 1933–1945*. New York: Oxford University Press, 1990.

Grau, Günter, ed. *Hidden Holocaust? Gay and Lesbian Persecution in Germany, 1933–1945*. Translated by Patrick Camiller. London: Cassell, 1995.

Hayes, Peter. *Industry and Ideology: IG Farben in the Nazi Era*. New York: Cambridge University Press, 2000.

Heilbronner, Oded. *Catholicism, Political Culture and the Countryside: A Social History of the Nazi Party in South Germany*. Ann Arbor: University of Michigan Press, 1998.

Hesse, Hans, ed. *Persecution and Resistance of Jehovah's Witnesses during the Nazi-Regime, 1933–1945*. Bremen: Edition Temmen, 2001.

Jehovah's Witnesses Stand Firm against Nazi Assault. 1 hr. 45 min. Watchtower Society, 1995. Videocassette.

Kluger, Ruth. *Still Alive: A Holocaust Girlhood Remembered*. New York: Feminist Press, 2001.

Opfermann, Charlotte. *The Ides of November*. Unpublished manuscript, 1999.

Phayer, Michael. *The Catholic Church and the Holocaust*. Bloomington: Indiana University Press, 2000.

Quack, Sibylle, ed. *Between Sorrow and Strength: Women Refugees of the Nazi Period*. Washington, D.C.: German Historical Institute; New York: Cambridge University Press, 1995.

Rigg, Bryan Mark. *Hitler's Jewish Soldiers*. Lawrence: University Press of Kansas, 2002.

Sofsky, Wolfgang. *The Order of Terror: The Concentration Camp*. Translated by William Templer. Princeton, N.J.: Princeton University Press, 1997.

Steinhoff, Johannes, Peter Pechel and Dennis Showalter, eds. *Voices from the Third Reich*. Washington, D.C.: Regnery Gateway, 1989.

5. Experiments in Brutality, 1939–1940: War Against Poland and the So-called Euthanasia Programme

Adelson, Alan and Robert Lapides, eds. Łódź *Ghetto: Inside a Community under Siege*. New York: Viking, 1989.

Aly, Götz. *'Final Solution': Nazi Population Policy and the Murder of the European Jews*. Translated by Belinda Cooper and Allison Brown. London: Arnold, 1999.

Arad, Yitzhak. *Ghetto in Flames*. New York: Holocaust Library, 1982.

Arendt, Hannah. *Eichmann in Jerusalem*. New York: Viking, 1963.

Bartov, Omer. *Hitler's Army: Soldiers, Nazis and War in the Third Reich*. New York: Oxford University Press, 1991.

Bauman, Zygmunt. *Modernity and the Holocaust*. Ithaca, NY: Cornell University Press, 1989.

Cornwell, John. *Hitler's Pope: The Secret History of Pius XII.* New York: Viking, 1999.

Dobroszycki, Lucjan. *The Chronicle of the Łódź Ghetto, 1941–1944.* New Haven, Conn.: Yale University Press, 1984.

Gerlach, Christian. 'Failure of Plans for an SS Extermination Camp in Mogilev, Belorussia'. Translated by Deborah Cohen and Helmut Gerlach. *Holocaust and Genocide Studies* 11, no. 1 (1997): 60–78.

Gotfryd, Bernard. *Anton the Dove Fancier and Other Tales of the Holocaust.* New York: Washington Square Press, 1990.

Gross, Jan. *Neighbors: The Destruction of the Jewish Community in Jedwabne, Poland.* Princeton, N.J.: Princeton University Press, 2001.

Harvey, Elizabeth. *Women and the Nazi East,* New Haven, Conn.: Yale University Press, 2003.

Hilberg, Raul. *The Destruction of the European Jews.* Rev ed. 3 vols. New Haven, Conn.: Yale University Press, 2003.

Hilberg, Raul, Stanislaw Staron and Josef Kermisz, eds. *The Warsaw Diary of Adam Czerniaków: Prelude to Doom.* Translated by Stanislaw Staron and the staff of Yad Vashem. New York: Stein and Day, 1979.

Klein, Gerda Weissmann. *All But My Life.* New York: Hill and Wang, 1995.

Knappe, Siegfried and Ted Brusaw. *Soldat: Reflections of a German Soldier, 1936–1949.* New York: Orion Books, 1992.

Kogon, Eugen, Hermann Langbein and Adalbert Rückerl, eds. *Nazi Mass Murder: A Documentary History of the Use of Poison Gas.* Translated by Mary Scott and Caroline Lloyd-Morris. New Haven, Conn.: Yale University Press, 1993.

Lukas, Richard C. *Did the Children Cry? Hitler's War against Jewish and Polish Children.* New York: Hippocrene, 1995.
Out of the Inferno: Poles Remember the Holocaust. Lexington: University Press of Kentucky, 1989.
The Forgotten Holocaust: The Poles under German Occupation, 1939–1944. Rev. ed. New York: Hippocrene, 1997.

Melson, Robert. *False Papers: Deception and Survival in the Holocaust.* Urbana, Il.: University of Illinois Press, 2000.

Noakes, Jeremy and Geoffrey Pridham, eds. *Nazism 1919–1945: A Documentary Reader.* 4 vols. Exeter: University of Exeter Department of History and Archeology, 1983–1998.

Polonsky, Antony, ed. *'My Brother's Keeper?': Recent Polish Debates on the Holocaust.* London: Routledge, 1990.

Rossino, Alexander. *Hitler Strikes Poland: Blitzkrieg, Ideology, and Atrocity.* Lawrence, Kans.: University Press of Kansas, 2003.

Tec, Nechama. *Defiance: The Bielski Partisans.* New York: Oxford University Press, 1993.

Yahil, Leni. *The Holocaust: The Fate of European Jewry.* Translated by Ina Friedman and Haya Galai. New York: Oxford University Press, 1990.

6. Expansion and Systematisation: Exporting War and Terror, 1940–1941

Aronson, Shlomo. *Hitler, the Allies, and the Jews.* New York: Cambridge University Press, 2004.

Bartoszewski, Wladyslaw. *The Warsaw Ghetto: A Christian's Testimony.* Translated by Stephen G. Cappellari. Boston: Beacon, 1987.

Bartov, Omer. *The Eastern Front, 1941–1945: German Troops and the Barbarisation of Warfare.* London: St. Martin's, 1985.

Borowski, Tadeusz. *This Way for the Gas Ladies and Gentlemen.* Translated by Barbara Vedder. New York: Penguin, 1976.

Breitman, Richard. *Official Secrets: What the Nazis Planned and What the British and Americans Knew.* New York: Hill and Wang, 1998.

Browning, Christopher. *Fateful Months: Essays on the Emergence of the Final Solution.* New York: Holmes and Meier, 1985.

Dallin, Alexander. *German Rule in Russia 1941–1945: A Study of Occupation Policies.* 2nd ed. London: Macmillan, 1981.

Dobroszycki, Lucjan and Jeffrey S. Gurock, eds. *The Holocaust in the Soviet Union.* Armonk, N.Y.: Sharpe, 1993.

Dwork, Debórah. *Children with a Star: Jewish Youth in Nazi Europe.* New Haven, Conn.: Yale University Press, 1991.

Eliach, Yaffa. *Hasidic Tales of the Holocaust.* New York: Vintage, 1988.

Fonseca, Isabel. *Bury Me Standing: The Gypsies and Their Journey.* New York: Knopf, 1995.

Frank, Anne. *The Diary of a Young Girl.* New York: Doubleday, 1995.

Friedländer, Saul. *When Memory Comes.* The New York: Farrar, Straus and Giroux, 1979.

Friedman, Henry. *I'm No Hero: The Journeys of a Holocaust Survivor,* Seattle: University of Washington Press, 1999.

Gellately, Robert. *Backing Hitler: Consent and Coercion in Nazi Germany.* New York: Oxford University Press, 2001.

Goda, Norman J.W. *Tomorrow the World: Hitler, Northwest Africa and the Path toward America.* College Station: Texas A&M University Press, 1998.

Herf, Jeffrey. *The Jewish Enemy. Nazi Propaganda during World War II and the Holocaust.* Cambridge, Mass: Harvard University Press, 2006.

Hirschfeld, Gerhard, ed. *The Policies of Genocide: Jews and Soviet Prisoners of War in Nazi Germany.* London: Allen and Unwin, 1986.

Longerich, Peter. *The Unwritten Order: Hitler's Role in the Final Solution.* Stroud: Tempus, 2003.

Mazower, Mark. *Inside Hitler's Greece: The Experience of Occupation, 1941–1944.* New Haven, Conn.: Yale University Press, 1993.

Megargee, Geoffrey. *Inside Hitler's High Command.* Lawrence: University Press of Kansas, 2000.

My Knees Were Jumping: Remembering the Kindertransports. Directed and produced by Melissa Hacker. 1 hr. 16 min. National Center for Jewish Film, 1996. Videocassette.

Ramras-Rauch, Gila. *Aharon Appelfeld: The Holocaust and Beyond.* Bloomington: Indiana University Press, 1994.

Sachse, William, ed. *English History in the Making: Readings from the Sources.* Vol. 2 *Since 1689.* New York: Wiley, 1970.

Schek, Raffael. *Hitler's Forgotten Victims: The German Massacre of Black French Soldiers in 1940.* New York: Cambridge University Press, 2006.

Schulte, Theo J. *The German Army and Nazi Policies in Occupied Russia.* Oxford: St. Martin's, 1989.

Steinberg, Jonathan. *All or Nothing: The Axis and the Holocaust: 1941–1943.* London: Routledge, 1990.

Steinert, Marlis. *Hitler's War and the Germans: Public Mood and Attitude during the Second World War.* Athens: Ohio University Press, 1977.

Tec, Nechama. *Dry Tears.* New York: Oxford University Press, 1982.

Toll, Nelly S. *Behind the Secret Window: A Memoir of a Hidden Childhood during World War Two.* New York: Dial, 1993.

Tolstoy, Nikolai. *Stalin's Secret War.* New York: Holt, Rinehart and Winston, 1982.

Weinberg, Gerhard L. *A World at Arms: A Global History of the Second World War.* 2nd ed. New York: Cambridge University Press, 2005.

7. The Peak Years of Killing: 1942 and 1943

Améry, Jean. *At the Mind's Limits: Contemplations by a Survivor on Auschwitz and Its Realities.* New York: Schocken, 1986.

Blatt, Thomas (Toivi). *Sobibor: The Forgotten Revolt.* Issaquah, Wash.: H.E.P., 1998.

Bauer, Yehuda. *A History of the Holocaust.* New York: F. Watts, 1982.

Browning, Christopher R. *Nazi Policy, Jewish Labour, German Killers.* Cambridge: Cambridge University Press, 2000.
   Ordinary Men: Reserve Police Battalion 101 and the Final Solution in Poland. New York: HarperCollins, 1992.

Cesarani, David, ed. *The Final Solution: Origins and Implementation.* London: Routledge, 1994.

Dean, Martin. *Collaboration in the Holocaust: Crimes of the Local Police in Belorussia and Ukraine, 1941–1944.* New York: St. Martin's, 2000.

Delbo, Charlotte. *None of Us Will Return.* Translated by John Githens.
    Boston: Beacon, 1967.

Donat, Alexander, ed. *The Death Camp Treblinka: A Documentary.* New
    York: Holocaust Library, 1979.

Felstiner, Mary Lowenthal. *To Paint Her Life: Charlotte Salomon in the Nazi
    Era.* New York: HarperCollins, 1995.

Fenelon, Fania. *Playing for Time.* Edited by Marcelle Routier. Translated by
    Judith Landry. Syracuse, N.Y.: Syracuse University Press, 1976.

Friedländer, Saul. *Kurt Gerstein: The Ambiguity of Good.* Translated by
    Charles Fullman. New York: Knopf, 1969.

Ginaite-Rubinson, Sara. *Resistance and Survival: The Jewish Community in
    Kaunas, 1941–1944.* Oakville, Ontario.: Mosaic, 2005.

Goda, Norman J. W. 'Black Marks: Hitler's Bribery of His Senior Officers
    during World War II'. *Journal of Modern History* 72, no. 2 (2000): 413–52.

Goldenberg, Myrna. 'Different Horrors, Same Hell: Women Remembering
    the Holocaust'. In *Thinking the Unthinkable: Meanings of the Holocaust,*
    edited by Roger Gottlieb. New York: Paulist Press, 1990.

Greif, Gideon. *We Wept Without Tears. Testimonies of the Jewish Sonderkommando
    from Auschwitz.* New haven, Conn.: Yale University Press, 2005.

Hackett, David A. *The Buchenwald Report.* Boulder, Colo.: Westview, 1995.

Heger, Heinz. *The Men with the Pink Triangle.* Translated by David Fernbach.
    Boston: Alyson Publications, 1980.

Herbermann, Nanda. *The Blessed Abyss: Inmate #6582 in Ravensbrück
    Concentration Camp for Women.* Edited by Hester Baer and Elizabeth R.
    Baer. Translated by Hester Baer. Detroit: Wayne State University Press,
    2000.

Herbert, Ulrich, ed. *National Socialist Extermination Policies: Contemporary
    German Perspectives and Controversies.* New York: Berghahn Books, 2000.

Hillesum, Etty. *An Interrupted Life: The Diary of Etty Hillesum.* New York:
    Pocket Books, 1981.

    Letters from Westerbork. New York: Pantheon, 1986.

Hoess, Rudolf. *Commandant of Auschwitz.* Translated by Andrew Pollinger.
    Buffalo, N.Y.: Prometheus, 1992.

Hoffmann, Peter. *The History of the German Resistance, 1933–1945.* 3rd ed.
    Montreal: McGill-Queen's University Publishing, 1996.

Horwitz, Gordon J. *In the Shadow of Death: Living outside the Gates of
    Mauthausen.* New York: Free Press, 1990.

Klee, Ernst, Willi Dressen and Volker Reiss, eds. *The Good Old Days: The
    Holocaust as Seen By Its Perpetrators and Bystanders.* Translated by Deborah
    Burnstone. New York: Simon and Schuster, 1991.

Klemperer, Victor. *I Will Bear Witness: A Diary of the Nazi Years, 1941–1945.*
    Vol. 2. Translated by Martin Chalmers. New York: Random House, 1999.

Korczak, Janusz. *Ghetto Diary*. Edited and translated by H. Goldsmitz. New York: Holocaust Library, 1978.

Laks, Szymon. *Music of Another World*. Translated by Chester A. Kisiel. Evanston, Ill.: Northwestern University Press, 1989.

Lanzmann, Claude. *Shoah: An Oral History of the Holocaust, The Complete Text of the Film*. New York: Pantheon, 1985.

Lindeman, Yehudi. *Shards of Memory: Narratives of Holocaust Survival*. Westport, Conn.: Praegar, 2007

Lower, Wendy. *Nazi Empire Building and the Holocaust in Ukraine*. Chapel Hill, NC: University of North Carolina Press, 2005.

Laska, Vera. *Women in the Resistance and the Holocaust*. Westport, Conn.: Greenwood, 1983.

Levi, Primo. *Survival in Auschwitz*. New York: Collier, 1958.

Millu, Liana. *Smoke Over Birkenau*. Translated by Lynne Sharon Schwartz. Evanston, Ill.: Northwestern University Press, 1991.

Muller, Filip. *Eyewitness Auschwitz*. Edited and translated by Susanne Flatauer. Chicago: Ivan R. Dee, in association with the U.S. Holocaust Memorial Museum, 1999.

Noakes, Jeremy and Geoffrey Pridham, eds. *Nazism 1919–1945: A Documentary Reader*. 4 vols. Exeter: University of Exeter Department of History and Archeology, 1983–1998.

Nomberg-Przytyk, Sara. *Auschwitz: True Tales from a Grotesque Land*. Translated by Roslyn Hirsch. Chapel Hill: University of North Carolina Press, 1985.

Przyrembel, Alexandra. 'Transfixed by an Image: Ilse Koch, the 'Kommandeuse of Buchenwald'. Translated by Pamela Selwyn. *German History* 19, no. 3 (2001): 369–99.

Ringelheim, Joan. 'Women and the Holocaust: A Reconsideration of Research'. *Signs* 10 (1985): 741–61.

Rittner, Carol and John Roth, eds. *Different Voices: Women and the Holocaust*. New York: Paragon, 1993.

Scholl, Inge. *The White Rose*. 2nd ed. Translated by Arthur R. Schultz. Hanover, N.H.: Wesleyan University Press, 1983.

Scrase, David and Wolfgang Mieder, eds. *The Holocaust: Introductory Essays*. Burlington: Center for Holocaust Studies at the University of Vermont, 1996.

Sereny, Gitta. *Into That Darkness: An Examination of Conscience*. New York: Vintage, 1983.

Shoah. Produced by Les Films Aleph and Historia Films. Directed by Claude Lanzmann. 9 hrs. 30 min. Paramount Home Video, 1986. Videocassette.

Spiegelman, Art. *Maus: A Survivor's Tale*. 2 vols. New York: Pantheon, 1986.

Stabholz, Thaddeus. *Seven Hells.* Translated by Jacques Grunblatt and Hilda
    R. Grunblatt. New York: Holocaust Library, 1990.
Steinbacher, Sybille. *Auschwitz: A History.* Translated by Shaun Whiteside.
    London: Penguin, 2005.
Stoltzfus, Nathan. *Resistance of the Heart: Intermarriage and the Rosenstrasse
    Protest in Nazi Germany.* New York: Norton, 1996.
Szwajger, Adina Blady. *I Remember Nothing More.* Translated by Tasja
    Darowska. New York: Pantheon, 1990.
Tec, Nechama. *When Light Pierced the Darkness.* New York: Oxford
    University Press, 1985.
Troller, Norbert. *Theresienstadt: Hitler's Gift to the Jews.* Chapel Hill:
    University of North Carolina Press, 1991.
Tydor, Judith Baumel. *Double Jeopardy: Gender and the Holocaust.* London:
    Vallentine-Mitchell, 1998.
Wood, E. Thomas and Stanislaw M. Jankowski. *Karski: How One Man
    Tried to Stop the Holocaust.* New York: Wiley, 1994.

8. Death Throes and Killing Frenzies, 1944–1945

Aly, Götz. *Hitler's Beneficieries: Plunder, Racial War and the Nazi Welfare
    State.* Translated by Jefferson Chase. New York: Henry Holt, 2006.
Braham, Randolph L. *The Politics of Genocide: The Holocaust in Hungary.*
    Condensed ed. Detroit: Wayne State University Press, 2000.
Braham, Randolph L. and Scott Miller, eds. *The Nazis' Last Victims: The
    Holocaust in Hungary.* Detroit: Wayne State University Press, 1998.
Elias, Ruth. *Triumph of Hope: From Theresienstadt and Auschwitz to Israel.*
    Translated by Margot Bettauer Dembo. New York: Wiley, 1998.
Fein, Helen. *Accounting for Genocide: National Responses and Jewish
    Victimization during the Holocaust.* Chicago: University of Chicago Press,
    1984.
Goldhagen, Daniel Jonah. *Hitler's Willing Executioners.* New York: Knopf,
    1996.
Gutman, Israel and Michael Berenbaum, eds. *Anatomy of the Auschwitz
    Death Camp.* Bloomington: Indiana University Press, 1994.
Hellman, Peter, Lili Meier and Serge Klarsfeld. *The Auschwitz Album: A Book
    Based upon an Album Discovered by a Concentration Camp Survivor.* New
    York: Random House, 1981.
Hoffmann, Peter. *Stauffenberg: A Family History, 1905–1944.* 2nd ed.
    Montreal and Kingston: McGill-Queen's University Press, 2003.
Ioanid, Radu. *The Holocaust in Romania: The Destruction of Jews and Gypsies
    under the Antonescu Regime, 1940–1944.* Chicago: Ivan R. Dee, 2000.

Isaacson, Judith Magyar. *Seed of Sarah: Memoirs of a Survivor.* Urbana: University of Illinois Press, 1990.

Klein, Gerda Weissmann. *All But My Life.* New York: Hill and Wang, 1957.

Moltke, Helmuth James von. *Letters to Freya 1939–1945.* Edited and translated by Beate Ruhm von Oppen. New York: Knopf, 1990.

Perel, Solomon. *Europa, Europa.* Translated by Margot Bettauer Dembo. New York: Wiley, in association with the U.S. Holocaust Memorial Museum, 1997.

Rotem, Simha. 'Kazik'. In *Memoirs of a Warsaw Ghetto Fighter*, translated by Barbara Harshav. New Haven, Conn.: Yale University Press, 1994.

Sereny, Gitta. *Albert Speer: His Battle with Truth.* New York: Knopf, 1995.

Siegal, Aranka. *Grace in the Wilderness.* New York: Puffin, 1985.

Speer, Albert. *Inside the Third Reich: Memoirs.* Translated by Richard Winston and Clara Winston. New York: Macmillan, 1970.

Volavkova, Hana, ed. *I Never Saw Another Butterfly: Children's Drawings and Poems from Terezin Concentration Camp, 1942–1944.* 2nd ed. New York: Pantheon, 1994.

Wallenberg, Raoul. *Letters and Dispatches: 1924–1944.* Translated by Kjersti Board. New York: Arcade, 1995.

Wells, Leon Welickzer. *The Janowska Road.* New York: Macmillan, 1999.

Wiesel, Elie. *Night.* Translated by Stella Rodway. New York: Bantam, 1960.

Epilogue: The Legacies of Atrocity

Abzug, Robert H. *Inside the Vicious Heart: Americans and the Liberation of Nazi Concentration Camps.* New York: Oxford University Press, 1985.

Baldwin, Peter, ed. *Reworking the Past: Hitler, the Holocaust and the Historians' Debate.* Boston: Beacon, 1990.

Brenner, Michael. *After the Holocaust: Rebuilding Jewish Lives in Postwar Germany.* Princeton, N.J.: Princeton University Press, 1997.

Dinnerstein, Leonard. *America and the Survivors of the Holocaust.* New York: Columbia University Press, 1982.

Friedländer, Saul. *Reflections of Nazism: An Essay on Kitsch and Death.* New York: Harper and Row, 1982.

Langer, Lawrence. *Holocaust Testimonies: Ruins of Memory.* New Haven, Conn.: Yale University Press, 1991.

Preempting the Holocaust. New Haven, Conn.: Yale University Press, 1998.

Levi, Primo. *The Drowned and the Saved.* Translated by Raymond Rosenthal. New York: Summit, 1988.

Mankowitz, Zeev W. *Life Between Memory and Hope: The Survivors of the Holocaust in Occupied Germany*. New York: Cambridge University Press, 2002.

Marrus, Michael. *The Nuremberg War Crimes Trial 1945–46: A Documentary History*. Boston: Bedford Books, 1997.

Miller, Judith. *One, by One, by One: Facing the Holocaust*. New York: Simon and Schuster, 1990.

Myers, Margarete. 'The Jewish Displaced Persons: Reconstructing Individual and Community in the U.S. Zone of Occupied Germany'. *Leo Baeck Institute Yearbook* 42 (1997): 302–24.

Naimark, Norman. *The Russians in Germany: A History of the Soviet Zone of Occupation, 1945–1949*. Cambridge, Mass.: Belknap, 1995.

Niewyk, Donald. *Fresh Wounds: Early Narratives of Holocaust Survival*. Chapel Hill: University of North Carolina Press, 1998.

Novick, Peter. *The Holocaust in American Life*. Boston: Houghton Mifflin, 1999.

Rubenstein, Richard. *After Auschwitz*. Baltimore: Johns Hopkins University Press, 1992.

Trials of War Criminals before the Nuremberg Military Tribunals under Control Council Law No. 10, October 1946–April 1949. 42 vols. Nuremberg: U.S. Government Printing Office, 1947–1949.

List of Illustrations

1. Illustration from a 1938 German children's book. USHMM, courtesy of published source (Ernst Hiemer, *Der Giftpilz: Erzählungen* [*The Poisonous Mushroom: Stories*]. *Der Stürmer*, c. 1938.)
2. Antisemitic poster for *Der Stürmer*. USHMM, courtesy of Deutsches Historisches Museum GmbH.
3. A German race scientist, accompanied by a policeman, questions a Gypsy (Roma) woman. Bundesarchiv Koblenz (R165-244-71).
4. The morning after the *Kristallnacht* pogrom. USHMM, courtesy of Bildarchiv Preussischer Kulturbesitz. Photographer: Paulmann.
5. Identity card issued in September 1939 in British-controlled Cyprus. USHMM, courtesy of Lily Haber.
6. German passport stamped with a red 'J' to indicate that the bearer was Jewish. USHMM, courtesy of John and Harriet Isaack.
7. Inside pages of enemy alien registration identity card. USHMM, courtesy of Lily Haber.
8. 'Gurs II', by Gert H. Wollheim (1893–1974. USHMM, courtesy of Museum Purchase.)
9. A chart of prisoner markings used in German concentration camps. USHMM, courtesy of KZ Gedenkstaette Dachau.
10. Nuns walk along a road with patients in August 1940. Stiftung Liebenau, Ressort Kommunikation [neg. 10564].
11. Doctors and patients at the Liebenau 'euthanasia' facility stand outside a bus. Stiftung Liebenau, Ressort Kommunikation [neg. 10564].

12. Children in the Łódź ghetto waiting in line for the soup kitchen. USHMM, courtesy of Juedisches Museum der Stadt Frankfurt; Photographer: Walter Genewein.
13. A group of boys in the Łódź ghetto. USHMM, courtesy of Juedisches Museum der Stadt Frankfurt; Photographer: Walter Genewein.
14. A woman and two children in the Łódź ghetto. USHMM, courtesy of Juedisches Museum der Stadt Frankfurt; Photographer: Walter Genewein.
15. An open-air market in the Łódź ghetto. USHMM, courtesy of Robert Abrams; Photographer: Walter Genewein.
16. Izak Lefkowizc, a ghetto postman. USHMM, courtesy of Robert Abrams; Photographer: Walter Genewein.
17. Ink drawing of a Łódź ghetto policeman by Kurant (?), dated 20 January 1941. USHMM, courtesy of Bernat Berk.
18. A merchant at his stall at the outdoor market of the Łódź ghetto. USHMM, courtesy of Juedisches Museum der Stadt Frankfurt; Photographer: Walter Genewein.
19. Jews board a passenger train during a transport action in the Łódź ghetto. USHMM, courtesy of Robert Abrams.
20. A ration card issued to the Jewish Council of Rzeszow. Photo Credit: USHMM, courtesy of Jack J. Silverstein.
21. 'Vendor of Jewish Stars', drawing by Halina Olomucki. USHMM, courtesy of Halina Olomucki.
22. View of the Gypsy camp in the Łódź ghetto. Photo Credit: USHMM, courtesy of Robert Abrams; Photographer: Walter Genewein.
23. Street scene from the Lublin ghetto, June 1941. Deutsches Historisches Museum, neg. (6620); Photographer: Max Kirnberger.
24. A German poster from after 7 December 1941. USHMM Photo Archives.
25. Illustrated page of an Italian child's diary, written in a Swiss refugee camp in 1943-44. USHMM, courtesy of Bruna D'Urbino.
26. A special issue of Serbian stamps bearing antisemitic and anti-Masonic themes. USHMM, courtesy of Morris Rosen.
27. German propaganda poster from 17 September 1941. USHMM, courtesy of Museum Purchase.
28. Watercolour by Nellie Toll entitled 'Peasant Family Eating at a Table'. USHMM, courtesy of Nellie Landau Toll.
29. Watercolour by Nellie Toll entitled 'Teacher with Children Wearing Black Uniforms'. USHMM, courtesy of Nellie Landau Toll.
30. Painting by Halina Olomucki, *Le camp les litieres dans le bloc*. USHMM, courtesy of Halina Olomucki.

31. One page of an illustrated album produced by Gyorgy Beifeld. USHMM Collection, Gift of Ivan Marko, Harold Wheen Tebbutt, Gabriella Teichner and Judith Uri.

32. Another page of Gyorgy Beifeld's illustrated album. USHMM Collection, Gift of Ivan Marko, Harold Wheen Tebbutt, Gabriella Teichner and Judith Uri.

33. View of the entrance to Auschwitz-Birkenau from inside the camp. USHMM, courtesy of Bildarchiv Pruessischer Kulturbesitz.

34. Untitled drawing of Birkenau by Franz Reisz, an Austria Jewish artist born in 1909. USHMM, courtesy of Aleksander Kulisiewicz.

35. Drawing by an unidentified artist of camp guards watching prisoners die in a gas chamber. USHMM Photo Archives.

36. Interior view of a gas chamber at Majdanek, showing a blue stain from Zyklon B. USHMM, courtesy of Archiwum Panstwowego Muzeum na Majdanku.

37. German civilians conscripted by U.S. troops dig mass graves. USHMM, courtesy of William O. McWorkman; Photographer: William O. McWorkman.

38. Former prisoners assemble in front of a barracks in the newly liberated Dachau concentration camp. USHMM, courtesy of Colonel Alexander Zabin.

39. Postwar view of the site of the Warsaw ghetto. USHMM Photo Archives

40. Survivors gathered outside Buchenwald concentration camp. USHMM, courtesy of Patricia A. Yingst; Photographer: Lieutenant Colonel Parke O. Yingst

41. An American soldier stands near a wagon piled high with corpses. USHMM, courtesy of Patricia A. Yingst; Photographer Lieutenant Colonel Parke O. Yingst

42. An American soldier stands among the corpses exhumed from a mass grave. USHMM, courtesy of Seymour Schenkman; Photograph Seymour Schenkman

43. David Greenfield sits in the centre of a large Star of David. USHMM, courtesy of Joseph and Rachel Greenfield

44. Survivors from Norway in the newly liberated Buchenwald concentration camp. USHMM, courtesy of Joseph Mendelsohn; Photographer: Joseph Mendelsohn

45. 'Aftermath', by Ernu Homanye-Grytze. USHMM, courtesy of Erwin Kieckhefer

46. View of the main camp at Auschwitz. USHMM Photo Archives

47. Cover page of 'Jidisze Bilder' USHMM, courtesy of Jack Sutin; Photographer: Jack Sutin

48.   A group of religious Jews goes on a kayaking excursion in Poland in the 1930s. USHMM, courtesy of Marilka (Mairanz) Ben Naim, Ita (Mairanz) Mond and Tuvia Mairanz.

49.   German Jewish soldiers celebrating Hanukkah in the field during World War I. USHMM, courtesy of Zydowski Instytut Historyczny Instytut Naukowo-Badawczy.

50.   The Jewish proprietor of a kosher butcher shop in Danzig. USHMM, courtesy of Betty Speier April.

51.   Children at the Jewish elementary school in Essen. USHMM, courtesy of Henry Straus.

52.   Members of the German boxing club 'Sparta' in 1929. USHMM, courtesy of Hans Firzlaff.

53.   A Gypsy encampment in Haarlem. USHMM, courtesy of Nederlands Instituut voor Oorlogsdocumentatie.

54.   A scene from around 1929 in the Eldorado, a nightclub frequented by the Berlin homosexual community. Photo credit: USHMM, courtesy of Schwules Museum.

55.   A lecture slide used during the 1930s at the national eugenics institute in Berlin. USHMM, courtesy of Irmgard Nippert.

56.   Portraits of the offspring of a union between an African woman and a white man. USHMM, courtesy of Bezirkskrankenhaus Kaufbeuren.

57.   A filmstrip of the Reich Propaganda office titled, 'The Terrible Legacy of an Alcoholic Woman'. USHMM, courtesy of Roland Klemig.

58.   A 1941 poster titled 'The Jewish Conspiracy'. USHMM, courtesy of Paul Flacks

59.   A 1933 poster depicting the Nazi view of Freemasonry and its purported links to a Jewish world conspiracy. USHMM, courtesy of Hans Pauli.

60.   Adolf Hitler and Heinrich Himmler review SS troops during Reich Party Day ceremonies in September 1938. USHMM, courtesy of Estelle Bechoefer.

61.   Hermann Göring delivers a speech at the District Party Day rally in Weimar in April 1931. USHMM, courtesy of James Sanders.

62.   Joseph Goebbels by renowned photographer Alfred Eisenstaedt. Alfred Eisenstaedt/Pix Inc./TimePix.

63.   Hitler on vacation, pictured with Helga Goebbels. USHMM, courtesy of Richard Freimark.

64.   Members of the League of German Girls. USHMM, courtesy of Foto-Willinger Collection, Hoover Institution Archives.

65.   Photo montage by German Artist John Heartfield entitled 'The Gallows Greeting'. John Heartfield, 1933.

66. A woman emerging from a Jewish-owned business in violation of the April 1933 boycott. USHMM, courtesy of Der Stuermer Archive, Stadtarchiv Nuremberg.

67. Heinrich Himmler at the entrance to the Dachau concentration camp during a 1936 inspection. Bundesarchiv Koblenz (152-09-25).

68. Watercolour by Johannes Steyer, a German Jehovah's Witness. Hans Hesse, ed., *Persecution and Resistance of Jehovah's Witnesses during the Nazi Regime 1933-1945*. Bremen, Germany: Edition Temmen, 2000. Used by permission.

69. Watercolour by Johannes Steyer, a German Jehovah's Witness. Hans Hesse, ed., *Persecution and Resistance of Jehovah's Witnesses during the Nazi Regime 1933-1945*. Bremen, Germany: Edition Temmen, 2000. Used by permission.

70. Himmler speaks to an inmate at Dachau in 1936, during an SS inspection of the camp. USHMM, courtesy of KZ Gedenkstaette Dachau.

71. 'Kauft Gasmasken' (Buy Gas Masks), an etching from 1934 or 1936 by Lea Grundig. USHMM, courtesy of Ladengalerie Berlin

72. A member of the Reich Department of Health, Racial Hygiene and Population Biology visits a Roma family in Vienna. Bundesarchiv Koblenz (146/87/111/21).

73. A Jewish woman washes clothes in the Zbaszyn refugee camp in Poland. USHMM, courtesy of Michael Irving Ashe.

74. The synagogue in Ober Ramstadt, Hesse is destroyed by fire. USHMM, courtesy of Trudy Isenberg; Photographer: Georg Schmidt

75. Children watch the Ober Ramstadt synagogue burn. USHMM, courtesy of Trudy Isenberg; Photographer: Georg Schmidt.

76. SS men march Jewish men through Baden-Baden. USHMM, courtesy of Lydia Chagoll.

77. An official visit by Hitler to the Sachsenhausen concentration camp around 1938. USHMM, courtesy of Instytut Pamieci Narodewej.

78. Prisoners of Sachsenhausen at forced labour. USHMM, courtesy of Gedenkstatte und Museum Sachsenhausen.

79. A carnival parade in February 1939 in the south German town of Neustadt mocks Jews. USHMM, courtesy of Stadtarchiv Neustadt.

80. A float in the Shrove Tuesday parade in the German Catholic town of Singen am Hohentwiel in February 1939. Photo credit: USHMM, courtesy of Stadtarchiv Singen am Hohentwiel.

81. A group of children from the Catholic institution for the disabled in Ecksberg board a bus that will transport them to a killing facility. Katholische Nachrichten Agentur Pressebild GmBH.

82. Hajj Amin al-Husayni, the Grand Mufti of Jerusalem, poses with German officials at a reception in Berlin. USHMM, courtesy of George Birman.

83. Poles seized during the 'pacification' of Bydgoszcz (Bromberg) in September 1939. USHMM, courtesy of Gertrude Adams.

84. SS personnel lead Polish women into the forest to be killed. USHMM, courtesy of the Main Commission for the Prosecution of the Crimes against the Polish Nation.

85. The execution of Piotr Sosnowski, a Roman Catholic priest. USHMM, courtesy of the Main Commission for the Prosecution of the Crimes against the Polish Nation.

86. A postcard showing the entrance to the Łódź ghetto in 1940 or 1941. USHMM Photo Archives.

87. Rabbi David Lifszyc and another man pose in front of a cabinet full of Torah scrolls that were smuggled out of the Polish city of Suwalki. USHMM, courtesy of Chaya Lifshitz Waxman.

88. Norbert Swislocki and his parents celebrate Passover with other refugees in April 1940 in Vilna. USHMM, courtesy of Norbert Swislocki.

89. Women prisoners gather by the barbed wire fence surrounding a North African internment camp. USHMM, courtesy of Hans Landesberg.

90. Prisoners gather outside their barracks in a North African internment camp. USHMM, courtesy of Hans Landesberg.

91. Two German Jewish refugee women stand behind the counter of the Elite Provision Store in Shanghai in 1939 or 1940. USHMM, courtesy of Ralph Harpuder.

92. Joseph Fiszman poses with four Chinese children in a store in Shanghai. USHMM, courtesy of Joseph Fiszman.

93. A Polish Gentile woman and two Polish Jewish men are forced to walk together, probably to an execution site, sometime in the 1940s. USHMM, courtesy of the Dokumentationsarchiv des Oesterreichischen Widerstandes.

94. A public execution in occupied Poland. USHMM, courtesy of Dokumentationsarchiv des Oesterreichischen Widerstandes.

95. A German soldier searches a Gypsy in Poland, probably in 1940. USHMM, courtesy of Harry Lore.

96. A German soldier stands guard in front of a castle. USHMM, courtesy of Rita Prigmore.

97. A Jewish soldier in the Dutch army poses astride his motorcycle. USHMM, courtesy of Robert Krell.

98. The ruins of Rotterdam after its bombing by the German air force on 14 May 1940. USHMM, courtesy of Instytut Pamieci Narodowej.

99. French colonial troops and their German captors in an unidentified POW camp. USHMM, courtesy of Instytut Pamieci Narodowej.

100. A Gypsy woman with a group of children in the Rivesaltes internment camp in 1942. USHMM, courtesy of Jacqueline Levy.

101. A Serbian gendarme escorts a group of Gypsies to their execution. USHMM, courtesy of Muzej Revolucije Narodnosti Jugoslavije.

102. A young girl in the Loborgrad concentration camp in Croatia. USHMM, Memorijalni Muzej Jasenovac (Collections: 2002.537.4).

103. The body of a Jewish doctor hangs on an electric pole in front of a bank in Sabac, Yugoslavia, in August 1941. USHMM, courtesy of Jewish Historical Museum of Yugoslavia.

104. Germans pose near the bodies of recently murdered Serbian civilians in 1941. USHMM, courtesy of Mrs. John Titak III.

105. German troops stand at the edge of a trench used as a mass grave for the bodies of Jews and Gypsies. USHMM, courtesy of Dokumentationsarchiv des Oesterreichischen Widerstandes.

106. Germans shoot a group of Poles in Lithuania in 1941 or 1942. USHMM, courtesy of Dokumentationsarchiv des Oesterreichischen Widerstandes.

107. A column of Soviet POWs moving toward a German internment camp near Kharkov. USHMM, courtesy of National Archives and Records Administration, College Park.

108. Soviet POWs in the 'Sonderlager' (special camp) at Sachsenhausen. USHMM, courtesy of Gedenkstatte und Museum Sachsenhausen.

109. A column of Soviet POWs heading toward the rear and internment. USHMM, courtesy of Archiwum Dokumentacji Mechanicznej; Photographer: Heinrich Hoffmann/Studio of H. Hoffmann.

110. A man filling a bucket from a standpipe in the Lublin ghetto. USHMM, courtesy of Instytut Pamieci Narodowej; Photographer: Otto Roesner.

111. Shmuel Grosman recites the morning prayer service in his bed in the Łódź ghetto. Beit Lohamei Haghetaot; Photographer: Mendel Grosman.

112. A woman selected for 'deportation' communicates with her son through the fence of the central prison in the Łódź ghetto. USHMM, courtesy of YIVO Institute.

113. A young Jewish woman in the Łódź ghetto writes a last letter before being transported to the killing centre at Chelmno. USHMM, courtesy of Leopold Page Photographic Collection.

114. Local Gypsies remove corpses from the Iasi-Calarasi death train during a stop in Targu-Frumos. USHMM, courtesy of Serviciul Roman De Informatii.

115. A group of Roma sits in an open area near the fence at Belzec in late 1941 or 1942. USHMM, courtesy of Archiwum Dokumentocji Mechanizney

116. Clandestine photograph of a Polish political prisoner and medical experimentation victim in Ravensbrück, October 1944. USHMM, courtesy of Anna Hassa Jarosky and Peter Hassa.

117. Christmas card given to Jadwiga Hassa in December 1942 by a fellow inmate of the Ravensbrück concentration camp. USHMM, courtesy of Anna Hassa Jarosky and Peter Hassa.

118. Dr Bigula Vajs attending to a sick child in Yugoslavia during the war. USHMM, courtesy of Jewish Historical Museum of Yugoslavia.

119. Dutch-Jewish children brought from the crèche to a children's home by the Dutch underground. USHMM, courtesy of Hilde Jacobsthal Goldberg.

120. Jewish partisan Bronia Szyr. USHMM, courtesy of Brenda Szyr Senders.

121. Stjepan Filipovic calls on the people of Serbia to fight just before his execution. USHMM, courtesy of Muzej Revolucije Narodnosti Jugoslavije.

122. Jewish Partisan Sara Ginaite. USHMM, courtesy of Sara Ginaite.

123. Georges Herz leads a pair of oxen on the grounds of the Chateau La Hille. USHMM, courtesy of Walter Reed.

124. Two little girls in the Kovno ghetto wearing Stars of David. USHMM, courtesy of Henia Wisgardisky Lewin.

125. A sick child in a crib in the Kovno ghetto hospital. USHMM, courtesy of George Kadish/Zvi Kadushin; Photographer: George Kadish/Zvi Kadushin.

126. Two young boys wearing Jewish badges in the Kovno ghetto. USHMM, courtesy of Shraga Wainer; Photographer: George Kadish/Zvi Kadushin.

127. Drawing made in December 1943 by Anatoli Garnik depicting the exhumation and burning of corpses at the Ninth Fort near Kovno. Ninth Fort Museum (DFMGEK 430), courtesy of USHMM.

128. Willem Arondeus and friends dancing at a garden party. USHMM, courtesy of Toni Boumans.

129. Jewish women and children see their fathers, husbands and sons as they are driven away from the deportation assembly point in Ioannina, Greece. Bundesarchiv (101-I-179-1575-15).

130. Jewish women and children assembled for transport in March 1944 from Ioannina, Greece. Bundesarchiv (101 I-179-1575-19.

131. Assembly for deportation at the railroad station of Koszeg, Hungary, May 1944. USHMM, courtesy of Magyar Nemzeti Muzeum Torteneti Fenykeptar.

132. Jews in the Westerbork camp in the Netherlands light Hanukkah candles. USHMM, courtesy of Yad Vashem Photo Archives; Photographer: Rudolf Werner Breslauer.

133. The main rail entrance of Auschwitz–Birkenau. USHMM, courtesy of YIVO Institute; Photographer: Stanislaw Mucha.

134. Jews get off a train and assemble on the ramp at Auschwitz–Birkenau. USHMM, courtesy of Yad Vashem (Public Domain); Photographer: Bernhardt Walter/Ernst Hofmann.

135. Jewish women and children await selection on the ramp at Auschwitz–Birkenau in May 1944. USHMM, courtesy of Yad Vashem (Public Domain); Photographer: Bernhardt Walter/Ernst Hofmann.

136. Women and children from Subcarpathian Rus on the ramp at Auschwitz–Birkenau. USHMM, courtesy of Yad Vashem (Public Domain); Photographer: Bernhardt Walter/Ernst Hofmann.

137. On the ramp at Auschwitz–Birkenau. USHMM, courtesy of Yad Vashem (Public Domain); Photographer: Bernhardt Walter/Ernst Hofmann.

138. Jewish brothers from Subcarpathian Rus on the ramp at Auschwitz–Birkenau. USHMM, courtesy of Yad Vashem (Public Domain); Photographer: Bernhardt Walter/Ernst Hofmann.

139. Women and children walk toward the gas chambers at Auschwitz–Birkenau, May 1944. USHMM, courtesy of Yad Vashem (Public Domain); Photographer: Bernhardt Walter/Ernst Hofmann.

140. Jewish women and children from Subcarpathian Rus walking toward the gas chambers in May 1944. USHMM, courtesy of Yad Vashem (Public Domain); Photographer: Bernhardt Walter/Ernst Hofmann.

141. SS Sturmbahnführer Richard Baer at the table of a hunting lodge. USHMM, courtesy of Anonymous Donor.

142. SS officer Karl Hoecker lights a candle on a Christmas tree. USHMM, courtesy of Anonymous Donor.

143. Karl Hoecker shakes hands with his dog Favorit. USHMM, courtesy of Anonymous Donor.

144. SS officers and women auxiliaries on a wooden bridge in Solahütte. USHMM, courtesy of Anonymous Donor.

145. Members of the SS Helferinnen and SS officer Karl Hoecker turn over their bowls to show they have eaten all their blueberries. USHMM, courtesy of Anonymous Donor.

146. A survivor looks out a barred window at the Hadamar Institute. USHMM, courtesy of Rosanne Bass Fulton; Photographer: Troy A. Peters.

147. A survivor in front of a barred window at the Hadamar Institute. USHMM, courtesy of Rosanne Bass Fulton; Photographer: Troy A. Peters.

148. Jewish youth liberated at Buchenwald lean out the windows of a train as it pulls away from the station. USHMM, courtesy of Robert Waisman.

149. Ruins of the Kovno ghetto, photographed in August 1944. USHMM, courtesy of George Kadish/Zvi Kadushin; Photographer: George Kadish/Zvi Kadushin.

150. German civilians watch a film about the atrocities of the Bergen-Belsen and Buchenwald concentration camps. USHMM, courtesy of Imperial War Museum.

151. German civilians exit the cinema where they were forced to see a film showing atrocities perpetrated in Buchenwald and Bergen-Belsen. USHMM, courtesy of Imperial War Museum.

152. Marion Kaufmann with the Gypsy family that hid her for a month in the Netherlands. USHMM, courtesy of Marion I. Cassirer.

153. Jewish displaced women pose with Red Army officers. USHMM, courtesy of Lilly Rosenzweig Wolnerman.

154. Ernst Mettbach testifies as a witness at the 1946-1947 Doctors Trial. USHMM, courtesy of National Archives and Records Administration, College Park.

155. Halina Mosinskis of Lithuania is presented with a certificate by Yad Vashem. USHMM, courtesy of Yad Vashem Photo Archives

156. Europe on the Eve of the Second World War. Map by Michael J. Fisher, cartographer.

157. The Division of Poland. Map by Michael J. Fisher, cartographer.

158. Map of killing centres and concentration camps. Map by Michael J. Fisher, cartographer.

Index

Abel, Theodore, 76
Africa, 30–1, 70–1, 112, 238–9;
    North Africa, 238–9
African soldiers, in occupation of
    Germany after First World War,
    31–2; as victims of killings in
    1940, 200–1
Afro-Germans, 8, 14, 68, 71, 87
Against the Jews and their Lies, 17
air raids: Allied: 220, 235, 273–4;
    German: 198–9, 203–6. See also
    Blitzkrieg; Luftwaffe
Albania, 240
Algeria, 239
Allied forces/Allies, 198–206; and
    Jews, 232–3, 237, 264–5; in the
    last year of war, 270, 271, 273,
    279, 285, 288–9;
-in post-war: 289–93. See also
    Britain, Soviet Union, United
    States, Second World War
Alsace-Lorraine, 39
Alten, Mark, 130–1

Americans. See United States
Amsterdam, 200
Anschluss (annexation of Austria),
    97–8, 208. See also Austria;
    Germany
Anti-Gypsyism, 25–7
antisemitism, 11, 13–7, 98, 122; as
    centre of Nazi ideology, 8, 14;
    history of, 14; Hitler's, 45–8;
    linked to other Nazi prejudices,
    28–9, 33–4, 37; outside Germany,
    99–100, 135–9, 221–3, 288–9;
    redemptive antisemitism, 8, 51
anti-Slavic attitudes, 32–4, 136
Antonescu, Ion, 221–3
appeasement, 100–1
Appelfeld, Aharon, 222
Ardennes Offensive. See Battle of
    the Bulge
Arendt, Hannah, 129, 139
Argentina, 294
armistice agreement, German-
    French, 201

Article 66, Weimar Constitution, 62–3

Article 304, Treaty of Versailles, 39

'Aryans', 236; as a constructed category, 50–1, 86, 210, 228, 235, 260

'asocials', 34, 69, 75, 244; in concentration camps, 256, 259–60

Augspurg, Anita, 111

Auschwitz (and Auschwitz–Birkenau), 134, 226, 228, 246, 249, 257, 294; at the end of the war, 242, 280–3, 289; Hungarian Jews in, 122–3, 251, 280–1; other Jews in, 126, 132–3, 200, 204, 242–3, 270; resistance in, 265; Roma in, 271, 282; Soviet POWs in, 224–5. See also killing centres

Australia, 74, 112, 202, 293

Austria, 39, 42–5, 59, 108; Anschluss, 97–100; Jews from, 114, 201, 247

Austria-Hungary, 32, 59

Axis, Rome-Berlin, 109, 240

Babi Yar, 218

Badoglio, Pietro, 240

Baeck, Rabbi Leo, 74

Balkans, 209, 211. See also Greece; Yugoslavia

Baltic States, 109, 122, 206, 212. See also Estonia; Latvia; Lithuania

Bartov, Omer, 211

Battle of Britain, 203–5.

Battle of the Bulge, 284

Battle of Stalingrad, 233–7

Bavaria, 47, 283

Beer Hall Putsch, 47, 54, 61–2, 102

Belaya Tserkov, 219

Belgium, 58, 196, 200, 227

Belgrade, 209

Belorussia, 134, 140, 212, 217, 229, 273–4. See also Soviet Union

Belzec, 245–6, 249, 263. See also killing centres.

Bergen-Belsen, 200, 256, 281, 288. See also concentration camps.

Berlin, 57, 95–6, 225–6, 246, 272, 276, 286; concentration camps nearby, 104, 105; gay community, 35, 86, 265–6; Hitler and, 117, 285; Jews in, 102, 111, 201, 235; T– programme, 142–3

Berlin-Plötzensee, 276

Bessarabia, 206

Bialystok, 129, 265

Bielski partisans, 140

Bielski, Tuvia, 140

Binding, Karl, 24–5

Bismarck, Otto von, 197

black market, 274

Blaskowitz, Johannes, 125

Blitzkrieg, 117, 197. See also Germany, Poland.

Blomberg, Werner von, 92–3

Bolsheviks/Bolshevism, 33, 137, 216–7, 224. See also communism, communists; Russia; Soviet Union

Bosnia, 209, 210. See also Yugoslavia

Bouhler, Philipp, 113, 142, 144

boycott, anti-Jewish, 71–3

Brandt, Karl, 113, 142, 144

Brauchitsch, Walter von, 92

Braun, Eva, 286

Braunau am Inn, 43

Brazil, 294

Brecht, Bertolt, 78, 111

Breitman, Richard, 56

Brest Litovsk, Treaty of, 38–9

Britain, 73, 104, 196–9, 206, 209, 239; Battle of, 203–5; final stages of war, 284, 289–90; First World War and, 39, 59, 90; as imperial power, 28–9, 31, 202; Jews and, 103–4, 201–2, 204, 225, 239–40,

263–4; navy, 108–9, 198; as occupying power, 295; partisans and, 209, 268; pre-war relations with Germany, 99, 109; Second World War and, 116, 196–200, 223–4, 239–40, 273–4

brothels, 120, 250–1, 256–7, 262

Brüning, Heinrich, 63

Buchenwald, 214, 256–7, 261. See also concentration camps.

Budapest, 280–2

Bug River, 222

Bukovina, 206

Bulgaria, 205–6, 209, 279

Buna rubber works, 249

Bydgoszcz (Bromberg), 143–4

Canada, 202, 264; as a destination for refugees and fugitives, 74, 112–3, 292–4

Caribbean, 293

Catholic Church, 44, 214; in Germany, 36, 69, 78–9, 106; protest against and legitimation of Nazi measures, 75, 120, 124, 145, 219, 232, 251. See also Christianity; Clemens August von Galen; Pius XII; protest; Vatican

Caucasus, 233–4

Centre Party, 66

Chamberlain, Neville, 100

chaplains, military, 219, 232

Chelmno (Kulmhof), 128–9, 243–5, 253. See also killing centres.

children: of concentration camp personnel, 250; Germanisation of, 229–30, 232, 268; Jehovah's Witnesses' taken away, 106; Jewish children, 250, 253–4; post-war, 289–90, 293–6; Jewish children rescued and

hidden, 203–4, 254, 265, 295; Roma children killed, 260; in Volkssturm, 277

China, 111

Christianity, 19, 23, 50–1, 137, 203, 246; antisemitism and Jews and, 16–7, 85; Nazi suspicion of, 54–5, 105, 232, 246; role in protests against Nazi measures, 145, 260–1, 275–6. See also Catholic Church; Protestant church in Germany

Churchill, Winston, 203, 263–4

circumcision, 20, 254

code–breaking, 198, 264

collaboration, 198–9, 201, 269; against Jews and Gypsies, 216–8, 239–40, 255, 280; post-war fate of, 292

communism, 33, 67, 91–2, 213, 291; Hitler and, 51, 109; Jews and, 137–8; Jehovah's Witnesses and, 291; papacy and, 79, 124. See also Communist Party; communists; Soviet Union; Stalin

Communist Party, German, 33, 62, 64, 85; attacked under Nazism, 66, 68, 77–8, 105; resistance and obstacles, 110, 112, 266. See also communism; communists

communists, 14, 33, 61, 210, 221; resistance, 201; Soviet purges of, 110–1; as targets of Nazism, 225, 255–6, 260. See also communism; Communist Party; Soviet Union.

concentration camps, 30; in pre-war Germany, 67–8, 76–7, 86, 102, 104, 106–9, 246–7; in Second World War, 116, 121, 208–9, 254, 256, 258, 260–2

Concordat, with Vatican, 79–80, 105, 108–9. See also Catholic Church; Pius XII

Conti, Leonardo, 142

conversion/converts from Judaism to Christianity, 16–7, 72–4, 96, 132

Coventry, 204

Crimea, 232

criminals, imprisoned in concentration camps, 256–8. See also 'asocials'

Croatia, 59, 205, 210, 257. See also Yugoslavia

Cuba, 112

Czechoslovakia, 59, 99, 202–3, 229; German minority in, 33, 99; Jews from, 122–3, 201–2, 247; resistance in, 268, 284; Sudetenland crisis, 99–100

Czerniaków, Adam, 133, 254

D–Day, 271, 274–5

Dachau, 67, 77, 104, 106, 248–9, 257. See also concentration camps

Dante Alighieri, 259

Danzig (Gdansk), 118

death marches, 272, 283–4

de Gaulle, Charles, 201

dehumanisation, 242–3

Denmark, 109, 196, 198–9, 227; rescue of Jews from, 205

denunciations, 89, 217, 261, 265, 290

deportations, 123, 206, 241, 289. See also ghettos; killing centres; resettlement schemes

deserters, Wehrmacht, 232, 235, 262, 277

Dietrich, Marlene, 111

Dirlewanger, penal battalion, 262

disabled. See handicapped

displaced persons, 270, 291, 293

displaced persons camps, 270

Divine Comedy, 259

Dniester River, 222

Dönitz, Karl, 286

Dora-Mittelbau, 256–7

Dresden, 83, 96

Dubno, 217

Dunkirk, 200, 203

East Prussia, 111, 276

Egypt, 25

Eichmann, Adolf, 122–3, 226, 279, 294; visits to killing centres, 247–9

Einsatzgruppen, 216–22, 226, 238, 295. See also Order Police, SS

Einstein, Albert, 78, 111

Eisenhower, Dwight D., 239, 274

Eisysky, (Eishyshok), 218

El Alamein, 239

Eliach, Yaffa, 218

Eliot, T.S., 285

Enabling Law, 68

Engelmann, Bernd, 80

Estonia, 109, 122, 206, 212

ethnic Germans, 33, 228–30; as beneficiaries of Nazi measures, 139, 144, 219; involved in persecution and killing, 131, 217, 221, 257; in Poland, 109, 116, 119–23; post-war displacement, 293; resettlement plans for, 122, 228; in Sudetenland, 99

Ethiopia, 238

eugenics, 22–4.

Eulenburg–Hertefeld, Philip zu, 35

'Euthanasia', 115–6, 142–6; children's programme, 113–4, 142. See also handicapped; T– programme

exiles, 111

experiments, Nazi medical, 250–1,
    255, 262, 294

Fascists, Italian, 240. See also Italy;
    Mussolini
Finland, 205, 207, 279
First World War, 24, 54, 81, 201;
    effects of German defeat in, 14,
    17, 55–61, 223, 230–1; Hitler's
    experience in, 45–8; impact on
    Europe, 32–3, 90; Jewish veter-
    ans of, 20, 80–1; as precondition
    for Nazism, 37–40. See also
    stab-in-the-back myth; Treaty
    of Versailles
Flossenbürg, 225, 256, 283
Fonseca, Isabel, 222
Foreign Office, German, 126, 226
Four-Year Plan, 55, 119, 144
France, 102, 203, 208, 227; First
    World War and, 38–40, 57–9,
    61; invaded, 196, 199–200; Jews
    and Gypsies in, 27–8, 112–3,
    204–5, 249, 288; killing of black
    soldiers in, 200–1; resistance in,
    202, 262, 268–9; Rhineland
    and, 31, 71, 90–1; post-war,
    246, 293; Second World War
    and, 116–7, 196, 227, 239–42,
    273
Franco, Francisco, 92
Frank, Anne, 200
Frank, Hans, 118, 123, 226, 245.
    See also General Government
Frank, Otto, 198–9
Frankfurt, 200
Frankfurter, Felix, 264
Free French forces, 201
Freemasons, 34, 37–8
Freikorps (Free Corps), 32–4
Frick, Wilhelm, 66, 75
Friedländer, Saul, 8, 51, 201–2
Fritsch, Werner von, 92

Führer principle, 53
functionalists, 42–3

Galen, Clemens August von, 146,
    247
Galicia, 213
gas, use of poison: on handicapped,
    143; on Jews, 225, 245, 248–51,
    253–4; on Soviet POWs, 225,
    249; vans, 143, 243–5
Gay, Peter (Fröhlich), 20, 103
Gellately, Robert, 89, 207
General Government, 118, 122–3,
    137. See also Poland
General Plan East, 226–8
genocide, 8, 12, 30, 209, 233, 253
Gens, Jacob, 133
German African Corps, 238–9
German–Soviet Non-Aggression
    Pact. See Hitler-Stalin Pact.
Germanisation, 137, 229–30, 244,
    268
Germans, popular opinion among:
    in 1935 and 1936, 85–9; in
    1938, 99, 103–4; during war's
    end and post-war, 271, 284–5,
    287, 294; Nazi sensitivity
    towards, 72, 102–3, 232; pro-
    grammes against disabled, 114,
    144–5; regarding homosexuals,
    82; regarding Nazi revolution,
    80–3, 85–6, 94; and war, 96,
    117, 207–8, 232, 234–6, 273–5
Germany, 12–3, 20–1, 34–5, 205;
    anti–black and anti–Slavic atti-
    tudes in, 30–4; before Hitler,
    57–64; declarations of war on,
    117, 197, 202, 241, 279, 284;
    East Germany, 291; First World
    War and, 14, 35, 38–40, 52; as
    imperial power in Africa, 30–1,
    70; Jews in, 16, 71, 73–4, 104,
    243, 247, 293; Nazi revolution

and routinisation in, 66–90;
occupied, 291–5; pre-war
expansion, 96–102; rearmament,
80, 90–3; wartime condi-
tions in, 207–9, 230, 273–6;
West Germany, 275. See also
Germans; Second World War
Gerstein Kurt, 246
Gestapo, 55, 84, 89, 203; roles outside Germany, 128, 216, 232–3,
267
ghettos/ghettoisation, 16, 213,
232, 251, 254; Jewish Councils
and Jewish police in, 128–33;
in Poland, 125–9, 134, 138–9,
254; resistance in, 265–6, 267–9;
Roma and Sinti in, 129, 260
Gleichschaltung, 76
Globocnik, Odilo, 253
Goebbels, Joseph, 53, 54–5; death
of, 287; jokes about, 50, 88;
propaganda efforts of, 76, 91,
102, 104, 231, 235–6, 236,
273–5. See also propaganda
Goebbels, Magda, 55, 286
Göring, Hermann, 50, 54–5, 56,
92, 123; Four–Year Plan and,
91, 119; Luftwaffe and, 198,
204; war's end and suicide, 286,
294
Göttingen, 256
Goldenberg, Myrna, 251
Gotfryd, Bernard, 140
Gotthold, Helene, 107
Graebe, Hermann, 217–8
Graf, Willi, 267–8
Grafeneck, 143
Grand Mufti of Jerusalem (Hajj
Amin al-Husayni), 240
Great Depression, 62, 63, 74
Greece, 196, 209, 220, 241, 262;
murder of Jews from, 241, 247,
253
Grese, Irma, 258

Gross, Jan, 135
Gross-Rosen, 224, 256, 283
Grynszpan, Herschel, 101
guards, camp, 237, 252, 257–8;
at killing centres, 241, 243,
247, 270; at war's end, 280,
283, 289–90, 294. See also
concentration camps; killing
centres
Gürtner, Franz, 85
Gypsies. See Roma; Sinti

Habsburg Empire, 59
Hacker, Melissa, 203
Hadamar, 143. See also
'Euthanasia'; T-4 programme
handicapped, 11, 27, 68, 216;
1933 and 1935 laws, 75, 86;
attitudes toward, 22–3; children
killed, 113–4; as first victims
of killing programme, 8, 225;
killed in T–4 programme, by
Einsatzgruppen, and in gas vans,
115–6, 141–6, 203; protests
against killing, 145–6, 246
Harvest Festival, 238–9
Hasidism, 20, 218
Heck, Alfons, 88–9, 94, 95, 102,
208
Helmbrechts, 283
Herero, 30, 55
Herzegovina, 210
Heuaktion (hay action), 229
Heydrich, Reinhard, 84, 215, 268;
and deportation and resettlement schemes, 120, 122;
and Einsatzgruppen, 216; and
Wannsee Conference, 225, 247
Heymann, Lida Gustava, 111
Himmler, Heinrich, 123, 225, 247,
280; as architect of genocide, 56,
215, 231, 244, 248–51; attacks
on Jehovah's Witnesses, homo-
sexuals and Roma, 70, 106, 260,

261; SS and, 76, 80, 82–3, 117; at war's end, 283, 285, 292. See also SS

Hindenburg, Paul von, 38, 60, 63–4, 83, 84

Hirschfeld, Magnus, 36, 70

Hitler, Adolf, 13, 17, 21, 38, 54, 65, 88; biographical information, 43–9, 55, 235; consolidation of power, 66–9, 75–9, 81–3; inner circle, 54–6, 285; murder of handicapped and, 141, 143–4, 208–9; plot to assassinate, 275–7; preparing for war, 80, 93, 96, 100, 108, 110; pre-war foreign policy, 78–9, 90–1; progress of war and, 197, 201, 216, 239; promise to annihilate Jews, 110–1, 208, 240; response to protests, 125, 233, 236; rise to power, 56–7, 61, 64; significance of, 42–3, 66; Stalin compared to, 206; at war's end, 271, 276–7, 284, 286; worldview, 8, 49, 51–4, 116, 210–2, 231

Hitler, Alois, 43

Hitler, Klara, 44

Hitler-Stalin Pact, 109–10, 117–9, 137, 212

Hitler-Youth (Hitler Jugend, HJ), 77, 88, 94–5, 208

Hoche, Alfred, 24–5

Hoess, Rudolf, 225, 249–50

Holland. See Netherlands

Holocaust, 7–8, 12; legacies of, 288, 290, 292–3, 295–6

Home Army, Polish (AK), 139–40, 278. See also Poland; underground; Warsaw uprising

homosexuality/homosexuals: accusations used to discredit, 82, 93; in concentration camps, 105, 255–6, 259, 261; Nazi measures against,

8, 56, 68, 70, 77, 87, 280; prejudices against, 14, 34–5, 35–6, 291

Horthy, Miklos, 279

Huber, Kurt, 267

Hungary, 39, 205–6, 209, 216, 251, 273–4; Jews in, 21, 122–3, 271–2, 279–82, 290–1; Roma in, 27, 279; war after Stalingrad and, 236–7, 278, 280–1, 283–4, 290–1

IG Farben, 249

imperialism, 28–30, 71–2

incorporated territories, from Poland into Germany, 118–9, 122–3, 137, 244. See also Poland

India, 25–6, 49–50, 202, 260

inflation, 38, 58–9, 274

intentionalists, 42

International Military Tribunal, 294

International Red Cross, 289

international responses to Nazism, 86, 98–9, 101–3, 264–5. See also Allied forces

Irish Free State (Eire), 202, 226

Isaacson, Judith Magyar, 281

Israel, 74, 122, 139, 222, 240, 293, 295

Italy, 97, 273–4; Jews and, 135, 241, 243; military cooperation with Germany, 92, 109, 205, 210–1, 238; war in, 136, 233, 240–2, 285

Japan, 111, 205–6

Jedwabne, 135–6

Jehovah's Witnesses, 8–9, 14, 34, 36, 70, 84, 291; in Nazi concentration camps, 105, 107–8, 255–6, 259–61

Jewish Councils (Judenräte), 129–31, 133, 245, 253–4. See also ghettos

Jewish Fighting Organisation, Warsaw (ZOB), 265–6, 269. See also resistance

Jews, 7, 11, 260, 279, 287; 1933–1935 situation in Germany, 70–1, 73–5, 85; in Austria after Anschluss, 97, 100; in concentration and labour camps, 256, 258–9; defined and marked, 50, 52–3, 85, 208–9, 244, 260; diversity among, 18–20, 22; in ghettos, 126–9, 233–4; in hiding, 213–5, 254–5, 295–6; history of, 19–21; Hitler, Nazi ideology and, 49, 50, 52, 109–10, 227–8; Hungarian Jews killed, 271–2, 279, 281; killed by Einsatzgruppen, 196, 216–9, 231; killing centres and, 225, 243–52; Kristallnacht and, 101–3, 108; linked to communism, 33, 137; as partisans, 140; in Poland, 119, 120, 123, 124, 125–34, 135–40, 226, 243–51; post-war, 289, 290, 293; as refugees, 111–2, 202, 203, 205; repercussions of war on, 240–1; resistance among, 265–6, 268, 282; in Yugoslavia, 209–10

Judaism, 20, 21, 23, 37, 86, 102, 232

justice, post-war, 293–4

Justin, Eva, 105

kapos, 141, 258–9, 281

Karski, Jan, 263–4

Katyn Forest massacre, 235–6

Kershaw, Ian, 53

KGB (People's Commisariat for State Security), 206

Kiev, 218

killing centres, 74, 237, 290; described, 243–4; knowledge of, 252–4; opened, 226–7; transports from ghettos to, 260, 267

Kindertransports, 202–3

Klemperer, Victor, 83, 96–7

Kluger, Ruth, 99–100

Knappe, Siegfried, 197

Knauer baby, 113

Koch, Ilse, 258

Koch, Karl, 258

Kovno, 254

Krakow, 120, 225

Kristallnacht pogrom, 101–4, 108

Kusserow, Wolfgang, 107

labour camps, 126, 131, 206, 255; combined with killing centres, 248–50; Jews in, 266, 279; new ones in last year of war, 271, 283; in Poland, 119, 250

Lang, Fritz, 111

Langer, Lawrence, 296

Latter-day Saints, Church of Jesus Christ of, 106

Latvia, 109–10, 122, 212, 217, 257; Soviet takeover, 206

Laval, Pierre, 201

Law for the Prevention of Hereditarily Diseased Offspring (Sterilisation Law), 75, 105. See also eugenics; handicapped; sterilisation

Law for the Protection of German Blood and Honour. See Nuremberg Laws.

League of German Girls (Bund deutscher Mädel, BDM), 76

League of Nations, 58, 79

Lebensraum, 49, 115, 212–3, 216, 228

Leipelt, Hans, 267

Leitner, Isabella, 251

Lendvai, Karoly, 280

Lenin, Vladimir Ilyich, 33, 59

Leningrad, 278

lesbians, 35, 69, 111, 257. See also homosexuals; women

Levi, Primo, 241–3, 259

Libya, 239

Lidice, 268

Lindeman, Yehudi (Rudy), 255

Linz, 45

Lithuania, 109, 134, 212, 254; Jewish partisans in, 218, 265; Soviet takeover, 206

Łódź, 118, 121, 213, 243; ghetto in, 126–9, 132, 238, 245–6

London, 201, 204, 263; governments–in–exile in, 118, 140, 199, 263

London, Jack, 78

Lublin, 21, 120, 123, 125, 224, 253; ghettos in, 128–31; killing operations near, 238, 245, 248

Ludendorff, Erich, 38, 47, 60

Lueger, Karl, 17, 45

Luftwaffe, 55, 91, 116, 209; use of in the west, 197, 199, 206

Luther, Martin, 17

Luxembourg, 128, 196–7, 199

Lvov (Lwow, Lemberg, L'viv), 212–5, 219, 246

Madagascar plan, 126

Majdanek, 120, 140, 223, 248, 270

Malicious Practices Act, 89, 207, 267–8

Mann, Heinrich, 78

Mann, Thomas, 78, 111

Marx, Karl, 19

Marxism, 42

Marzahn, 88, 95, 104–5

Maschmann, Melitta, 76

Masons. See Freemasons

Mauthausen, 108, 225

May, Karl, 48

medical doctors, 85, 113–4, 142–4, 229, 250–1

Mein Kampf, 43, 44, 47, 82; and Hitler's antisemitism, 51, 69; and Hitler's view of Lebensraum in East, 212, 216

Mengele, Josef, 250, 293–4

Mennonites, 218

Merin, Moishe, 132–3

Michalowsky, Zvi, 218

Middle East, 205, 293–4. See also Egypt; Grand Mufti of Jerusalem; Israel; Palestine

Minsk, 134

Mischlinge, 86, 235

mixed marriages, Jewish–Christian, 236. See also Klemperer; Rosenstrasse incident

Moltke, Helmuth James von, 276

Molotov–Ribbentrop Pact. See Hitler–Stalin Pact

Monowitz, 250. See also Auschwitz

Montgomery, Bernard L., 238–9

Morley, Ruth, 203

Morocco, 31, 239

Moscow, 278

Münster, 145–6

Munich, 46–8, 84, 267

Munich Conference, 99–100

Mussolini, Benito, 62, 92, 97, 209, 238; collapse of Fascist regime and, 240

Nama, 30, 55

Namibia. See Southwest Africa

Naples, 240

Napoleon, 17, 60, 210

National Socialist German Worker's Party (NSDAP, Nazi Party), 11, 12, 34, 54, 56, 84; in the 1920s, 49, 62–3; in the 1930s, 63–4, 67, 69; in wartime, 224, 232

Naval Agreement, German-British, 108

Nazi ideology, 198, 227; centred on antisemitism, 8, 25; homosexuals in, 261; Jewishness considered 'race', 72, 85; Roma and Sinti in, 259–60; Slavs in,

135, 228. See also Hitler; race and space; war

Nazi revolution, 57–82, 98, 105

Nazi terminology, 49

Nazism, 207

Nero Order, 277–8

Netherlands, 136, 227, 274; German conquest of, 196, 199, 202; Jews in, 18, 112, 222, 247, 255

Neurath, Constantin von, 92

New Zealand, 202

Nietzsche, Friedrich, 46

Night of Long Knives. See Röhm Putsch

Nisko, 123

NKGB. See KGB

NKVD (People's Commissariat for Internal Affairs), 206. See also Soviet Union

Nomberg–Przytyk, Sara, 259

non–aggression pacts, 79, 108, 109

'non-Aryans', 142. See also Afro-Germans; Jews; Nuremberg Laws; Roma; Slavic peoples

Normandy, 274. See also D–Day

North Africa, 238–40

Norway, 136, 196, 198–9, 202, 227

Nuremberg, 86–7; Nuremberg Laws, 85–7, 106; Nuremberg Trials, 286, 294–5

Odessa, 221

Olympic Games, 1936 in Berlin, 88, 90, 106

Omdurman, Battle of, 29

Operation Barbarossa, 211–3, 272

Operation Overlord, 274

Operation Reinhard, 247. See also killing centres

Operation Sea Lion, 204

Operation Torch, 239

Order Police, German, 216–7, 238, 264. See also Einsatzgruppen

orchestras, in camps, 257–8

Oswiecim, 249. See also Auschwitz

Pact of Steel, 109

Pale of Settlement, 19

Palestine, 75, 141, 240, 293

Pan-Germanism, 45

Papen, Franz von, 64

Paragraph 175 (German criminal code), 69, 87. See also homosexuals

Paris, 101, 201, 206, 274, 278

partisans, 211, 230, 231, 241; Jewish, 140–1, 264–5, 267–8; Yugoslavian, 209–10, 284

Pauli, Harry, 262

Paulus, Friedrich, 234

Pavelic, Ante, 210

penal units, 262

Penner Ilona, 203

Penner, Kurt, 203

Pétain, Henri Philippe, 201

'phoney war', 197–8

photographs, uses of, 290, 296; from killing sites, 210

pink triangle, 258. See also homosexuals

Piotrkow Trybunalski, 132, 253

Pius XII, 124, 145. See also Catholic Church

Plaschow, 120

plot of 20 July 1944, 271, 275–6

Plymouth, 204

Podchlebnik, Mordechai, 245

pogroms, 16, 21, 101–2, 131, 214, 217, 222, 291

Poland, 59, 212–3, 227, 243–4, 273; effects of war, 287, 289–90, 292–3; established as state after First World War, 32, 59; German invasion and occupation of, 116–26, 197, 211; German crimes against, 119–24, 209, 233;

German plans for, 49, 119–24, 228–9, 244; German–Soviet arrangement regarding, 109–10, 117–8, 137–8, 212–3; government–in–exile, 118, 140, 263, 278; handicapped murdered in, 143, 145; Jews in, 19–20, 21, 111, 125–41, 213, 222, 245, 253, 259, 263–4, 291; pre–war relations with Germany, 79, 101, 108; rescue of Jews and resistance, 139, 215, 253, 263; Soviet crimes against, 235, 291; underground army in, 118, 139, 278; particularities of situation in, 134–9

Pomerantz, Jack (Yankel), 21, 22, 117, 138

Portugal, 205

Prague, 74, 202, 262, 268, 284

priests, Roman Catholic, 120, 124, 254. See also Catholic Church

prisoners of war, 118, 201, 224, 240, 248, 263, 292; black POWs shot by Germans, 200; captured by Allies, 239, 288; Soviet POWs, 8, 197, 216, 224–5, 248–9, 280, 288

Probst, Christoph, 267

propaganda, Nazi German, 76–9, 91, 94, 101–2, 109; and German war effort, 209, 234–5, 272–3, 276–7

protest and non-protest: against killing handicapped, 145–6, 246–7, 260; against killing Jews, 241, 245; against killing Polish priests, 124; against killing Roma, 260. See also Germans; international response; resistance

Protestant church in Germany, 36, 70, 73, 100; conflict and cooperation with Nazi regime, 108, 144, 221, 232. See also Christianity

Protestant Reformation, 17

Quisling, Vidkun, 199

race and space, ideology of, 7, 12, 49, 97; implemented in war, 110, 125, 167, 227–8, 237, 275

Racial Hygiene and Population Research Centre, 260

racism: anti–black racism, 28–31, 70–1; and killing of French black soldiers, 201; against Jews, 49–52. See also Afro–Germans; antisemitism; Nazi ideology

Radom, 140

Radu, Drina, 222

Radzyn, 21, 117

Rassenschande, 106

Raubal, Geli, 48

Ravensbrück, 96, 104, 256–8, 284. See also concentration camps; women

Reck-Malleczewen, Fritz Percy, 47, 64

Red Army, 138, 206, 230, 239–40; advancing in 1944–1945, 240, 269, 271, 272, 278, 281, 283; Battle of Stalingrad and, 234, 237; prisoners of war from, 223–5; at war's end, 291–2; Warsaw uprising and, 278

refugees, 201–2, 205, 291, 293. See also displaced persons

Reich Citizenship Law. See Nuremberg Laws

Reich Committee for Scientific Registration of Serious Hereditarily- and Congenitally-Based Illnesses, 114

Reich Department of Health, Racial Hygiene and Population Biology Research. See Racial

Hygiene and Population Research Centre
Reich Representation of the German Jews, 74
Reich Security Main Office (RSHA), 120, 122
Reichenau, Walter von, 220
Reichstag, 63–4, 67–8, 90–1, 110; Reichstag fire, 67–8, 77, 93
Reiprich, Doris, 71
Remarque, Erich Maria, 235
reparations, post-First World War, 38–40, 57–9. See also Article 304, Treaty of Versailles
reprisals, German use of in Second World War, 209, 231, 267
rescue: of Danish Jews, 204; hiding Jews, 253–4; of Hungarian Jews, 279–80; of Jews in Poland, 138. See also protest, resistance
resettlement schemes, 122, 137, 292; of ethnic Germans, 121–2, 128; Soviet post-war plans, 291
resistance, 230, 262–70; in camps and killing centres, 247, 255, 282–3; in Germany, 267–9, 275–7; Jewish, 131–3, 218, 265–6, 267–70; obstacles to, 268; in Poland, 139; among Roma and Sinti, 281–3. See also partisans; protest
Rhineland, 31, 71, 89–90
Ribbentrop, Joachim von, 92, 285
Riefenstahl, Leni, 87
Riga, 132
Ritter, Robert, 105
Robota, Roza, 282
Röhm, Ernst, 81–2. See also storm troopers
Röhm, Putsch, 81–2, 85
Roma (Gypsies), 8, 25, 209, 215; in concentration camps, 255, 257, 259, 261; Einsatzgruppen killings and, 216, 218, 221, 222; in ghettos and internment camps, 88, 95, 128, 131, 245, 281; history of, 25–8; in killing centres, 245, 247, 248, 250, 255, 270, 271; post-war problems, 291; prejudices against, 11, 13, 25–8, 35, 55, 69; pre-war measures against in Germany, 75, 87, 88, 103, 105; resistance, 282
Roman Catholic Church. See Catholic Church
Romani language, 28, 260. See also Roma
Romania, 205, 206, 209; Gypsies in, 27, 222, 291; Jews from, 221–2; after Stalingrad, 234, 237, 278
Rome, 79, 92, 109, 240
Rommel, Erwin, 238–9
Roosevelt, Franklin D., 264, 272, 275, 284
Rosenberg, Otto, 88, 96, 105
Rosenstrasse incident, 236, 260. See also Germans; mixed marriages; protest; resistance
Rotterdam, 199
Royal Air Force, 204, 272
Rumkowski, Chaim, 132–3, 245
Russia, 33, 39, 59. See also Soviet Union
Russian Revolution, 33, 40

Sachsenhausen, 96, 104, 261, 284
Sartre, Jean-Paul, 133
Schieder, Theodor, 228
Schleicher, Kurt, 82
Scholl, Hans, 267
Scholl, Sophie, 267
Schmorell, Alexander, 267
Scholtz–Klink, Gertrud, 56
Schuschnigg, Kurt von, 97
Scientific Registration of Serious Hereditarily- and Congenitally-

Based Illnesses, Reich
Committee for, 114
Second World War, 227; final phase,
278–85; impact in Germany,
207–9; in Italy, 240–1; legacies
of, 286, 288–96; in North Africa,
238–40; in northern and western
Europe, 196–203; outbreak of
in Poland, 116–9; relationship to
Holocaust, 7; in Soviet Union,
211–2, 233–5; in Yugoslavia and
Greece, 209–10
secrecy, of mass killing operations,
247, 252–4, 263–5
Security Services (SD), 89, 219, 234
Serbia, 210, 257. See also Yugoslavia
Sevastopol, 232
sexual slavery, 257. See also brothels
Shanghai, 111
Sheptitisky, Andreas, 213
Siberia, 111, 137, 206, 213, 281, 289
Sicily, 239
Siegal, Aranka (Piri Dawidowitz),
21
Silesia, 122, 132
Sinti, 26, 70, 75, 88, 104. See also
Roma
slave labour, 216, 228–31, 239, 250,
272, 273, 280; post-war situation,
288, 292
Slavic peoples, 8, 14, 48, 228; anti-
Slavic attitudes, 32–3, 136, 215,
224, 227. See also Poland; Soviet
Union; Ukraine
Slovakia, 100, 205, 241, 249
Sobibor, 247, 252, 265, 293, 295
Social Darwinism, 18, 23, 38, 285.
See also Nazi ideology
Social Democrats, German, 62, 68
soldiers. See Allies; Red Army;
Wehrmacht
Sonderkommandos, Jewish, 244,
247, 283. See also killing centres

South Africa, 202, 293
South America, 293
Southwest Africa (later Namibia),
30, 55, 71
Soviet Union, 33, 52, 58, 59, 92,
202, 204; Baltic states and, 206;
communist exiles in, 73, 109–11;
German invasion of, 145, 204,
209, 210–4; German plans for,
49, 51, 120; Jews and, 137–9,
232, 247, 264, 288; nature of war
in, 215–21, 227; Poland and, 137,
234–5, 292; prisoners of war
from, 8, 197, 216, 223–5; resistance, 262; slave labourers from,
228–30; war's end, 273, 278, 281,
282, 283, 286–90, 291–2
Spain, 16, 17, 200, 205; civil war in,
92, 95, 201
Special Operations Executive, 262,
268
Speer, Albert, 273–4, 278, 280
Spielberg, Steven, 120
SS (Schutzstaffel), 55, 76, 79, 82, 83,
230, 257, 284; concentration
camps and, 104, 257; ghettos and,
266, 269; at killing centres, 243,
246, 249, 250; mass killings and,
143, 219, 224, 225, 232; in Poland,
118–20, 124; at war's end, 237,
284–5, 221–2. See also Himmler
St Louis (ship), 112
Stab-in-the-back myth, 40, 51, 60,
68, 198. See also First World War
Stabholz, Thaddeus, 269–70
Stalin, Josef, 212, 234, 238; abuses of
regime, 109–11, 205–7, 230, 278,
288; pact with Hitler, 109–11,
137. See also Soviet Union
Stalingrad, 234; Battle of Stalingrad,
233–7
Stangl, Franz, 247, 252–3, 292–3
Stangl, Teresa, 252–3

Stauffenberg, Claus Schenck von, 276–7. See also plot of 20 July 1944

sterilisation, 24, 71, 75, 79, 87, 105, 229–30, 259. See also Law for the Prevention of Hereditarily Diseased Offspring

Stoltzfus, Nathan, 236

Stopes, Marie, 24

storm troopers (Sturmabteilung, SA), 62, 67, 78, 80; attacks on homosexuals, Jews and Poles, 69, 71, 102, 121; Röhm, Putsch and, 81–3, 84, 93

Strasser, Gregor, 82

Strength through Joy, 77, 127

Stutthof, 256. See also concentration camps

Sudan, 29

Sudetenland, 99–100, 104, 108, 208, 292. See also Czechoslovakia

Sweden, 21, 199, 205, 226, 246; Jews and, 205, 281

Switzerland, 111, 205, 241, 264

Szerynski, Josef, 131

T-4 Programme, 141–5, 225, 243, 247, 252, 292. See also 'Euthanasia', handicapped

Tec, Nechama, 140

Theresienstadt (Terezin), 74

Thimme, Annelise, 93

Thimme, Friedrich, 93

Third Reich, 65. See also Germany; Hitler

Three-Power Pact, 205

Tiso, Josef, 100

Tito, Josip Broz, 209, 284

Tokyo, 92

Toll, Nelly, 213–5

Transnistria, 134, 222–3

Treblinka, 248, 252, 265, 266, 270–1, 294

Triumph of the Will, 88

tuberculosis, 128, 245

Tucholsky, Kurt, 78

Tunis, 239

Tunisia, 239–40

Turin, 241

Turkey, 39, 205, 226, 293–4

twins, experiments on, 250

Ukraine, 21, 134, 212–3; camp guards from, 244, 257; mass killings in, 138, 212–4, 217–8, 219, 222, 231; post-war, 291–2; slave labourers from, 274. See also Soviet Union

unconditional surrender, 284, 287

underground: Czech, 268; Dutch, 295; Jewish, 131, 263–5; Polish, 138–40, 263. See also resistance

United Nations, 292

United Nations Relief and Rehabilitation Administration, 292

United States, 24, 63, 90, 199, 202, 224, 270, 281; destination of refugees, exiles and survivors, 20, 73, 111, 203, 215, 292; and Jehovah's Witnesses, 36, 105; and Jews, 232, 263–4; as occupying power, 292; and Second World War, 108, 238, 284, 289

United States, Air Force, 272

United States Holocaust Memorial Museum, 113

universities, German, 72, 267

Ural Mountains, 229

Ustasha, 210. See also Croatia; Yugoslavia

V–weapons, 256, 274

van der Lubbe, Marinus, 67

Vatican, 79–80, 105, 108, 124, 246, 293. See also Catholic Church

Versailles, Treaty of, 38–9, 78, 80, 90, 97–8, 101, 108. See also First World War

Vichy, 201; Vichy France, 200, 134, 241. See also France

Vienna, 45–6, 92, 284; Jews in, 98–9, 122, 203

Vilna (Vilnius), 133, 268

Vistula River, 278

Volga River, 234

Volksdeutschen. See ethnic Germans

Volkssturm, 277

Volkswagen, 77

Voltaire, 17

Wagner, Richard, 45, 285

Wallenberg, Raoul, 281

Wannsee Conference, 226, 243, 248; construction of killing centres and, 225, 245, 248

war: accelerating dynamic of, 227; cover for killing of handicapped, 144, 208; German preparations for, 79, 96, 99, 108–9; in Hitler's worldview, 51, 198, 227; outbreak in September 1939, 116–7. See also Hitler; Nazi ideology; race and space; Second World War

war criminals, 205, 245, 292

Warsaw, 118, 140, 247, 269; Warsaw ghetto, 126, 128, 131, 132, 247, 253, 263, 265, 269; Warsaw ghetto uprising (1943), 265, 269; Warsaw uprising (1944), 278

Wehrmacht (German military), 79, 89, 91, 99, 121, 124, 128, 232; bribery of officers, 233; chaplains in, 219, 232; at end of war, 273, 277, 284; establishment and nazification of, 79, 85, 91–2; invading, 98, 116, 199–200, 209, 211–2; mass killings and, 210–1,

216–7, 219–21, 224–5; morale in, 124, 146; target groups and, 214, 220–1, 261, 278. See also Germany; Luftwaffe, Second World War

Weimar, 57, 104

Weimar Republic, 35, 57–61, 63, 81

Weinberg, Gerhard, 215

Werewolf organisation, 277

Wessel, Horst, 78

Westerbork, 200, 295

White Rose, 267. See also resistance

Wiesel, Elie, 281

Wilhelm II, Kaiser, 35

Winter War, 207

Wirth, Christian, 246

Wisgardisky, Henny (Henia Lewin), 255

women: Gentile women as victims, 104, 111, 230, 268, 284; Germanisation and, 229; Jewish women, 216, 219–21, 232, 250–1, 281–4; Nazi ideas about, 51–2, 69; Nazi racial laws and, 71, 85–7; as partisans, 140; as partners and beneficiaries of Nazism, 56, 207–8, 211, 250–3, 258; as rescuers, 236, 295; sexual abuse of, 120, 124, 257, 293; vote and, 57. See also Germans; Jews; lesbians; resistance

Yad Vashem, 139

Yiddish language, 19, 22

Yugoslavia, 196, 209–10, 240–1, 284; end of war for, 279, 286, 293; partisans and resistance in, 161–2, 284

Zacharias, Karin (Pardo), 111

Zegota, 139

Zionism, 75, 106, 132, 293

Zyklon B, 225, 246, 249, 270